# Frank Lovell's World W

## The European War Theater Years
## June 6, 1944 to September 14, 1945

The Private Diaries of a Chief Warrant Officer, Personnel Section,
60th Field Artillery, 9th Infantry Division
Written by Frank Lovell
Edited by Mary Lovell
Assistant Editor: Yuri Beckers

*Frank Lovell's World War II Diaries: The European War Theater Years, June 6, 1944 to September 14, 1945* is a diary of the author's experiences. Some names may have been changed, places are actual, and events are recorded from the author's daily experiences and have been verified to the editors' ability.

Published in the United States by WWIIDiaries

ISBN: 978-1-937588-66-3

# We dedicate this book...

From Mary:
As the daughter of Frank Lovell, I would like to dedicate this book to my Father, his "Army buddies," and to all the soldiers that have served in the 9th Infantry Division, both in conflict and in peacetime.

From Yuri:
To all the men who served with the 9th Infantry Division during World War II. A special mention here to those who served in any of the four Field Artillery Battalions. Often overlooked, these men also participated in eight battle campaigns, and helped the 9th Infantry Division to successfully give back freedom to many. I will be forever thankful to all these men and will always remember them and the price of freedom.

# Table of Contents

# Biography

Frank Lovell was born on April 1, 1917, in Boston, Massachusetts and was raised in Houghs Neck, Quincy, Massachusetts. His mother Julia Sweeney, was an Irish immigrant from Killarney, Kerry. Frank's father, Walter Franklin Lovell, was descended from an early New England family. He worked as a Chauffeur and car mechanic, specializing in Rolls Royce cars. Other family members included a sister Helen, and a brother Walter.

Frank grew up playing baseball for the local youth league. After graduating from Quincy High School, in the middle of the Great Depression, he worked alongside his brother Walter as a clam digger. Later he worked for the U.S. Post Office as a Mailman and a Postal Clerk. During the late 1930s Frank traveled around the country trying out for major league baseball teams; he played for the Minor league team the Utica Braves, in the 1939 -1940 season.

In February 1940, Frank was drafted into the U.S. Army and his military service began. Initially he was at Fort Bragg, North Carolina, in A-Battery, 60th Field Artillery Battalion, 9th Infantry Division. Later he became a clerk and was transferred to Headquarters (HQ) Section, 60th

Field Artillery Battalion, 9th Infantry Division. Later his title was changed to Military Personnel Officer. By completion of his service, on November 1, 1945, Frank's highest rank was Chief Warrant Officer.

Prior to landing in Normandy, Frank participated in all the 9th Division campaigns. These included the invasion of Morocco as well as action in Algeria and Tunisia. This was followed by the invasion of Sicily. His unit then rested and refitted at Camp Barton Stacey in England. On June 10, 1944 he landed with his Battalion at Utah Beach, Normandy, France and proceeded during the next 15 months to cross into Belgium and Germany.

In July 1945 Frank was transferred, in preparation for his transfer home, to the 666th Field Artillery Battalion and was stationed in Austria.

Wedding picture of Frank Lovell and
Patricia (Patsy) Donnellan, October
1946

In October 1945 Frank met his future wife, Patricia Anna Donnellan (Patsy), at an Officer's dance in Boston. He recognized her from his mail route in Hough's Neck, Massachusetts, where Patsy's family had a summer cottage. They married a year later, in October 1946. Patsy Donnellan was 22 years old and Frank Lovell was 29 years old.

After living in Brighton, Massachusetts, in 1962 they moved to West Roxbury, Massachusetts. They had 5 children. After the war Frank worked for 30 years in the U.S. Post Office as a clerk.

Frank Lovell passed away January 25, 1996.

Lovell Family circa 1962 – Kathy pictured to side as Mom was still pregnant with her during the time the family photo was taken

# The Diaries

The earliest Frank Lovell diary found was from 1940. It is unknown if he kept one prior to this time. But we do know that from the date, January 1, 1940 until his death in January 1996 Frank kept a diary.

Even though it was against U.S. Army regulations to keep a diary, or military documents, or processed uncensored photos, Frank Lovell did all three.

Story of the Three Diary Manuscripts.

There are actually three diary manuscripts.

1) As seen in the photo above, the original handwritten diaries are the original "source" document. These are the actual diaries written at the time of occurrence by Frank Lovell.

2) There is a typewritten manuscript in which Frank Lovell takes the source document and adds/edits some material in it. We call this Frank Lovell's Memoir manuscript.

The added material includes things such as a remembered story, hometowns of the soldiers, and some descriptive data. Many of the fragmented sentences have been altered to make them flow better for easier reading

The edits include things such as names censored in instances of soldier misbehavior or suicide. Other edits are actual events or thoughts that may reflect poorly on a soldier or the author himself. Overall there are very few edits that were made.

3) The third manuscript is the one you are reading now. Both editors have worked on this manuscript to have it reflect, as closely as possible, the content of the original source document.

We want to be as forthcoming and honest as possible in identifying how this manuscript differs from the source document and why any changes were made. Here is a list of how it differs.

- As many abbreviations as possible have been spelled out.
- Some fragmented sentences have been altered to make them flow better for easier reading.
- A few – only (3 to 4 paragraphs) have been extensively rewritten by the editors. These were done for clarity reasons. An example is June 18, 1944, the day the $9^{th}$ Division fought their way their way across the Cotentin Peninsula, cutting the Germans in the north off from their divisions in the south, thus creating a wedge dividing the German army in two. The source document wording was found to be unclear to many readers.
- Names of soldiers that were accused of misbehavior have been censored.
- In a few instances of soldier's misbehavior, the incidents have been described in less explicit terms than in the source document.
- Additional material added, to this version of the diary, have been taken from Frank's Memoir manuscript in order to clarify what is written in the source document.
- Corrected spelling of soldier's names.

- Corrected spelling of towns and cities.

Again it is the intent of the editors to make it clear what this manuscript is. Some of the entries are exactly like the source document and some are changed to make it easier reading or to edit out a name or incident.

The editor, Mary Lovell, and assistant, Yuri Beckers, wrote each chapter's historical overview.

We have given much thought into what to call this book. Should it be called a diary, a journal, or a memoir? After much thought and consideration we feel that the term "diary" best reflects the manuscript you are reading.

The photos and captions, except as noted, are from Frank Lovell's personal collection.

# Chapter one: June 1944

June 6, 1944 to June 30, 1944

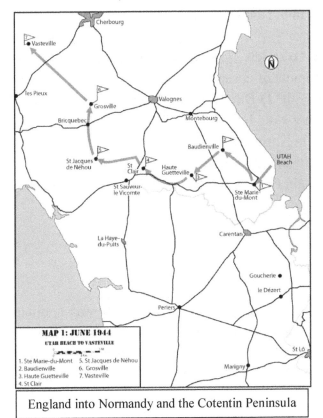

England into Normandy and the Cotentin Peninsula

June 1944 Historical Overview
June 1944 Corps Assignments:
First Army, 12th Army Group
June 4 to June 30, 1944 – VII Corps

General Overview

On June 6, 1944 the Allied invasion, what was commonly referred to as D- Day, began in Normandy, France.

9th Division Overview: The Allied command, knowing there would be massive amounts of casualties, kept some veteran divisions out of the first waves of the D-Day Invasion. The 9th Division was one of them.

On D-Day + 4, June 10, 1944, the 9th Division began landing on Utah Beach in Normandy.

During the month of June, the 9th Division moved westward and cut off the Cotentin Peninsula. They then drove north to capture the port of Cherbourg.

*** 

*June 6, 1944*
Camp A, Barton Stacey, England
D-Day

I got up for breakfast about 7:30 a.m. I was coming back when Captain Rockwood came by and told us that the people of France, who live within 35 miles of the coast, had been warned to move. I listened to the radio, and the British Broadcasting Corporation (BBC) is reporting that the Germans say the invasion has started. They say the Allies are landing crafts off Le Havre and there is some fighting there. They say Dunkirk and Calais have been heavily bombed and paratroopers have been dropped on the Normandy Peninsula.

The sky overhead is full of planes, some in huge formations headed for France. The Allied Supreme Command confirmed that the invasion is on. It started about 10 a.m. The radio is blaring away about it.

We worked on passenger lists all morning, then packed up everything and loaded the trucks. We left for the Marshaling Area at 6:15 p.m., and everyone is in good spirits. We have been waiting for this moment for a long time. We know that we have to be in it, so the sooner we get in, the

2

sooner it will be all over.

We moved slowly and went about 15 miles to the Road Convoy Reception Point (RCRP), # 3 Camp, # 8 White Block. This camp is in between Winchester and Southampton. We parked, walked to camp, and then we drew cots and blankets. We slept in pyramidal tents.

## June 7, 1944

Road Convoy Reception Point (RCRP), # 3 Marshaling Area, England
D-Day +1

Road Convoy Reception Point (RCRP), # 3 Marshaling Area, England

We got up about 7 a.m. and dressed; there are Captains Gray and Rockwood, Lieutenants Obeldobel, Gaffney, and Hall, Warrant Officer Williams (9th Signal Corps) and me. We had breakfast in one of those English tents, but it was American food. It was about a half-mile away.

I took a shower and we got orders to move immediately. We didn't have time to get briefed but know we are to land on the Normandy Peninsula, near Sainte- Mere-Eglise. We put on our impregnated clothes (they are soaked in a greasy chemical to repel gas), in the event of a gas attack. Then we turned in the cots and blankets and had a lunch. There was some trouble turning in our money and getting partial pay. We got French francs for it.

About 1 p.m. we went to the trucks and sat there until 5 p.m., we ate supper in the field, served to us by the American Services of Supply (SOS). We hung around until 11 p.m. and then only moved up the road about 500 yards.

## June 8, 1944

D-Day + 2
Marshaling Area to Dock Area, Southampton, England

We moved from the road about 2 a.m. There was an air raid alert but nothing happened. We went toward Southampton. The truck behind us smashed into us, smashing the trailer against our truck. It snapped my head giving me a little whiplash. We arrived at the dock area about 4 a.m. and were given hot coffee and doughnuts. There are some Seabees here, the first I have ever seen. They sure had huge backpacks.

I went aboard the ship. It is a Liberty ship named "James Caldwell". I washed and shaved but still feel crummy, as we have to keep the same impregnated clothes on. The men are sleeping in the warehouse nearby, so I went over. I hung around for a while and sat in the front of the Air Observation Post truck and got a couple hours of sleep.

Colored soldiers loaded the trucks aboard the ship. We had Mass in the warehouse, there was General Absolution and I went to Communion. I met Mathewson from the Palmer Street area, Quincy, MA, who I had played basketball against. He is in the 9th Division, in our 47th Infantry Regiment. The SOS put out another dinner.

We all boarded the ship at 2 p.m., and got bunks in the hold with the enlisted men. We ate K-rations for supper. The ship left the dock at 7 p.m. and anchored in the channel.

## June 9, 1944
Aboard S.S. James Caldwell
D-Day + 3

I slept pretty well in my impregnated clothes and borrowed blankets. There are many boats and ships all around, as far as you can see. There must be a thousand of all types. I got up at 10:30 a.m. and I feel pretty dirty; I shaved and cleaned in the crew's quarters.

We were given a hot meal in the wardroom, and it was good. I hung around on my bunk in the afternoon. We lifted anchor and moved out about 8 p.m. passing between the Isle of Wight and the mainland. It was cold on deck. We all talked and drank coffee until midnight. I groped my way back to bed.

## June 10, 1944
Aboard S.S. James Caldwell (En route to France)
D-Day + 4

We are headed for France. We were alerted to report on deck at 4 a.m. There were white and red flares all around. A ship was burning in the distance; it was hit by a plane. We were alerted again at 4:45 a.m. There are huge convoys in all directions. Our convoy has about 10 ships.

We had a breakfast of fried eggs.

We are in sight of France now. There are loads of boats at each beachhead. A body just floated by. Many ships are sunk all around us, including a destroyer, a Liberty ship, and some Landing Ship Tanks (LSTs). I took a quick shower and shaved. The coast is pretty high in spots. We came to anchor and I ate dinner. Occasionally a shell whistles over and lands in the water, once in a while one lands on the beach.

We got off the ship about 3 p.m. and went ashore on a tank lighter. We had to wade ashore waist deep. The fellow in front of me disappeared under the water after stepping in a shell hole. Someone managed to find him and pulled him up.

The beach had been the scene of heavy action. We walked up the beach and the beach workers are all in foxholes. The land adjacent to the beach is under water. We put on our packs and started hiking inland. We met the Nurses from the 128th Station Hospital (we had come over from Sicily on the same ship with them). They were hiking along too, although some of them were invited to ride, by hanging on the sides of the tanks. I had a short talk with them, some of whom I knew.

It was hot, we were wet, and the impregnated uniforms weighed a ton. As we hiked along a General roared by in a jeep blasting everybody. He yelled, "Single File" and also "Indian File," and "Spread out and hike on both sides of the road." We had hiked about five miles, and there were wrecked gliders and parachutes strewn all over the fields along the way. The forced laborers had erected poles in all the fields so the gliders would smash up when they tried to land.

There are vehicles moving up and down the road, especially tanks, which threw up clouds of dust and dirt. We are now filthy dirty. The 82nd Airborne and the 101st paratroopers had landed all around here.

5

We have now gone about six miles, so we pulled into a field for the time being. We seem to be the first ones to stop in this area. We have no food or bedding. We scouted around and collected parachutes, equipment, and gear. We salvaged food left by the paratroopers. We found plenty of K-rations, which we ate. We will sleep in the parachutes. Some of the B-Battery arrived. The paratroopers used green camouflaged chutes for jumping, and white ones for medical supplies.

I looked in the next field and found a burned C-47. I found two burned and dismembered bodies, but no identification. There were other torsos, arms, and legs, strewn around.

Our planes were hustling over on missions, up until about 10:30 p.m. Then after that some Jerry planes came in. One was shot up and he came down in a ball of fire. You could see our tracers ripping into him. He crashed in a field a little ways over in a huge burst of flames. There were many other Jerry planes around. The flak started to come down heavy. The Jerry planes started to zero in on us now. From the craters in the next field we estimated they were at least 2000 pounders, it was terrific, and I felt the concussions. One of the Officers and I had to lie in the mud in a ditch to get cover. Bennett of Headquarters Battery was hanging on my legs. The Officer was hanging on my arm. He is just returning to us from England after being all shot up in Africa.

Jerry planes were over on and off all night. He dropped flares right over us, and it was like broad daylight out. He dumped his personnel bombs on us. It almost seems like he has a bushel-basket full. They saturate the area and find every nook and cranny. Jerry really hit the beach area tonight. I wrapped up in a parachute and fell asleep.


## June 11, 1944
3 Miles Northwest of Sainte-Marie-du-Mont, France

I slept fairly well between the parachute and a canvas cover. I slept on my left side, edgeways, and didn't move all night, even though there were air raids now and then.

About 8 a.m. I washed and shaved. I ate a breakfast of K-rations, thanks to the paratroopers. We will have to eat these until our gang comes in. We hung around all morning and then moved a little further up along the banking. I had a K-ration dinner. The rest of the Batteries got in this afternoon.

There was a strafing raid by three Jerry planes this afternoon. They hit some of the Medics over a few fields from us.

The 34th Field Artillery Battalion (155 mm Howitzer), who are behind us down the road a little bit, opened up and everyone jumped. I walked over and visited A- Battery of our 60th Field Artillery Battalion. The 60th Infantry Regiment moved by us, heading for the front.

We had a heated 10-1 ration for supper. I retired pretty early. Jerry bombed a few times in the evening, just up a ways. There is a lot of our anti-air craft (Ack-ack) in action.

## June 12, 1944
3 Miles Northwest of Sainte-Marie-du-Mont, France

I got up at 8:30 a.m. after having a fair night's sleep. Jerry bombed in the distance a few times and there was local anti-aircraft fire. All in all it was a quiet night. Our own (Personnel) trucks came in this morning.

I heated some water by the brook and shaved. We unloaded the truck and put our equipment in two trailers. I rearranged my own things. I got my camera and with Gene Skoczlyas, Tony Wisniewski, and Noel Galfo went over to the burned C-47 and took some pictures. I snapped some pictures of the gliders. I reported the findings of the C-47 bodies to the 9th Division Military Police. Jack Markowitz found blood plasma and other medical supplies lost in the drop. We turned them over to the 9th Medics and they were very grateful for them. I found two pigeons that were supposed to send messages back. I fixed my bedroll and equipment.

We had two casualties today. McElhatton had his hand blown off and

7

Froelicher was hit in the face, when they picked up a booby trap.

After supper (personnel are cooking their own, as are other sections), I went up to Battalion and they were having fire missions. Our guns were blasting right over our heads as we came in. The S-3 section was very busy. I talked with Sergeant Major Urban and Sergeant Rousse. Some German 88s come whistling in, and all Headquarters took to the foxholes. The 34th Field Artillery was firing counter fire like mad in the field right beside us. It was real noisy here.

We brought Charlie Nagy back with us. We got on the wrong road and found ourselves headed for the beach. We turned around and came back to our field. It was hot and dusty. The Corp Artillery is firing constantly, and it is terribly noisy. The 84th Field Artillery Battalion came in today.

I fixed my bedroll and have a nice white silk parachute for a sheet. I

June 12, 1944. Sainte-Marie-du-Mont, France. Parachutes.

**June 12, 1944. Sainte-Marie-du-Mont, France. Gliders.**

June 12, 1944. Sainte-Marie-du-Mont, France. Gliders. Tony Wisniewski.

June 12, 1944. Sainte-Marie-du-Mont, France. Crashed C-47.

have my Navy blankets back, so I gave away the Army ones. German artillery is hunting for some of our big guns as their shells are whistling over us to the rear.

Jerry planes were over a few times during the night bombing, coming close once.

## June 13, 1944
3 Miles Northwest of Sainte-Marie-du-Mont, France

I got up at 9:45 a.m. and dressed. I ate breakfast and then wrote a letter. I caught up with my diary. It rained all afternoon so we fixed up a canopy.

The guns are booming all day. Occasionally an enemy artillery shell whistles by and lands in the distance. Around 6 p.m. we got March Order and so we got everything in order.

It is clear now. We moved to a more open area and we are a couple of fields behind the Battalion. It is very dirty here as troops have been here. There is a rubbish pile left by a Clearing Company, full of bloody clothes. We carried our stuff to another field and built up the wadi with logs. We then camouflaged it. There are some 155 mm rifles around us, and they are only one or two fields away and firing over our heads. The noise is terrific. La Rock of A-Battery was wounded in the stomach today.

We are now one mile northwest of Baudienville.

## June 14, 1944
1 Mile Northwest of Baudienville, France

We didn't get much sleep, as it was noisy. The 155 mm rifles were booming all morning. They lift you off the ground and lay you down again and shake dirt in your face.

I got up at 10 a.m. and we had breakfast. We gather around and cook it ourselves over lighted cans of gasoline. I signed a few things today.

La Rock came back to duty (Wounded in Action yesterday).

There are plenty of German prisoners being marched by. The 39th Infantry captured them.

We are drinking water out of a well, but I put Halazone tablets in it, especially after you see some of the things floating dead in the wells.

Gerry Tempesta came by today and we talked for a while. He used to be in A- Battery, 60th Field Artillery Battalion, with us, but is now a lieutenant in the 4th Infantry Division. He looks the same as ever.

June 14, 1944. Baudienville, Normandy. Paratrooper grave. He hit the farmhouse roof and was killed.

The second priority gang came in today.

The German Nebelwerfer (six-barrel mortar) shells were landing around us. It is a weird, screeching sound. I hung around all day and then dug a rubbish hole and straightened out my sleeping place.

We turned in about 11:30 p.m., after I dug a rubbish hole and straightened out my sleeping place. Jerry was over before long. The ack-ack opened up as he came in low and dropped some bombs. A piece of shell or flak landed beside my foot. It came humming through the air and hit with a thud. Jerry airplanes were over very low during the night. The 155 mm rifles fired occasionally during the night.

Piece of shrapnel that landed at Frank's feet.

## June 15, 1944

1 Mile Northwest of Baudienville, France

I got up at 9:30 a.m. just as Sergeant Nix came by and said that we are to get March Order. I found the piece of shrapnel that fell at my feet

10

last night. It is fairly large and as sharp as a razor. I can understand when they say it goes into you small and comes out the other side a pound of meat.

We ate breakfast. We are waiting for the Battalion to move. They began about noon and we got all ready. The colonel told us to stay here, so we sat down and had a snack about 2 p.m. We sat around and then I walked out to the road. I was talking to two of the Service Battery men when 2 G.I.s came along on a German motorcycle, and they were side swiped by some G.I.s in a German jeep, right at my feet. I saw that one of the men on the motorcycle had a bad cut on his hand. I tore open my first aid kit, sprinkled some Sulfadiazine on the open cut and started to bandage it when he passed out on me. The other fellow was okay. The guys nearby took him to an Aid Station. The guys came by later and said he was okay.

We had the 155 mm rifles right over us, and it is nerve wracking. We had a pretty good air raid later on and a lot of ack-ack.

## June 16, 1944
1 Mile Northwest of Baudienville, France

I awoke early this morning with rain sprinkling in my face. I got up and put my shelter half over the log roof while I was in my underwear. I went back to bed for a while. I got up at 8 a.m. as I had some work to do. It was still sprinkling and my bed was all wet on the outside. I got some things from the trailer. We set up a little shelter to work under. Charlie Nagy did the typing. I took a bath and took off my impregnated clothes, which are filthy.

We got March Order about 7 p.m. We rushed and stacked everything on a truck and left. We traveled about eight miles to Haut Gueutteville and are in the area vacated by the Battalion. There are dead cows and horses all over the place. We fixed up holes to sleep in. We are in front of the 34th and 26th Field Artillery guns. They are firing right over us, as well as the 155 rifles.

11

## June 17, 1944
1/4<sup>th</sup> Mile West of Haut Gueutteville, France

It was a very noisy night as the guns fired intermittently and the shells are going right over us. Jerry planes were over and the ack-ack was firing. One plane was just skimming the treetops. We did not hear any of them bomb but just sweated them out.

I got up at 10:30 a.m. and had some black soluble coffee and crackers. We walked up the road and saw two dead Jerries. One was just a kid and had been hit badly around the legs. He hadn't started shaving yet. The other was face down and plenty ripe, his face was green. I took two pictures. There was a dead American nearby. The Grave Registration Service put him on a truck and covered him. The 79<sup>th</sup> Infantry Division pulled into the area.

We walked to another field where there was an American lieutenant (90<sup>th</sup> Infantry Division) dead, with a hole through his head. He had been writing in a notebook: "The mortars are closing in." His wallet was strewn around, money taken, and only his family photos left. There were four dead G.I.s and four dead Jerries lying there at this hedgerow. They must have been fighting hand to hand when mortars hit the trees and killed them. They are a pitiful sight. There are dead cattle everywhere.

The 79<sup>th</sup> boys are firing Jerry rifles and machine guns in the area. They are green and don't understand what the sound of a German weapon means to other soldiers. They will find out the hard way when a pocket of Jerries is bypassed.

I went to bed about 11:30 p.m. but I could still see those bodies. I did not sleep very well and there were planes overhead and the ack-ack fired at them. A piece of flak came singing by and landed in the woods nearby. There were heavy concentrations of Artillery fire. A 155 mm rifle unit moved into the next field and opened up a little later, almost knocking us out of bed.

**June 18, 1944**

Near Saint-Clair, France

I got up at 7:30 a.m., as we are supposed to move. We packed and moved at 8 a.m. We went through a town, which was in utter ruins (Pont l' Abbe). There were a few dead Jerries and American dead along the road shoulder. We moved into the 60th Field Artillery Headquarters' area; this is Saint-Clair.

There is firing all around. Our combat team, which consists of the 60th Infantry Regiment and the 60th Field Artillery Battalion, has wedged our way in between the German lines to the west coast of the Cherbourg Peninsula. Jerry by machine gun fire was able to break through our wedge at the rear of the Infantry, cutting us, the 60th Field Artillery Battalion, off from our 60th Infantry Regiment. Our 60th Field Artillery Battalion packed and pulled back. The Infantry came back and cleared them out, so things are back to normal for a while.

There are guns firing all around us. The Battalion (Headquarters Battery) took 13 prisoners. It turned out to be a German maintenance section that fell in with the Headquarters convoy by mistake in the mix up.

In the dark of the early morning, Medic Henry Shimkowski was shaken awake. It turned out to be a German soldier who said to Henry, "You my prisoner." He finally stammered, "No, you my prisoner." The German said, "You stay here in field," and he went into the woods. Henry took off in the other direction. It is so mixed up nobody really knows where the front lines are.

My section is feeling kind of rough and some are sick. Skoczylas ran into a doughboy patrol about 200 yards away. The German ack-ack is firing at our fighters and they are not too far from here. They shot down a P-47, which crashed not too far away. Some guns were firing below us, and we could see the high bursts not too far away. We are evidently in a narrow strip, splitting the German army apart. Lieutenant Obeldobel said that we aren't even supposed to be here, as it is considered enemy territory.

We had a make-shift supper. We watched the P-38s and P-47s bomb and strafe Jerry and watched their ack-ack (not so very far away). I fixed up a ditch and dug into it a bit to sleep in. We had some coffee. We no sooner got to bed than it began. There was a terrific barrage of guns until 2 a.m. It was evidently a German counter attack. There was small-arms fire and machine-gun fire just to one side of us. I was a bit jumpy as I thought they might break through, as the fire was so close. Bennet, Headquarters Battery, came by all packed and ready to take off. Not much sleep tonight.

## June 19, 1944
Near Saint-Clair, France

I was awakened early and told that we are to get ready to move out. It was 7:15 a.m., the gang and I arose, and we packed. We brewed some coffee and waited. Hot coffee deserves the Legion-of-Merit award. It is so reliable. It is the main factor in our lives. Without it I don't know what we would do. We are all confirmed coffee drinkers now.

We moved out about 10 a.m. We traveled through Sainte-Colombe (it was in complete devastation), and continued on for about six miles. We saw a few dead Jerries in the ditch and there were dead cows and horses everywhere. There were whole herds (15 or more in a group) dead. There was a lot of Jerry equipment around. We arrived about 10:30 a.m. and took our things off the truck. We are now located one mile east of Saint-Jacques-de Nehou. We had a K-ration dinner at 12 noon and it began to rain, so we just hung around. I leveled off a piece of ground to sleep on. There was a German 88 mm gun and a German truck burned nearby. There are two dead Jerries also. One is in the ditch and the other in the field.

Jack and I ran down to Division Forward, G-1, and turned in a report. They aren't too far away. We saw about 13 truckloads of German prisoners go by. In some of the trucks there were Russians and

Mongolians. They were in civilian clothes and were used as forced labor battalions. I went to bed about 11:30 p.m. and it was windy but had stopped raining. There were some planes overhead a couple of times, but not too many. The big guns rumbled in the distance. The Battalion is about 15 miles away.

Private Robert Carter was killed yesterday and Private Joseph P. Bonura wounded.

## June 20, 1944

1 Mile east of Saint-Jacques-de-Nehou, France

Sergeant Nix awoke me this morning and said that Captain Tooley is looking for an area to move to. I got up 9 a.m., and dressed. We had a slip-shod breakfast, and then I shaved and cleaned up.

Charley Nagy and I walked up to Saint-Jacques-de-Nehou. There are refugees coming by and there were some Russian Labor workers in the 9th Division Prisoner of War Camp. We came back and I was writing when we got March Order. We moved about 12 miles in all, near Grosville. It is pretty country and the houses were unmolested by the war. Every now and then on the main road there were burnt spots where German vehicles had been hit, burned, and cleared away.

We passed a garage with a couple of German 88 mms in front of it. There were plenty of dead animals around and one horse had his head completely severed. We moved our trailer over by the second field. I walked up and around the little town but there wasn't anything there. They were making coffins as two bombs killed 25 people in the town. They were digging graves in the churchyard.

The boys got some cider (hard). We were told that we had better be ready to move back at a minutes' notice. This means that they may have to retreat fast. This has happened to the Battalion once or twice before. We were on the alert and told to man the hedgerows with our guns drawn. The Service Battery guys captured five Jerries and earlier had grabbed two Russian Laborers. The Russians have to be cleared, and

15

probably Okayed, and sent back to Russia when it's all over.

A Frenchman called the guys and said there were Germans in a house nearby. Some of the Service Battery guys got them but had to go into the bushes to get two of them. We all slept close by and in our clothes as we have to be prepared to move out in a hurry if need be. I had a good night's sleep.

## June 21, 1944
½ mile North of Grosville, France

We got up about 9:45 a.m. and had breakfast. The boys got some of their things out and did some of their back work. The alert seems to be over. It is actually chilly, so we built a fire and cooked our meals on it. I had a glass of cider and a drink of Cognac. We hung around all day. I walked out to the road in the evening. We were talking and some German 88s came singing through the air and were landing not too far away, on the other side of the area. They appear to be hunting for the 155 mm rifles of ours over there.

Two Jerry Prisoners rode by in a 47th Infantry Regiment jeep; one was wounded and bloodied up. I stayed out by the road and talked and watched people go by. The German Nebelwerfer (six-barreled mortar) landed a few close to us, a few times during the day.

We listened to our phonograph. I went to bed about 11:30 p.m. and it was still daylight.

Technical Sergeant Clayton was wounded today.

## June 22, 1944
½ Mile North of Grosville, France

I had a great night's sleep and awoke to Sergeant Ferguson's voice. He's down here to get some orders cut. I got up about 10 a.m. and had a 10-1 breakfast, as usual. I walked up by Service Battery and sat on the ammunition boxes, watching the Battery's 5th section load.

We are to attack Cherbourg at noon today. The Americans have dropped leaflets telling the Germans to give up or be bombed. Eight German planes flew over. They strafed the new Corp dump and we could hear the ammunition exploding. They went over the second time and there are now about 12 of them. Four of them came streaking towards us. They bombed our Battalion area and the ack-acks were firing at them. They came right overhead and seemed to be almost marked like ours; in fact they looked like P-47s. The fellows in a better angle said that they were German.

Our planes laid it into Cherbourg about 1 p.m. and the whole place is smoke and dust. It is smoky all through our area.

We went to bed about 11:30 p.m. The German planes started coming over. I didn't sleep any too well.

## June 23, 1944
½ Mile North of Grosville, France

I got up about 9:30 a.m. when I heard Sergeant Burrows say that Captain Tooley was going back to the Division Rear Echelon. I hurried about and got dressed and ate quickly. We went to Ordnance first and then on to Division through Grosville, Bricquebec, and Saint-Jacques-de-Nehou. They are about five miles from here and about 19 miles from us. We passed fields of dead cows and Jerries, and the summer sun is beginning to take its toll. We now know most of the bad spots. As we approach, we hold our nose and the driver floors the jeep. We hold our breath as long as we can. One cow had a hole in its stomach and its intestine hanging out and it is listing badly. When we returned later it was on its back with four legs sticking up in the air. A lot of the cows are moaning badly as they have not been milked. This terrible smell is what is known as the "Perfume of Battle."

At Division I went to the Adjunct General, talked, and did my business. They are located in a villa. I visited Frank Page who was nearby while I was here. We came back about 1:30 p.m., ate dinner, and washed my jacket. I signed and checked some papers.

Private Villereal was horsing around (he is the Battery bugler). He blew the Charge call for the fun of it. Immediately after this the German guns all opened up and a shell whistled over our head. The guys kiddingly said they were going to kill him. He quit and lay down in a safe place.

Lieutenant Kelly was wounded pretty badly this afternoon; and a few of the men got nicked. I went back about four miles looking for the Clearing Company that probably would handle his case, to find out his condition. No luck.

We heard that one of the A-Battery gun crews had a muzzle burst. Lizon was killed (decapitated and hand severed). Barhight and Corbett were wounded.

## June 24, 1944
½ Mile North of Grosville, France

I got up about 9:15 a.m. and did some work. We have to get out reports, so I decided to go to Battalion to get the information. I did not have transportation so I sat by the road and got a ride with a C-Battery jeep. The Battalion is about seven miles up. I walked from C-Battery to A-Battery and spoke to some of the fellows. I went to Headquarters Battery and the Medics. C-Battery had some casualties when one of the guns had a premature burst. It killed Loftin and knocked Phelps arm off and hit about four others. The colonel wanted to see me so I went over there. He is going to write decorations, and I have to make them out.

I got on the back of a ration truck and came back. We stopped at C-Battery on the way. I talked with my former roommate (in England), Tatt Pritchard, and Captain Parish. I picked up Loftin's personal effects. A few Jerry shells whistled over and down the valley.

After getting back, I picked up my mail. We had the Rosary, Confession, and Communion at Service Battery by Father Connors. Some Jerry shells were whistling by and landing close for about 15 minutes. We had a parachute alert tonight.

Private Gonzales was wounded today.

## June 25, 1944

½ Mile North of Grosville, France

I got up at 8:15 a.m. and got ready to go to church, as it is Sunday. I cleaned up and had some cereal, dressed in olive drabs, and went to the 9 a.m. Mass at the local church with Captain Tooley. The women have funny hats; they remind me of the ones worn by the Dutch. They are starched and colored black and white. Mass was short and a bird flew up and down during it all. There were about 50 people, all old women and young kids. Also there were about eight G.I.s.

June 25, 1944. Grosville, Normandy, France. They brought us flowers and eggs. We played the phonograph for them and gave them candy.

Harry Hammer and French children

We came back to the area and did some work. In the afternoon four little kids visited us. There were three girls and a boy. We fed them, played records for them and they had a good time. I took a picture of them.

It began to sprinkle. We hung around in the evening talking with Service Battery guys. There was plenty of noisy artillery during the night.

## June 26, 1944

½ Mile North of Grosville, France

I got up as it was raining. It was about 9 a.m. I dressed, rolled up my stuff, and covered it over. It was pouring by then. The fellows were all under their canvasses. Sergeant Nix, Harry Hammer, and I put up the tarp and we got soaking wet.

I had some material to read and then we had breakfast. It rained throughout the day. We pulled the trailer to the tarp, and the fellows worked out of it. We did quite a bit of work today, despite the rain. We had a rush job to do for the colonel, on awards. We got some mail as Carter (Mail Clerk), sorted it out here when he returned from the Post Office.

## June 27, 1944
½ Mile North of Grosville, France

I didn't sleep any too well as it was raining. I covered up so I wouldn't get sprayed. In the morning the sun began to break through. Sergeant Burrows came around and told us to dry our stuff and get ready to move this afternoon. We had breakfast and packed everything. It is nice out now and we were ready to move out at 2:30 p.m.

Our truck could not make the narrow turn, so we went to Grosville to turn around. We got a big brick between our dual wheels and had to stop in town and take the wheel off to knock it out. Raymond Rust (Rusty) was our driver. There is a big crowd of people watching us.

We went to the new area by ourselves. We took the back way, as I knew the road. We pulled in to the area (near Vasteville), and we are in enemy artillery range. There are some of our 155 Howitzers firing over our head. There is a German 280 mm dud in the next field. It plowed the dirt but didn't explode. Shells are whistling over and landing nearby. I dug a sleeping hole.

## June 28, 1944
½ Mile West of Missent near Vasteville, France

I didn't sleep well at all, as there was ack-ack and planes overhead during the night. A shell or something came screaming over and we all sweated it out.

I ate breakfast and then got a truck to go to Division Rear at Saint-Jacques-de-Nehou. We started out and I made out pretty well on the right way to turn. We went through Grosville and Bricquebec to Saint-

Jacques-de-Nehou. When I got to Division I found out they moved. There were all kinds of traffic and we kept asking Military Policemen for directions and finally found a sign saying, "To the Rear." We were then beyond Grosville, heading for Les Pieux. A Military Policeman sent us on the wrong road. We finally found them in a castle, by the sea, in Flamanville. I accomplished a few things and we came back.

We traveled 70 miles in all. I ate and then went up to the Battalion, about five miles ahead. I spoke to the colonel and the boys. I fixed a few things up. It was quiet up there. I came back and dug my sleeping hole a little wider and deeper.

## June 29, 1944
½ Mile West of Missent near Vasteville, France

I didn't sleep any too well. There were occasional ack-ack bursts at planes over head. The 155s fired off and on during the night and especially early in the morning. We are all working this morning and afternoon.

Zimmer, who use to work for me in the Command Post in England as a runner, was killed at the Observation Post. Szczygiel was injured and a 180 shell hit Private Jenkins.

It rained like heck all afternoon. Just before it began, we watched our planes strafe the enemy. We could see the planes machine guns spit fire.

My tent stayed fairly dry, considering the rain. We sat around reading newspapers and listening to the phonograph in the evening. It was still raining.

## June 30, 1944
½ Mile West of Missent near Vasteville, France

I had a fair night's sleep, although there was a little ack-ack fire at a few planes. The Germans threw a lot of star shells (illuminating shells) up in the distance.

I got up at 9 a.m. and the sun was out. I cooked bacon, canned ham, eggs, and coffee. It became overcast with rain clouds. The sun came out occasionally. I hunted around for transportation to the Rear Echelon, but I couldn't get any. The Battalion moved up a few miles. I finally got a ride to Division Rear with Captain Tooley and we stayed there a couple of hours. I completed most of my business. I even had to type out a Pay Transfer Account on a killed in action (KIA) at Finance.

We got back about 4 p.m. and I ate something. I then hitched a ride with the Medics to Battalion to straighten out some things. A-Company of the 39th Infantry was moving up as we went. The Batteries were firing occasionally.

I went to C-Battery and they said the Battalion had a rough time of it last night. I came back and it began to rain. We played records.

Propaganda flyer dropped
behind enemy lines.

# Chapter two: July 1944

### July 1, 1944 to July 31, 1944

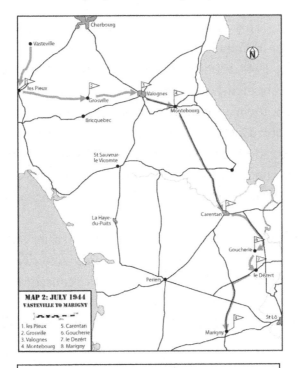

Cotentin Peninsula and Northern France

July 1944 Historical Overview
July 1944 Corps Assignments:
First Army, 12$^{th}$ Army Group
July 1 – July 31, 1944 - VII Corps

General Overview

After the successful capture of the Cotentin Peninsula, the Allies spread out into Northern France. The terrain here consists of fields separated by hedgerows. This time is often referred to as "Battle of the Hedgerows", or in French "bocage."

On July 20, 1944 a failed attempt on Hitler's life took place. The conspirators were high-level German military Officers.

Sainte-Lô, a town in northern France, was of military importance because it occupied a place of strategic crossroads. The Battle of Sainte-Lô took place during July 1944 and included a massive Allied bombardment, both from the air and ground. The massive aerial bombardment from thousands of Allied aircraft was called Operation Cobra.

Operation Cobra began on July 25, 1944. Disaster struck when the bombs fell short, falling on their own allied American troops. The reason for this error has been debated, but the consequences were not. Many casualties resulted, including General McNair. The bombing caused almost complete destruction of the town of Sainte-Lô.

9th Division Overview: The month begins with a rest period in Les Pieux, France. After this short rest, the 9th Division moved out of the Cotentin Peninsula and into central and northeastern France. They participated in the Battle of the Hedgerows and the Battle of Sainte-Lô.

On July 25, 1944, the 9th sustained many casualties because of Operation

\*\*\*

*July 1, 1944*

½ Mile West of Missent near Vasteville, France

I had a good night's sleep in the tent and got up about 9:30 a.m. It is overcast. I got the dope for the Officers' partial pay. I am busy as heck and the boys are working on the payrolls and figures. We worked most of the day on records that are to go out.

The Cotentin Peninsula is completely ours now. Only stragglers and snipers are left. Sanders, Noverio, and Caton went souvenir hunting. A sniper shot Caton through the arm three times.

In the evening we sat around talking. The Battalion is moving back tomorrow to a rest area near Les Pieux. It is raining out.

## July 2, 1944
½ Mile West of Missent near Vasteville, France

It rained all night. I got up about 4:45 a.m. and packed my stuff. It is drizzling out and everything is wet. We packed the truck and trailer and we moved out in the road to await the rest of the Battalion. We ate breakfast while on the side of the road waiting. We moved about 7 a.m. We had been delayed because someone had screwed up the convoy (34th Field Artillery?). We moved about eight miles. The boys threw out cigarettes, candy, and everything else they could think of as we went.

We stopped in Les Pieux a short while and the guys are throwing out everything. The people were sticking their heads out of the windows. They threw things to the second story even. One woman got up out of the tub to look out of the window to see what was going on. We pulled into the new area. It is beside some homes and there are some Polish families here. The boys are speaking to them, as Skoczylas and Wisniewski and a few others speak Polish fluently. It is drizzling so we set up a tarp and the boys put up their tents in a nice orchard. We also put up the pyramidal tent. We took most of the day to get organized.

We went to Sunday Mass in a farmhouse held by Father Connors. This new area is near Les Pieux.

## July 3, 1944
2 Miles West of Les Pieux, France

I had a good night's sleep. We have a lot of work to do as we have the payroll and various other things to get out. The colonel is screaming bloody murder about awards and other things that are supposed to get out. I think he is blaming me for some of it. But a lot of it isn't my work anyway, so I don't care. I have enough personnel work to keep me more than busy. Most of the boys finished their payrolls.

I took the Officers' payroll to Finance at Flamanville and took some pictures of their castle. Napoleon stayed here at one time. It has towers and a moat and even some palm trees. We came back and had to finish up some recommendations for awards. We worked until 1 o'clock in the morning.

## July 4, 1944
2 Miles West of Les Pieux, France

I got up about 7:10 a.m. as we are alerted that we may move today, and they want us to clear up various things before we move. I kept away from the Battalion area as the colonel is still screaming bloody murder over the awards not getting out. The enlisted men's payroll was turned in the afternoon.

We have a band concert this afternoon - or should I say this evening - at 7 p.m. Our own Division band put it on and they are very good. Some civilians were also there. I went to it and talked with some of the

July 4, 1944. Les Pieux, France. Field Artillery Band.

officers. Corporal Hamburger wanted to talk to me. He is concerned that his mother will hear of his being wounded (second time) and will be worried. I told him what would happen and put his mind at ease. I went to the movies in the barn and it was good. We all sat on the straw floor.

P.S. Corporal Hamburger was killed 16 days after this on July 20, 1944.

## July 5, 1944
2 Miles West of Les Pieux, France

I got up about 8:30 a.m. I had a good night's sleep. There were some planes over low last night. One you could almost hit with your hat. They (Germans) bombed Cherbourg.

Today is payday for the Officers and men. I worked on various things and we are trying to clean up everything. I inventoried Lieutenant Kelly's effects and a couple of other hospitalized men's effects. It sprinkled for a short while but turned out to be a swell day.

There was a live stage show at Battalion in the afternoon. It was pretty good. There were French chorus girls and clowns.

I ran the personal effects back to Quarter Master at Grosville and then I took the payrolls back to Finance in Flamanville. I looked up some circulars for the colonel in the evening. I talked with Major Elliott, Lieutenant Tom Gaffney, and Captain Williams while in the Battalion Command Post area.

## July 6, 1944
2 Miles West of Les Pieux, France

I had a good night's sleep, only awakening once or twice when planes were going overhead very low. There is the rumble of cannonading in the distance.

I got up about 8:40 a.m. and cleaned up. I cooked myself some powdered eggs (German) with bacon, coffee, and German powdered milk, and it was tasty. I cleaned up some work and answered a few telephone calls at Service Battery. I stripped down to the waist and went over to the orchard and caught up with my diary.

In the late afternoon I took down some Pay Transfer Accounts and Soldier's Deposits (about $6,000 dollars) to Finance at Flamanville. I came back and hung around for a while and then went to the movies at the barn. I went to bed about midnight.

## July 7, 1944
2 Miles West of Les Pieux, France

I got up at 9:30 a.m. and cleaned up. I cooked bacon and canned ham and eggs. It was sprinkling out. I cleared up the morning work and then ate dinner. I cleaned my mess equipment and did some work in the afternoon.

I was going to the movie at 6 p.m. but the generator broke down. I came out and met Captain Tooley and Lieutenant Obeldobel; we went to Mass at the 34th Field Artillery area. I came back and hung around the tent. All the French kids were here and the Polish girl. The Polish girl is actually a pretty young woman, whose French husband has been taken by the Germans. They use them as forced laborers.

We played ball with the kids. One of the kids said four American soldiers came to their house last night and demanded cider. They didn't get any, so they took the grandmother's watch. I sent a note to Captain Tooley. He had a formation and the guilty party confessed, before the woman identified them.

## July 8, 1944
2 Miles West of Les Pieux, France

I got up about 9:15 a.m. and had a little breakfast. One of the young women came over to give us a live rabbit but we couldn't cook it so we didn't take it. I cleaned up and did some work. I worked most of the day on various things which kept me pretty busy. One of our lieutenants was sent back to Division Rear to be reclassified. I talked with the little French kids.

I went to Division Rear in Flamanville about 5 o'clock and turned in Lieutenant Kelly's Silver Star and some Pay Transfer Accounts to Finance. As we were coming back we noticed C-Battery striking tents. We got back at 6:30 p.m. and got March Order at 7:30 p.m. We packed and knocked down everything. All the people are watching us, including a couple of pretty girls. Big formations of our planes went over. We moved about five miles to one mile south of Les Pieux.

## July 9, 1944
1 Mile South of Les Pieux, France

I did not sleep well as there were all kinds of airplanes overhead all night. I got up about 6:40 a.m. and packed my things. We had a little breakfast, lined up, and left the area about 8 a.m.

We hustled right along. We went back through Les Pieux to Grosville and on to Valognes. Valognes is sure shot up and some of the downtown section is just blocks of rubble. We went through Montebourg and Carentan. We pulled into our area a few miles beyond, near Carentan. The 30th Infantry Division is here somewhere. We set up the pyramidal tent and our own kitchen. We had dinner and sent out a few reports. It is sprinkling. The cannonading and machine gun fire is not too far away. We hung around; most of us are sleeping in the big tent. We retired about 10:30 p.m., and then Rusty came in and talked for a while.

## July 10, 1944
4 Miles South East of Carentan, France

I had a fair night's sleep; I awoke suddenly once when the 90 mm, 40 mm, and a machine gun opened up on a plane overhead.

I got up about 9:15 a.m. and cooked some powdered eggs and coffee. I got out some reports and censored some mail. It is drizzling off and on. I wrote in my diary and cleared up some paper work. It was chilly but I wanted to get clean, so I took a lightning sponge bath and washed my clothes.

We got a form to fill out from the colonel, and we all filled it out. We got some papers and booklets on France. We went to bed about 11 p.m. Once during the night the ack-ack opened up on a plane. The ack-ack guns are nearby and the shells whistle overhead and break. A piece of flak whistled in nearby, so I put my helmet on.

## July 11, 1944
4 Miles South East of Carentan, France

Sergeant Nix came around about 7 a.m. and said that they didn't know whether they are going to move out or not. I was tired so I rolled over and finally got up about 8:30 a.m. It took a while to cook breakfast. We all cook our own.

I walked down to Service Battery Orderly Room. I borrowed a jeep to go back to the Rear Echelon. I left about 11:15 a.m. We took a left on the hard road and were traveling right along. We passed the Artillery Battalions and were coming to the Infantry. We decided that we were going in the wrong direction. We went back through Carentan to Bosville and then to Division Rear at Hiesville. I went to Finance and then Adjunct General. I stopped at the Inspector General and the colonel gave me a song and dance on a Line of Duty case. I got back about 2:30 p.m. I ate and worked until suppertime. We ate on an improvised table of boxes. We retired at dusk, which is about 10:30 p.m.

## July 12, 1944
4 Miles South East of Carentan, France

I had a good night's sleep, only awakened once, when they opened up on a plane. Some flak fell close by; there was plenty of 90 mm action. I got up about 9 a.m. and cooked myself a pretty good breakfast.

I got the reclassification case thrown in my lap. Sergeant Nix has just left for Division Rear in a jeep. Now I have to go back. Charlie Nagy and I borrowed a little German vehicle, actually an English-made Standard. It was so light it was all over the road. We went through Carentan to Hiesville and Division.

I didn't get any cooperation from Division Adjunct General. They were blaming me for a couple things that I didn't have anything to do with. We met Sergeant Nix there. We started back but had forgotten to stop in at the Inspector General. We turned around and started sliding sideways. The rear wheels were in the gutter and we almost turned over. The car won't go in gear so we pushed it into a field. I bummed a ride to Division Headquarters and from there bummed a ride to Noisy Observation Post. From here they took me back to Service Battery. I returned back to the car in a wrecker and we towed it back.

July 12, 1944. Near Carentan, France. Our captured vehicle we almost turned over and had to be towed back.

I hung around after supper. We had a raid by two German planes about 11:30 p.m. and they came in low, right overhead. The 90s and everything else opened up on them. The flak whistled all around. They dropped a couple of bombs.

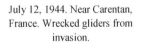

July 12, 1944. Near Carentan, France. Wrecked gliders from invasion.

## July 13, 1944

4 Miles South East of Carentan, France

I got up about 7:45 a.m. and hurriedly cleaned up. We ate a B-ration breakfast at Service Battery, for the first time in France. We had a good breakfast at that.

We got March Order about 10 o'clock. It was quite a surprise. We lined up and moved out about 11:30 a.m. We moved about five miles to Headquarters Battery's old area, near Goucherie. There are beaucoup dead cows and signs of where Jerry dug in all around. B-Battery is still in the next field.

We set up our pyramidal tent on one side of a hedgerow and B-Battery guns are firing on the other side. There are quite a few of our Artillery guns still behind us. We have a nice corner next to the Service Battery Command Post. (They have a radio). We had a B-ration dinner.

I helped Nagy fix up the lieutenant's reclassification case. We had a B-ration supper, after which Father Connors had Mass. I was busy and had to go to the Battalion (about 5 miles forward). I had the colonel fill out some papers and I settled some other business. I came back and read my mail and wrote. It is raining.

## July 14, 1944

1/3 Mile North of Goucherie, France

I did not sleep at all. The mosquitoes were fierce and it was too hot to get under the covers. It was noisy also as the guns were firing over us, the hollow sound of them speeding through the air keeps one awake. There were machine guns (ours and theirs), which sounded close. The Artillery fired all night.

I got up about 8 a.m. and had a good breakfast of cereal, pancakes, and coffee. I collected the reclassification case and worked with Charlie Nagy typing it up.

I ate dinner and then went with Lieutenant Freeman through Carentan to Hiesville to Division. The reclassified lieutenant has been sent back to England. I came out and went with Lieutenant Freeman to Isigny and the Officer's Post Exchange. It is all G.I. clothes. We came back to camp. By fixing up some papers I completed the reclassification case and filed it away. I had Charlie Nagy type a recommendation for an award.

Two Jerry planes (Focke-Wulf 190s) came over. They drew streams of ack-ack fire. I crouched in the ditch beside the hedgerow. A spent 50 caliber went singing by our tent, cut a branch off the tree and went through the cover of Sergeant Nix's foxhole, which was about five feet from us. There were nine planes in all but we only saw two of them. The anti-aircraft fire shot one of them. There was a Nebelwerfer and Jerry's artillery shells landing not too far away.

## July 15, 1944
1/3 Mile North of Goucherie, France

I got up at 8 a.m. and went to breakfast. The big guns have moved up right behind us now. I kept the mosquitoes off of me a little better last night.

I went to Battalion with Lieutenant Obeldobel. I got some information on Zeltwanger (who I understand was a good boxer, back in the states), and Stokes who were killed today. I wound up at B-Battery, then A-Battery where I talked with Joe Zuba (Pawtucket, R.I.), who was on the phones waiting for a fire mission. The gun crew had chalked on the shell; "To Adolph from Dark Joe" (he always had a deep tan). They slammed it in the breach block and pulled the lanyard, sending it on its way to the German lines.

I finally found C-Battery and Lieutenant Jenkins, who was with Zeltwanger and Stokes. He explained that they got a direct hit on them yesterday by a German 105 and the bodies were badly mangled and unidentifiable.

I came back to Service Battery, ate dinner, lied down at 2 p.m. and slept until 4:30 p.m. I then went up past the Battalion to the

Quartermaster, in an effort to locate the Graves Registration Office and identify the bodies. I did not see the Officer, so I left him a note. I came back by the Battalion and I saw two of the Observation Post parties leaving to go forward with the Infantry. There was Lieutenant Ragland of A-Battery, and Lieutenant Wilson of B-Battery, and their parties.

Corporal Norder was wounded yesterday.

## July 16, 1944
1/3 Mile North of Goucherie, France

I got up at 8 a.m. and ate. I got a ride to Quartermaster and saw the Graves Registration Officer. He didn't have any record of Stokes. I came back to Personnel and did some work.

Captain Thurtle was shot through the back two or three times, his arms creased and also his head, yesterday. Two Jerries sneaked into the Infantry Command Post and raked the room with machine pistols; they killed a few doughboys (one was Shopinski, that excellent boxer for the 60th Infantry). The other doughboys mowed them down.

Lieutenant Johnny Ragland was hit by a shell and had his leg blown off, the other leg will come off and he has wounds and a fractured arm. Captain Rockwood got a hole in his leg to the bone and a broken leg. Corporal Delaney of Headquarters Battery was killed. Humphries and Botsford have concussions.

I made out the Battle Casualty report. The doughboys are taking a beating. They only advanced 400 yards today. I ran up to Battalion and got some information on the casualties. I then went to Division Rear, who are now only five miles back.

I got back the reclassification case again, and some more information. I then returned to our area. I met Lieutenant Duncan of Division Artillery and he is requisitioning more officers for us.

After supper I borrowed a jeep and a driver and ran down to the Clearing Company. I checked all our Battle Casualties' dispositions. I went into the hospital next to the Clearing Company and saw Johnny

Ragland. He was the picture of death (Shock). He still had one foot on but it will come off. His eyes flickered open and he looked at me and then shut them. The nurse asked me if I wanted her to awaken him, I said, "No" (it was too heart rending), "He needs all his strength." There are some pathetic cases in here. There isn't enough that can be said for these wonderful nurses. God bless them.

Johnny Ragland died a little later; I guess I was the last of the gang to see him alive.

## July 17, 1944
1/3 Mile North of Goucherie, France

I got up about 8 a.m. and had breakfast and I have plenty of work to do. I worked all morning and then ran up to Battalion before dinner. I tried to locate the Graves Registration Office but couldn't. I checked things at Division Artillery.

I worked in the afternoon for a while. I ran up to Battalion again as I am still trying to establish Stokes' death. I got in touch with Adjunct General and was able to establish his death. In the afternoon I did some more work at Personnel. In the evening I went to Battalion and got the colonel's signature on various papers. I got back about dark.

## July 18, 1944
1/3 Miles North of Goucherie, France

I got up at 9:30 a.m. this morning and there were papers waiting for me to act on for the colonel. Jack Markowitz made breakfast (a 10-1). I had bacon, canned ham, and eggs.

I worked on the battlefield commission, for Dougher, C-Battery, with Galfo. I had to write it up. I was very busy on this and decorations and payrolls all morning. I had a snack for dinner and worked right up until 5:30 p.m. I got a ride to Battalion and went to C-Battery and got the papers signed. I went to the Command Post and had the colonel sign them.

Captain Prince is back with us now. I headed back and stopped at Message Center, Division Artillery. A German Messerschmitt 109 flew over while I was at the Command Post. Everyone around fired at it. I came back and ate supper and then read for a while. We are to move tomorrow. Some of the gun Batteries have moved away.

## July 19, 1944
1/3 Mile North of Goucherie, France

I had a good night's sleep and ate. They are to come after us about 10:30 a.m. We packed up everything and are ready to move. They came after us about 1 p.m.

We went beyond the old Battalion Command Post and beyond Quartermaster. We pulled into a dirt road. A Military Policeman told us to take it easy as Jerry sees the dust rising up and throws 88s in.

We put up our tent and there is a dead Jerry in the ditch nearby. We have to move out of this area as it is to be taken by the First Army.

I have an attack of Malaria. I am knocked out. We moved about 9:30 p.m. to the new area. It is the old Division Artillery Service Battery area and is near Le Desert. We set up the tent and everyone feels lousy and irritable. There is a dead Jerry here that stinks up the area.

We heard Jerry overhead and he hung flares up away and bombed. Our ack-ack was terrific and we all took to the foxholes. Some flak whizzed by so I left my clothes on to sleep.

## July 20, 1944
1 Mile South West of Le Desert, France

About 2:30 a.m. shells whistling overhead awakened me. They landed up away from us. I was half way out of bed ready to go the foxhole. There were about eight shells in all. Soon after, Jerry threw about the same number of shells over here on our side. They whistled right over us and I was sweating out his short rounds. About 4 a.m. he started again and we all took to the foxholes. They were whistling and landing very close now.

I still don't feel well and I threw up twice, the Malaria attack is still with me. I rested until 11:30 a.m., got up, and George heated me some coffee. I had crackers and then shaved and took some Atabrine. There are Corp concentrations off and on. We are just behind our small guns and in front of the 155s.

I went to Division Artillery and came back. The 1st Infantry Division and the 4th Infantry Division are on our flanks now. I rested for a while and dug my foxhole a little better and got some logs to cover it.

These three fields are full of dead Germans, killed in their foxholes. The shells hit the trees here and explodes splattering right straight down, so to stay alive you have to cover your foxhole with logs. We all retired about 10:30 p.m. It was pretty quiet.

Corporal Hamburger, B Battery was killed at the Forward Observation Post.


## July 21, 1944

1 Mile South West of Le Desert, France

There was an artillery duel between our 155s and Jerry about 2 a.m. Jerry's shells were landing below a good ways from us. About 2:30 a.m. I was dozing when one of Jerry's shells landed right beside us. I was half way out of my roll and into the mud and on the alert. I waited a second and then I could hear the whistle of another shell. I jumped into my foxhole, in the mud, in my stocking feet. I lay there and he threw in about two more. A couple of the guys were in the tent hunting for their helmets, raincoats, and shoes. I yelled at them to get into their foxholes as it won't do any good to find their helmet if their head is blown off. Jerry sent in about two more but further away. Some of the shrapnel fell in our area. I lay in the damp hole for a while and then I got out and so did the rest. We were all lying down dozing until about 4:30 a.m., when they began to whistle in below us. We all got back in the holes again. I stayed for a while and then came back to bed, all covered in mud. I slept until 10:30 a.m., and then had a little breakfast.

It is a miserable day as it is raining. I scraped the mud off of my clothes with a knife. We set up a few desks to work and it rained all day. A Warrant Officer Junior Grade, from the 957th Field Artillery came over for a little advice. I fixed up my foxhole.

The big drive (St Lo Breakthrough) is supposed to start tomorrow if the weather clears.

They (Germans) tried to kill Hitler today.

July 20s. Le Desert, France. Foxhole home.
Charlie Nagy.

**July 22, 1944**

1 Mile South West of Le Desert, France

I lay in the damp foxhole on top of some Quincy Ledgers (Newspapers), wrapped up in a shelter half, and wore my helmet for a pillow. The artillery was blasting away and Jerry was firing in rounds below us. Planes rumbled overhead and the ground shook. They kept going, thank goodness. I heard Warrant Officer Bob Ramsdell asking someone who yelled "Gas…What is going on?" as some of them were wearing gas masks.

I finally got out of the hole about 3 a.m., got my bedroll, and slept above ground. I got a pretty good sleep after this. I got up about 10:15 a.m. and then I ate.

It is sprinkling and damp out. The boys are working on payrolls this morning. We worked all day and it is overcast and damp out. I dug my foxhole a little bit better until bedtime. I have to be careful as the next foxhole (eight feet away), has a dead Jerry in it. I don't want to jump into that one by mistake.

I was aroused about 11 p.m. by Jerry throwing shells right near us. He threw about ten or twelve in all. Around midnight I was awakened by men all around yelling and by guns shooting. I was up immediately, as I feared the Germans had broken through. Then I heard them yelling "Gas." Still half asleep I held my breath and put on my gas mask. Charlie Nagy didn't have one but I remembered a spare under the seat of the truck. I ran and got it and gave it to Charlie. He shook my hand in gratefulness. It seems that no one was overly eager to test for gas, by pulling the side of your mask away from your face and sniffing the air. I kept mine on for a while and we found it was a false alarm. It seems that a new outfit was moving up the street, in convoy, when Jerry threw in some smoke shells. This green outfit thought it was gas and yelled up and down the column, and of course all the outfits billeted in the area heard it.

## July 23, 1944
1 Mile South West of Le Desert, France

About 1:30 a.m. the shells started coming over. I rolled over and crammed against the hedgerow. They landed fairly close, about 12 rounds in all. It was damp and dirty sleeping. I dozed off and on. About 2 a.m. they had some more yelling and shouting about gas. I got up and listened and then went back to bed. About 6:30 a.m. (daylight), Jerry really began to throw in shells. They were coming over in volleys of three and five, for about a half hour. They were high and had that cutting sound as they go through the air. Some landed nearby, I lay against the banking. He fired about 25 rounds.

I got up about 10 a.m. and had breakfast. Charlie showed up and had a dirt ring around his face from the dirty gas mask and he showed me the mask. There was a hole in the side of it as big as his fist. We all had a good laugh. I really worked today and fixed records, boxed the wounded Officer's personal effects (Thurtle and Rockwood), and signed many things.

Service Battery had a detail today (volunteers), to pick up all the dead German bodies that are all through our area, some in foxholes. They are beginning to smell real bad and are becoming a health hazard. Eisenstein (Baltimore, Maryland. Nightclub owner) lead about five men on the detail. They all donned gas masks and have a rope. They made out pretty well on most but "Eisey" tied a rope around the arm of one over ripe Jerry in a foxhole and when they pulled, only the arm came up, they had pulled it right off the body. The smell was terrible and "Eisey" walked away, ripped off the gas mask and threw up. He quit right there. They finished the detail clearing about 18 bodies.

Later in the evening it cleared for a while and our planes came over. They strafed and bombed Jerry. You can hear the strafing plainly.

## July 24, 1944
1 Mile South West of Le Desert, France

I had a fair night's sleep. Planes had been over and a few fired at them, they were high, and even a 50 caliber opened up.

I got up about 9:30 a.m. and had a good breakfast and then did some work. I had a bit of lunch and rode with Warrant Officer Bob Ramsdell to Division Rear and then to Isigny, to the Officer's Post Exchange. It sure was funny to see the American Services of Supply (SOS) and new units in field clothes. Most of them with white faces, clean clothes, and chin straps hanging down from their helmets. In our outfit, and especially when you are under General Patton's command, it is almost a court martial offence to have the straps hang down.

This morning has been one of the noisiest we have witnessed. There are 240 mms, 155 mm rifles and 90 mms firing. The 240s projectiles sound like a freight train going through the air. They keep you wondering whether, it is incoming or outgoing mail, as the rebels (Southerners) say.

It was clear enough today for our planes to bomb. The fighters come over first. We watched and one of them seemed to drop a bomb not too far from us, it might have been an empty wing gas tank. Later the heavies came and bombed, raising smoke and dust. The Jerries must be sweating this out. The planes dropped silver strips of paper that are intended to disrupt the German radar. The raid didn't seem too effective because as the Americans withdrew during the bombing Jerry advanced and was in a protective area. It seems that a lot of the bombs landed on empty areas.

There weren't any shells over tonight for a change.

## July 25, 1944
1 Mile South West of Le Desert, France
Beginning of the St Lo Breakthrough

It was about 10 a.m. when I awoke to the rumble of guns all around. I could hear plenty of planes going over and I could hear the fellows saying, "Look at them all." I got up and there were lots of P-47s going over. I watched them bomb and strafe.

One P-47 seemed to be waving his wings, but he was trying to shake free an empty wing gas tank. It finally freed itself and sailed down toward our Battalion area. They got alarmed and foolishly set off yellow flares (denoting friendly troops).

Soon the Liberators began to come over in huge flights. They were very low, not much more than 2000 feet. They were bombing very close, even to us, just over the hill. We could see it all until it became too smoky and dusty. There seemed to be no end to the Liberators. It seems that they, seeing the smoke (from flares), started the bombing from this point.

We saw one Liberator smoking and then he fell out of formation. It quit smoking for a minute and then nosed down. He broke into flames and crashed.

Some of the Liberator's bombs hit very close to our lines. We saw another Liberator break into flames and then come down in a ball of fire. We saw a few parachutes blossom out of these two planes. They seemed so small and we cheered and punched our arms in the air rooting them down, almost like rooting for a local football team.

Another Liberator nosed down and twirled around and around, snapping off a wing at the narrow point of the wing structure, and crashed. We saw more than one of these Liberators snap off their wing, at this narrow point, after they were hit, and fall to the ground. It almost seems to be a structural weakness.

The planes continually drop silver strips to break up the radar beams and they are falling all around. The big guns all around us opened up to keep the Germans off of their anti-air craft guns. There still was quite a bit of German ack-ack but there was less and less as the raid continued. The planes dropped smoke directors (streams of smoke) marking the target area for the planes that follow. The sky was full of ack-ack, planes, and smoke.

As the Flying Forts started coming over, Morrison, George, Goin, and Snead, came tearing back. They said that the P-47, which shook off his wing tank, landed near the 60th Field Artillery Command Post, but the 155 gang nearby were the ones that set off the flares. They put up ground flares. The Liberator planes thought it was their target and bombed. They said everyone up there was scared, as it was Hell up there. There were nine killed and 21 wounded in the 155 Command Post. A bomb knocked down our Battalion S-3 and the Command Post tents. It was a 500-lb. bomb and landed a few feet from them. No one was hurt but many were shaken. The 15th Engineers received a direct hit on a truck loaded with dynamite and 15 were killed and nine wounded. I saw the explosion and the smoke go up. They really beat up some of the 47th Infantry Regiment as they bombed right up through them. It is rumored that Lieutenant General McNair was killed, as he was here as an observer.

A colonel from the 9th Air Force, who is the air-to-ground coordinator, has been trying desperately to contact the planes to have them start their bombing a little further up and away from the American lines. He isn't having much luck

The planes keep coming; there must have been at least 3000 of them. There are medium bombers now. The large shells passing overhead are whirring from their wings. A shell whizzed over our head in the afternoon. Jerry's machine guns and our field pieces are still firing. The 4th Infantry

July 25, 1944. Le Desert, France. Watching liberators bomb and being shot down

43

Division and 1<sup>st</sup> Infantry Division are moving up.

I rode up to the battalion Command Post, 2 ½ miles up the road. The fighters are strafing and bombing all the time. It is sure noisy around. The guns fired and fired with no let up. I slept in the hole as I expected the Luftwaffe over in retaliation. The ground rumbles and the din of artillery is heavy. There are machine guns and tank duels up forward.

Private Griffith was killed today and Private First Class Sabo was wounded.

## July 26, 1944
1 Mile South West of Le Desert, France

I had little sleep as the guns around us fired all night. The ground rumbles and the din rings in your ears. There was increased fire up forward. It is either tanks or mortars. The tanks were on the move all night; the big drive is on.

I got up at 10:30 a.m. and had a little to eat and then cleared up some work. I checked personal effects of hospitalized men and Private Griffith from A-Battery; a shell up forward killed him. I worked all day and into the evening. I checked casualties for all Campaigns.

It was just dark when we heard planes and then the familiar, Whoom!! Whoom!! of their bombs. Our ack-ack opened up and I took to the foxhole. I fixed my bed while the planes were in the distance and went to bed in the foxhole. The ground rumbles when the guns go off.

## July 27, 1944
1 Mile South West of Le Desert, France

I got up about 10 a.m. and started eating breakfast but wound up reading circulars and other things. Tony cooked my breakfast while I was working. I worked all afternoon.

In the late afternoon I went to the Battalion, passing through Les Champs-de-Losque, and then to Division Artillery, and then came back. I had supper and then sat around. Someone got a speaker for the radio tonight and it is nice to hear a radio for a change. We heard, which confirms the rumor, that Lieutenant General McNair was killed here in Normandy.

I had my clothes out to dry that I had washed earlier. I decided to sleep out on the ground tonight.

## July 28, 1944
1 Mile South West of Le Desert, France

Shortly after 1 a.m. there were two airplanes over. I was on the alert but they passed over. A short while later there were more planes. Sergeant Nix took to his foxhole. I was alerted and in a few seconds he dropped about six flares not very far away. Everyone was yelling, so I got my shoes and jacket on and got into my foxhole. I no sooner got in and there was the familiar, ca-whoom!! ca-whoom!! of his eggs. The ack-ack opened up on them but not too intense. There were many planes now and they were diving over us. They would let their bombs (sounded like basketfuls of personnel bombs) go. They came whistling down and landed all around. They hung flares by the end of the next field to us. They bombed all around us. They were around for about 40 minutes. I got out of the foxhole and went back to bed.

I got up about 9:30 a.m. and ate breakfast. I worked all afternoon on the payrolls. I wrote after supper. The news on the American front is good.

About 11 p.m., we saw flares and heard ack-ack a short distance away. I took to the foxhole.

## July 29, 1944
1 Mile South West of Le Desert, France

It was drizzling for a while so I decided to sleep in the tent. I had to get out and into the foxhole three times in the early hours of the morning. Finally, during the third raid, I threw my bedroll in my foxhole in disgust. I had little sleep, as there were planes over all night. They dropped flares and drew beaucoup ack-ack. A piece of flak sung by me.

I got up about 8 a.m., and had a B-ration breakfast. We have March Order. We packed things up and left about 10 a.m. We shuttled up past the Battalion area and waited in a field for the Battalion. They went some other way, so we left by ourselves about 12:30 p.m. We went through a wooded area, the one hit by the 3000 planes. It was havoc, just like the pictures of Belleau Wood or Chateau Thierry of 1918. The towns are just piles of rubble. We passed knocked-out German Mark IIIs and Mark IV tanks. We moved to the other side of Marigny.

It is sprinkling, so we just sat around and ate a B-ration supper at 4:30 p.m. and at 7 p.m. a Messerschmitt 109 was shot down in a flurry of ack-ack, a little way over. The pilot bailed out in a parachute.

I dug a sleeping hole and got in it. It was dirty.

## July 30, 1944
1 Mile South of Marigny, France

I got up about 8:30 a.m. as we are having an ordnance inspection of small arms. The dirt fell on me as I got out of the hole. I feel miserable and dirty. The first thing I did was wash and shave, and then I cleaned my pistol.

The gang brought their guns to Service Battery to be inspected. We set up a tarp to do the necessary things and sat around most of the day. We worked on essential things, read, and listened to the radio. Our planes have been going over. Two Messerschmitts streaked across with Mustangs on their tail. We watched the dogfight and saw one of the German planes go down. Their machine guns could be heard easily.

We retired about 10:30 p.m. It was hardly dark when Jerry was around. I saw the first plane clearly. I fixed my bed and retired. The planes were over all night. They dropped flares all around and bombed close by. I sweated them out.

## July 31, 1944
1 Mile South of Marigny, France

I got up about 10 a.m., ate breakfast, and worked.

Today is payday for the troops. I answered the telephone and worked. It is sunny today. Major Elliott and Captain Thivierge were around getting records out of the safe.

There was a parade in the morning for awards. Colonel Adams, Lieutenant Jenkins, Corporal Hamburger (Posthumous), and Corporal Delaney (Posthumous), got the Silver Star. Siegal, Templeton, Shaffer, Crabbe, Leymarie, and Hines, got the Bronze Star. Schaussau got the Soldier's Medal. I had written a few of the citations.

I took a bath and cleaned up. We are busy. I got a bottle of Cognac from the colonel. He gave one to each of the Officers. There was a USO show, I saw a bit of it but didn't stay. I worked after supper. I split the Cognac up among the section and then made my bed. There have been planes over all day and two Messerschmitts 109s went across the area.

The gang is collecting Pay Transfer Accounts and there are plenty. I worked until late and then listened to the radio. I slept in the hole. There were planes hanging flares and bombing nearby.

# Chapter three: August 1944

## August 1, 1944 to August 31, 1944

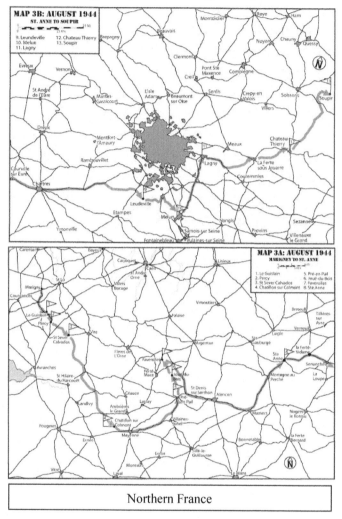

Northern France

August 1944 Historical Overview
August 1944 Corps Assignments:
First Army, 12<sup>th</sup> Army Group
August 1 to August 31, 1945 – VII Corps

48

General Overview

The Allies broke out of Normandy and made rapid advances south and southeast into France.

A large German force gathered in an area between Falaise and Argentan, France. During August 12 to August 21, 1944 the Allies attempted encircling maneuvers to cut off and capture these troops and prevent their escape toward the east. This became known as the Battle of the Falaise Gap.

Operation Dragoon, the Allied invasion in Southern France occurred on August 15, 1944.

Paris is liberated on August 25, 1944.

9th Division Overview: During the month of August, 1944 the 9th advanced eastward across France. They participated in the Allied closing of the Falaise Gap. The Falaise Gap refers to an area between Falaise and Argentan, France that was occupied by German forces. The Battle of the Falaise Gap occurred between, August 12 to August 21, 1944

By the end of August 1945 the 9th neared the border of Belgium.

\*\*\*

*August 1, 1944*

I Mile South of Marigny, France

I had a pretty good night's sleep but didn't get up for the B-ration breakfast. Instead I heated myself some coffee and had some crackers.

I went to work counting money and cleaning up the work. It is hot today. We got March Order to move at 1 p.m., but because we are so busy they are going to let us work and they will come back for us. We sat down to work and in about 20 minutes a Red Cross Club Mobile came into our field. They were just late, but we had coffee, doughnuts, and music. Three American girls operated it. We talked and ate until they came after us.

We went about 15 miles to the new area which is Le Guislain and it is a nice area. We set up the tarp over the trailers. We then all dug in. I started to sleep outside but the planes came over, so I got in the hole. It was too narrow, but I got in it each time the planes came over. I finally

August 1, 1944. Marigny, France. Red Cross Mobile.

gave up and just slept outside.

## August 2, 1944
Le Guislain, France

I slept fairly well after a while and got up at 8 a.m. We had a good breakfast. I came back and washed and shaved.

I went with Lieutenant George Obeldobel to Battalion. We drove along for about four miles. We passed the 47th Infantry Regiment marching along, and they are going into combat. They turned off the road and cut cross-country. We then passed a few Infantry Command Posts.

We then met some of our Headquarters Battery guys in a jeep checking wires, and they said we had better not go any further. So we turned around and located our Command Posts a mile or so back. I spoke to the colonel and picked up some papers at Message Center. We came back a ways to Division Artillery, then the Division Ammunition Officer (D.A.O.), and then on to Saint-Lo (22 KMs). Saint-Lo is just rubble; it is one of the worst beat up towns I have ever seen.

We got back in time for lunch. I counted the money for the Pay Transfer Accounts and it came to $13,000. We packed up our trailer, as we have to move at 7 a.m. tomorrow. There were enemy planes over all night and they dropped flares and drew ack-ack.

## August 3, 1944
Le Guislain, France

I got up about 6 a.m. after a good night's sleep. I dressed and had coffee. We had a little trouble loading but finally got everything on. We moved only about two miles and pulled into a temporary area, but ended up staying here. It is near Percy.

We set up a tarp against the ammunition truck. I puttered with my knife carving rungs for a camp chair while everyone else was fussing and fuming. In the afternoon, after a good dinner, we set up a few things and started a little work. It began to rain and it came down terrifically and it hailed also. The water wet everything, so I sat in the front of the truck.

We received word that Major Hochdoerfer was killed, the colonel wounded, and the driver Private First Class Hefter, Headquarters Battery, died at the Clearing Company. It seems they were in a jeep and they backed up to turn around when they backed over a Teller Mine. It blew the jeep upside down and made a mess of it. It is quite a loss.

I went to the Battalion to get the necessary information. I got the personal effects and talked to Captain Gray. We drove back in a damaged jeep. Captain Tooley and I are going to the hospital tomorrow.

## August 4, 1944
Near Percy, France

I got up about 7 a.m. and packed everything. We hurried and moved

51

out about 7:35 a.m. We moved down the road to the outskirts of Percy. We passed a dead G.I. (green) in the gutter. We pulled into an area. The first thing I did was wash and shave and the boys fixed my breakfast.

At 9:30 a.m. I took off with Captain Tooley. We went up to Division Artillery first and got some information. We then went back to the other bivouac area and picked up Colonel Adams' clothes. We took off for the hospital. We went through Saint-Lo and many other places. We got caught in the traffic there. We went almost to Bayeux. About 4 p.m. we found the hospital after many inquiries. We talked with the colonel. He will be all right. He has water on the elbow, a sprained hip and shoulder, and a few cuts. He expects to be back with us soon. We left and came back to camp. The traffic was heavy around Saint-Lo. We got back about 5:30 p.m.

I checked Major Hochdoerfer's things, ate supper, and put my cot and bedroll beside the hedgerow.

## August 5, 1944

Near Percy, France

I had a good night's sleep and got up at 9 a.m. I ate and had my things rolled up. It was about 11 a.m. when we were through, so I washed and waited to move at noon. It is hot and I stripped to the waist and bathed in the sun.

We finally moved out about 1 o'clock. We moved to the area that the Battalion had just left. It is about seven miles from here and near Saint-Sever-Calvados. We are down by the road with the ammunition train. The Orderly room is about one mile away. We put up a tarpaulin. I checked Pay Transfer Account slips.

The 34th Field Artillery is firing over our head and the 105s are just ahead. I put my cot up beside the hedgerow in the next field over. Jerry was over just after dark and also planes that sounded like ours. Jerry's shells landed just below us. I got a pretty good night's sleep.

August 5, 1944. Between Percy and Saint-Sever-Calvados, France. Convoy.

Harry Hammer pictured.

## August 6, 1944
Near Saint-Sever-Calvados, France

I got up about 8:30 a.m. and it is damp out. I had bacon and a fresh egg for breakfast. I got my things ready to move.

I worked all morning on Pay Transfer Accounts and signing papers. Then I got ready to go to Division Rear. I walked up to Service Battery Orderly Room, but there wasn't any transportation around. It is hot. We had a couple of good meals with fresh vegetables, (lettuce, onions), also butter and bread, and some 10-1 rations. I hung around all day but couldn't get a ride.

August 6, 1944. Near Saint-Sever-Calvados, France. Eating Dinner.

Frank Lovell eating dinner

53

Just after supper I went over to Supply. Father Connors said Rosary and Communion. I went to Confession also. Soon as it got dark a plane with a light patrolled around. The ack-ack fired at it. Planes are coming over low tonight.

August 6, 1944. Near Saint-Sever-Calvados, France. Open-air office.
Harry Hammer et al

August 6, 1944. Near Saint-Sever-Calvados, France. Getting dinner ready

George Neuhardt and Jack Markowitz

**August 7, 1944**

Near Saint-Sever-Calvados, France

About 1:30 a.m. planes dropped flares a short way over. The planes circled overhead, they bombed and drew ack-ack. I got out of bed, and the planes came over so low, I saw three of them just clearing the treetops, then I lay down. They were over all night long. I hardly slept and it is damp.

I got up early, as I have to have some information for the new Commanding Officer, Major Beets, out of the 26th Field Artillery Battalion. I worked all morning. About 1 p.m. I got a jeep, with King driving, and went in search of Division Rear around Marigny. We went through Saint-Lo and I took some pictures. We traveled a long distance and very fast. We couldn't find it. They must have moved.

I have the Malaria blues again but took Atabrine so it is in control.

August 7, 1944. Saint Lo, France

**August 8, 1944**

Near Saint-Sever-Calvados, France

I got up about 9 a.m. and ate breakfast.

I am real busy. I have $13,000 for Pay Transfer Accounts. I got everything collected and in the afternoon I got a ride to Division Rear, which is now in Saint-Sever-Calvados. I stayed in Finance from 3 p.m. until 5:30 p.m. I cleaned up all my business and came back. It is hot. I collected the Officer's pay and locked it up for the night.

Jerry was over and dropped flares and bombed in the distance. I didn't bother to get up.

### August 9, 1944
Near Saint-Sever-Calvados, France

I got up about 9 a.m. and ate.

I worked on the Officer's pay and got it all straightened out. I went to A-Battery on the way back on the ammunition truck. I walked toward the Battalion Command Post. I was sort of humming to myself when I gazed into the bushes and there were two German soldiers sort of staring at me. It startled me, but they were both dead.

I went to the Command Post and paid many of the officers. I was there until 5 p.m. I finally came back and did some work.

Jerry was over at night and dropped flares and bombed. They strafed close by but I didn't get up.

Sergeant Embry was wounded today.

### August 10, 1944
Near Saint-Sever-Calvados, France

I got up about 9 a.m. and feel a bit rough (the old Malaria).

I have a lot of work. I went to Battalion to see if I could do some good. I paid some of the officers and then went to the Batteries and did the same. I came to Personnel and worked. I wrote recommendations for promotions and awards. I checked money for Pay Transfer Accounts. I went to Battalion again and saw Major Beets, the new commanding officer.

I saw a P-51, who was strafing the enemy, come down in flames. The pilot bailed out and safely parachuted down.

I didn't get back to Service Battery until 10:45 p.m. I hung around for a while and then went to bed. About 3 German planes strafed nearby and also dropped flares in the distance. There was ack-ack overhead so I got up in my bare feet and sat by the foxhole. The planes dropped flares and bombed. I finally went to bed.

## August 11, 1944
Near-Saint-Sever-Calvados, France

I got up before 8 a.m. this morning, as I have to rewrite the recommendations for promotions. I rewrote them and typed half of one and then handed it over to the Battery Clerk.

I rode up to Battalion with the agent. I got a jeep and driver up there. I dropped in on B-Battery for information. I then went to Division Clearing Company, then to the 44th Medical, looking for Lieutenant Hall, who they say was wounded, but he was gone. I came back to Battalion, stayed for a while, and then came back to Service Battery with Tom Gaffney. I ate, got some work together, and then went to Division Rear at Saint-Sever-Calvados. I deposited money and sent $100 Pay Transfer Account home. I had a steak dinner there and it was good.

I came back to Service Battery, saw Major Elliott, and then finished some work. I brought out the half bottle of Gin and passed it around. A Jerry plane drew ack-ack nearby.

## August 12, 1944
Near Saint-Sever-Calvados, France

About 2 a.m. Jerry was around, he dropped his flares in the distance and bombed. I didn't get up. I got up about 9 a.m. and ate breakfast.

About 10:30 a.m. we got March Order, so we loaded up. We moved through Saint-Sever-Calvados and waited in a field. We did some work; the G-1 report, the morning reports, and a battlefield appointment to second lieutenant for Crabbe. We got March Order and moved out.

We were on the road all day. It was hot and dusty. We passed a field where they had a tank battle. There were about six Mark VIs and two of ours. For all the time we were on the road we only moved 45 miles. We passed the various

August 12, 1944. En route across France. Between Sainte-Sever-Calvados and Châtillon-sur-Colmont, France. Notice the puppy. It was a hot and dusty ride.

sectors, 28th Infantry Division, 4th Infantry Division, 35th Infantry Division, 1st Army Group, and the 2nd and 3rd Armored Divisions.

The 5th Rangers were hiking along the road. Who should I see but Harold Beston from the hometown, Houghs Neck, Quincy,

August 12, 1944. En route across France between Saint-Sever-Calvados and Châtillon-sur-Colmont. Mark 6 with 88. (mistakenly identified: Panzerkampfwagen V "Panther" (75mm)

Massachusetts. He saw me and yelled and just then our convoy stopped and the Rangers halted for a few minutes as they were turning off the road and into the woods. So I jumped out of the truck and we shook hands and had a chance to talk for a few minutes. Then our convoy moved out. We stopped after dark and bedded down in a field for the night. We are near Châtillon-sur-Colmont near Brittany.

**August 13, 1944**

Near Châtillon-sur-Colmont, France

I had a swell night's sleep. I only heard ack-ack once or twice. I got up about 9:15 a.m., dressed, and walked up to the truck.

I took a change of clothes and went down by the Service Battery Command Post. I got a pail and a half of cold well water and I took a nice bath. I came back and put up my bunk. I took pictures by the pool of people washing clothes. I washed my fatigues and went around in my shorts. It sure is hot and I am getting a burn. We didn't unpack anything. I bought some cider.

The news sounds good. We expect March Order tonight. We packed up and sat around until 9 p.m., and then we are supposed to move. At 11 p.m. they told us to go to bed but we would have to move out in a few hours. We are to follow the Armor and cut off the Germans.

August 13, 1944. Châtillon-sur-Colmont, France.
Typical French farming family. Kid has lollypop.

Harry Hammer

## August 14, 1944

Near Châtillon-sur-Colmont, France

There was ack-ack and a few planes in the early hours. I was up and headed for the trailer-once, I was going to get under it. The second time I stayed in bed but a piece of flak came singing by and I lunged against the bank. It landed close to me.

We got March Order about 4 a.m. and got loaded up and moved out at 5 o'clock. We traveled fast and got on the road to Paris. We were on a nice wide road and sped along. There aren't many signs of war around here. The Armored column evidently came through here. We pulled into a field for a while and then left a short while after. We pulled into a bivouac area across from the 60th Infantry, near Pre-en-Pail. We didn't unload. The Battalion and the 60th Infantry moved out later. The doughs are pretty well "cognaced." We had B-rations to eat. The Germans are giving up en-mass.

The local French people paid us a visit. We traded for butter, eggs, milk, cognac, and cider.

Some drunks in the 3rd Armored fired off their guns. We investigated it. We have a guard on duty as German stragglers are all around.

August 14, 1944. Near Pre-en-Pail. Captured vehicle.

**August 15, 1944**

Near Pre-en-Pail, France

I got a good night's sleep. We stayed packed up, as we didn't know whether or not we would move. We had B-rations and hung around all day. I received some messages.

I got a ride and went in search of Division Rear. I went through Javron and Couptrain and finally found them. I completed my work and I picked up a new officer assigned to us by the name of Bezold. I brought him back. I went to Battalion with him through Pre-en-Pail and Saint-Samson. I left him off and accomplished a little business while I was here. I came back to Service Battery and did some work before it got dark.

There is a Personnel Section beside us from the 87th Field Artillery, which is attached to the 3rd Armored Division. The Warrant Officer was talking to us. We met one of the guys in the Battery who used to be in our C-Battery, named Gasic. I remember he used to catch for us on the ball team when I played first base.

We packed everything up, as we are to move tomorrow.

**August 16, 1944**

Near Pre-en-Pail

I had a good night's sleep and got up about 6:30 a.m. We ate at 7 a.m. and moved out a short while later at 7:30 a.m. We went through Pre-en-Pail and Saint-Samson, past the old Battalion area. As we passed along I noticed in the gutter a German's leg from the hip down.

We pulled into a field a little way up. We are right beside the road. We put up the pyramidal tent and made a sign, which we put out on the road. We did quite a bit of work. We had B-rations all day.

There had been a Jerry in a nearby farmhouse, he left when we came in (according to a French woman). There are German stragglers wandering through the woods. Some of the fellows are hunting them. They got souvenirs only.

61

I was pretty busy all day. I fixed a foxhole and slept beside it.

The next town up is Joué-du-Bois. The Germans burned it down because the French resisted them.

## August 17, 1944

Near Joué-du-Bois, France

I got up at 8 a.m. after a good night's sleep. The fellows are out getting souvenirs (helmets and guns). We got word that we are to move at 1:30 p.m. We cleaned up most of the work and packed.

We moved through the burned town of Joué-du-Bois and there are beaucoup Jerry trucks knocked out. There were about four or five Jerries lying in the gutter. One bloated, green German is laying so close to the road that everyone is riding over his hand. We moved about five miles. We moved past the 84th Field Artillery guns, which were firing. We passed by the Artillery Battalions. We are in one respect in front of all Division Artillery guns.

We set up our tent in the corner of the field and this worried the Command Post boys. Jerry threw in some shells below us. We found out that they hit Lieutenant Jenkins, Lieutenant Kraft, Technician Fourth Grade Omasta, Private Lovett and also slightly, Householder, and Flipowitz. They were hit in the C-Battery chow line.

I dug a foxhole and Freddy Smart (from New Hampshire), helped me. I opened the ration bottle (quart of Red Label Scotch), and passed it around. Jerry pumped in some shells below us and they sure whistled.

## August 18, 1944

Near Faverolles, France

Jerry fired some more shells below us in the early hours of the morning. You can hear the "pung," as the shell leaves the gun, and shortly after that the whistle, and then K-Wham as it hits. It must be a tank. The boys could see the flash of the gun when it fired and the flash of the shell when it landed. I was on my elbows ready to dive into the foxhole if it came closer.

I had a good night's sleep. I got up at 7:50 a.m. and ate. I rode to the Rear Echelon (Division Rear) near Couptrain, in Supply's captured German vehicle. I came back and worked most of the day and later went to the 9th Clearing Company and the 42nd Field Hospital, to check on the casualties.

After supper I worked. The boys fixed Colonel Beet's German radio and we had some good music. There were planes droning over a few times after dark. Some planes had dropped flares and bombed in the distance. We believe that they are our planes.

The news has been good as the Americans are rumored near Paris.

## August 19, 1944
Near Faverolles, France

I had a good night's sleep and worked all morning and we are quite busy. I took a bath and changed into an olive drab uniform in the late afternoon.

We went to the Battalion (the Officers), and listened to our new General. He is the new Commander of the Ninth Infantry Division. His name is Major General Craig, brother of General Maitland Craig in the Pacific. Major General (our former commander), Manton S. Eddy, left this morning to be commander of the XII Corp.

I came back and inventoried the Officer's effects. It began to rain in the evening before supper. It rained on and off all night. I got out the cot and threw a shelter half over it and went to bed. It is hot and stuffy underneath and yet I get wet if I keep my head out.

## August 20, 1944
Near Faverolles, France

It rained pretty heavily and I felt uncomfortable. A plane droned around in circles overhead during the early hours. Some of my stuff got wet.

63

I got up at 8 a.m. and found out that my things are not wet. After breakfast I did a few things and then hopped in the Service Battery truck going to Mass (Sunday) in the church at Faverolles. It is about one and a half miles up the road. There is a shell hole just to one side of the altar and the head is knocked off the savior on the altar. Outside of that the church is nice. There was a good crowd. Sergeant Rouse rang the belfry bell. The rope almost pulled him up to the ceiling. Father Connors said the Mass, we had general absolution, and I went to Communion.

After dinner I got a haircut and washed some clothes. The sun came out good. It later became overcast and began to sprinkle. We all talked in the evening. We found out as we were going to bed that we are on a one-hour alert and are to move out early tomorrow morning. We slept in the pyramidal tent.

## August 21, 1944
Near Faverolles, France

It is still raining heavily; I got up and rolled up my bedroll. I put on my clothes and went to chow at 6:30 a.m. My raincoat was soaking and we are all wet. We came back and loaded the trailer and our bedrolls. We were all through about 7:30 a.m., and it was wet. I sat in the front of the cab with Rusty's dog, we just sat around waiting. We had dinner at 11 a.m.; they got March Order, so we had to rush through it. We moved out.

All along the road the people waved and some threw flowers. Some gave out drinks of cognac, cider, or calvados. They also gave out bottles of these things. Our boys got some calvados. We traveled a good distance, through Alençon and Montagne. Some are nice towns and not hit too heavily, especially Alençon. I never saw so many pretty girls as I did today. They were as pretty as a picture.

We traveled 72 miles to Sainte-Anne. I didn't pitch a tent. It began to rain so I went under the truck and I got drowned. I ended up in the cab of the truck with two blankets.

**August 22, 1944**

Near Sainte-Anne, France

I slept a little better than I thought in the cab of the truck, although I was a bit cramped. I opened the door of the cab and hung my feet out and slept this way for a while. I got up at 7:45 a.m. and had a good breakfast.

After breakfast I hung out my wet things. The sun came out and things began to dry. We set up the pyramidal tent. Everyone is drying out clothes.

We did a good deal of work. The clerks went to the Batteries and had the payrolls signed. I stripped to the waist and got some sun. We set up our radio. The kitchen is cooking the 10-1 rations. I saw some Jerry prisoners going by in a jeep.

At supper the yellow jackets were so thick you had to fight your way through to the plate. I put up my pup tent and a cot underneath it. We all sat around the radio and talked. I went to bed about 11 p.m.

**August 23, 1944**

Near Sainte-Anne, France.

I had a good night's sleep outside of the fact that the spiders were crawling over my face. We had breakfast at the kitchen at 8 a.m. We worked in the morning.

I walked over to the road and watched the traffic go by. I then signed and checked payrolls. I worked most of the day. In the afternoon the new colonel (Beets) had come around and checked on a few things. I started for the movies in the evening but found out that the bulb of the machine had blown out. We sat around and talked. It is raining fairly hard. We listened to the radio and the news is good. The underground has taken Paris, Marseille has also been taken, and Rumania has accepted Russian peace terms.

## August 24, 1944

Near Sainte-Anne, France

I had a good night's sleep even though it rained fairly hard. We have 10-1 rations to eat. I cooked an egg and bacon.

We packed up, as we are to move. As the time of 11 a.m. came to move, it began to rain heavily. They loaded the ammunition on and then we didn't have any space available to load our stuff on. Everyone is soaking wet and the fellows have to ride on top of all this, in the open. I am in the cab and so is Rusty's dog, Rita Cherbourg,

Near Melun, France. En route to Belgium. It was really hot. Raymond "Rusty" Rust with puppy, Rita Cherbourg.

who is between us. We rode about 20 miles in the rain. We passed a crashed Liberator, which was strewn all over the place. We pulled into a bivouac area near La Ferté-Vidame. We put up the pyramidal tent, in the mud and rain. It cleared up later and the sun came out. We cooked ourselves a good supper. I paid 200 francs ($4.00), for six-dozen eggs. We sat around after supper. It was clear and nice now. We watched an old Frenchman and his dog tend the cows. I slept on the cot beside the pyramidal tent, under the fly tarp.

## August 25, 1944

Near La Ferté-Vidame, France

I awoke to Sergeant Burrows saying we have to be ready to move by 11 o'clock. We had a breakfast of eggs and packed everything.

They came around and said that we have to wear olive drabs and helmets at all times. We are going to go about 100 miles. We started out, slowly at first. We traveled over a rough road for a good ways. Many of the trucks had to stop and repack. We traveled toward Chartres for a while and we passed many nice homes on the way. There were pretty girls and people crowding the roads, many were headed back to Paris. We were given tomatoes, cider, onions, and fruit. We threw cigarettes and candy to them. There were people waving all along the way. We stopped off and on and I talked to many girls along the road. The people are actually glad to see us. We pulled into an open field near Leudeville, pitched our bedrolls and went to sleep.

## August 26, 1944
Leudeville, France

About 7:30 a.m. they announced that we would have breakfast at the kitchen at 9 a.m. The puppy was chewing on my socks and jacket. I got up about 9 a.m. and cleaned up. We ate breakfast at 9:30 a.m. and then sat around.

We made our own dinner, cooking potatoes and eggs. We had tomatoes, onions, butter, cocoa, and crackers. It sure was a good meal. We sat around until about 1 o'clock or so and then loaded the truck on March Order. They changed their minds so we unloaded the truck. We had to unload it because Rusty has to leave with 5 other ammunition trucks. We just sat there with our stuff piled all over the ground. We finally got to move at 9 p.m. Before we moved, we talked with a Frenchman and his family. He spoke English, French, Italian, Spanish, and German. He was a card. We talked about Sicily.

It was dusk as we pulled out. We passed through the airfield, with all the burned Jerry planes. We drove through Arpajon and some other nice towns with tree-lined streets. It was dusty and hard black out driving. We traveled fifty miles and strained our eyes all the way.

## August 27, 1944
East of Melun, France

We got to bed about 2:30 a.m. and I slept beside the truck and a pile of cordwood. I awoke about 8 a.m. to the sound of March Order. I got

67

up and ate and walked around the mansion that was burned. The Germans used it to assemble airplane motors. Our incendiaries burned about six of the motors.

We moved out about 10:30 a.m. and passed through some towns such as Melun and Etampes. The people lined the streets and cheered, waved, shook our hands, gave us cider, cognac, and tomatoes. We crossed the Seine River and it was very pretty. We crossed on a pontoon bridge. We pulled into a field, just after we had passed the doughs again. We give them anything we have, candy, cigarettes and anything. They are lying beside the road, it is hot, and they are tired. They have their shoes off and are fixing their feet. As they lay on the bank they have their pants down, as

August 27, 1944 Melun, France.
Welcoming committee.

they are chafed from the uniform, it is so hot out. We waited in a field beside a burning granary. We pulled out and passed the doughs again. We finally pulled into an area and we are to stay here for the night.

## August 28, 1944

West of Melun, France

I awoke about 7:15 a.m. to an argument by someone. I got up and had some coffee and we have March Order. We left about 9:30 a.m. and cut this way and cut that way. We passed the doughs; they were loading on the sides of tanks instead of walking. We pulled into a field and they had a Jerry prisoner at the crossroads. The billeting party took him.

We started to cook dinner across from a beautiful mansion. They came around and told us that we were to get our guns and helmets and guard the hedgerow, as there were some German foot troops around. We did this for a while and then finished cooking the meal. We got March Order, to get out of the line of fire of the guns.

We heard that General Patton is in Germany or at least Luxemburg. We moved behind our guns and then we moved out of here. We passed through many towns and are evidently the first Americans to go through many of them. They gave us paper flags and eats. I got an apple from the old peoples' home; they were all outside with the nuns. We saw beaucoup pretty girls. We pulled into a small grove of woods and had supper here.

About 11:30 p.m. Jerry planes came over low. We all got up and watched them flare and bomb over away.

## August 29, 1944
Near Lagny

We are in a grove of woods. It is raining fairly hard this morning. I got up about 8 a.m. and had coffee and crackers for breakfast. We packed everything on the truck and then it stopped raining.

We got March Order about 10:30 a.m. We went through small towns and again are about the first Americans that they have seen. The people all wave and shake our hands and they throw flowers and other things to us. We throw them cigarettes and candy. We crossed the Marne River. It must have been the sector crossed by the English, Scotch, and Irish in WWI, as there was a large memorial to them in the town of La Ferté-sous-Jouarre.

We headed for Chateau-Thierry, of WWI fame. We saw German prisoners tended by the French. We pulled into a field about 15 kilometers from Chateau Thierry and ate. We moved to the tree line and are to bed down.

We started to eat and it began to rain. I had pitched my tent. I took the plate of potatoes, canned beef, bread and butter, peas, and tomatoes into the cab of the truck. I caught it on the camouflage net and spilled it all on the dirty floor of the cab. I just nibbled a little piece here and there. It reminded me of the story my cousin told me years ago. A friend of his, in France in WWI, got his first good meal in a long time. He dropped it in the mud and just stood there and cried.

Everything is damp.

## August 30, 1944
Near Chateau-Thierry, France

I had a good night's sleep. I awoke at 7 a.m. and we have to move out at 8 a.m. I didn't have time to eat, as we had to pack everything aboard.

We went through many small towns. They are poor farm towns and the former battle sites of the last war. Skoczylas is talking French and Polish with the people. There are many Polish families here (forced labor). We got tomatoes, apples, and plums. Tony Wisniewski is sick so I let him ride in the cab and I rode on top with the gang. I had a good time waving to the people and tipping my helmet like a politician in a parade. We got bouquets of flowers. We passed the site of the Second Battle of Marne. The people are rabid in their enthusiasm. They throw kisses and wave. The French Resistance (Underground) is all around with arms, patrolling against snipers and pockets of Jerries.

Just before we got caught in a traffic jam with some tanks, 45 Germans put up a fight ahead, but the doughs got them. I came back inside the cab, as I was too conspicuous (Officer's identification) to snipers. It began to sprinkle and the fellows got damp. We are still heading for Belgium. We passed a few signs of combat, a burned automobile with three burned Germans in it.

We bivouacked beside a canal, a couple of the boys went swimming and some rowed a boat. We are near Soupir.

**August 31, 1944**
Near Belleau Wood
Near Soupir, France

The German planes were over about 2 a.m. but they bombed a good ways over. We got March Order about 4 a.m. in the morning in the drizzle. I hadn't slept all night. As we stumbled around in the dark it began to pour. There was mud, darkness, and rain to make it miserable. We somehow or other got everything on. Everything was wet. We moved out at 6 a.m., all soaking wet and it was just getting light. It sprinkled as we went and we passed the doughs walking.

We went through Belleau Wood (what memories of the impressions of WWI it brings back). We were about the first elements through these towns. The tanks go through and we are right behind. The people are happy. They are lining the streets yelling, throwing kisses and flowers. The women are standing in the windows yelling and waving.

We passed an English Cemetery (WWI), with old zigzag trenches still across the field at Soissons. We met resistance a little ahead and the doughs and tanks went ahead to handle it. Our planes and guns took care of them. The boys spoke Polish to the refugees around.

One group of Resistance Fighters has a little car filled with Champagne. They are working from the rear of the convoy, throwing up to the guys bottles of Champagne. We got five quarts in our truck. It is from Reims and it is good. The boys are feeling happy.

Captain Tooley signaled a stop after we had moved about four miles. The guys are all bombed and staggering around. Captain Tooley was all shook up and had everyone go into the woods out of sight and bed down for the night.

**August 1944 Special Data**

The French are glad to see us. Most of the people here are imported forced labor by the Germans. There are a lot of Polish. Freedom to the French means they get their farms back. They in turn are kicking the Poles out. The Poles are hanging around wherever they can. They will probably be sent back to Poland after the war. Now they can have jobs on French farms, however. In Poland they had 15 minutes to pack and take their families here to France, sometimes in the middle of the night.

# Chapter four: September 1944

September 1, 1944 to September 30, 1944
France and into Belgium and Germany

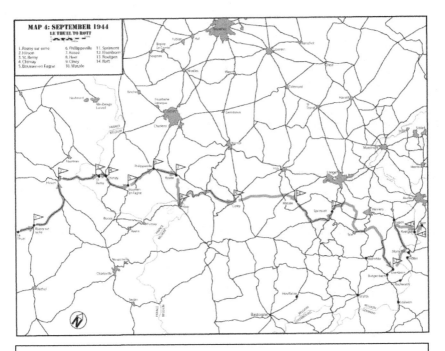

Northern France, Belgium, and Germany

September 1944 Historical Overview
Month of September 1944 Corps Assignments:
First Army, 12th Army Group
September 1 to 17, 1944 – VII First Army

General Overview

Allied troops are hampered in their forward movement by fuel shortages
The front is vast and includes Allied troops moving toward Germany from Italy, France, Belgium, and from the east, Russians.

September 1, 1944. The Allies enter Belgium.

September 13, 1944. The Allies reach the Siegfried Line in Germany.

September 17, 1944. Operation Market Garden in the Netherlands begins. This operation failed to meet its full objective of capturing a Bridge at Arnhem, but was able to liberate some Dutch towns.

The Battle of Aachen Germany begins.

9th Division Overview: The 9th was one of the first Allied troops to enter and liberate Belgium. They continued their onward easterly movement into Germany.

The Allied high command decided that while other Divisions would isolate and capture Aachen, the 9th Division would push south of Aachen, through the dense forest of the Hürtgen. This would be the beginning of what some would call "The Bloody Hürtgen Forrest Battle." It would rage on for months and include many American divisions. Yards of this heavily fortified woodland territory would be won and lost multiple times. Casualties, on both sides, were enormous.

\*\*\*

*September 1, 1944*

Le Thuel, France

We slept for the first morning in quite a while. I got up at 9 a.m., ate, washed, shaved, and got some sun. We got March Order at 12:30 p.m., went three miles and stopped in an apple orchard. We ate there and then moved on about four more miles. There were a few blown-out Jerry tanks and equipment along the way. There are enemy guns up ahead. We pulled into a field and stopped by a ravine. We sat around and had a good supper, then did some work. Private Hardy's orders came through, sending him to Officer Candidate School back in the states. He is a lawyer and has been accepted to the Judge Advocate General's Officers Candidate School.

I set up my cot in front of the truck. We are near Rozoy-sur-Serre.

## September 2, 1944
Rozoy-sur-Serre, France

About 2 or 2:30 a.m., I was lying in bed when I heard an awful droning sound. It was windy and chilly out. I could see all of the heads coming out of the bedrolls, as I was on a cot and could look down. There was a light coming through the air. At first I thought it was one of our night fighters with a light. As it got overhead there was another right beside it. They were very low and seemed to be gaining momentum. There was another right behind them, and then there was a horrible droning sound heard as they went overhead. It dawned on us that this was the "Buzz Bomb," or "Robot Doodle Bug." There were quite a few more, but the rest were to the side of us. Some of the gang watching them (we got up) saw the light go out on three "Buzz Bombs" and watched them as they fell. After they landed there was a huge red glow in the sky but no sound of an explosion. They are being launched not too far from here. The direction they are coming from and where they are going is unknown to us. We no doubt will hear later. They can be seen and heard for miles before they come and after they go. But I could not see any shape to them.

I got up about 9 a.m. Hardy came here on his way to the Rear Echelon, the first step on his way to the States. He is going back to the United States to get a commission in the Judge Advocates' Offices (he's a lawyer). Morrison, the driver, was here and he said a dud Buzz Bomb landed in the Jersey area.

We lined up to move at 11:30 a.m. and finally moved out at 1 p.m. We went through a few towns and finally stopped outside a town where we hear rifle fire. We waited while they fired. Evidently there were snipers there. We moved on again. As we passed through towns the people were coming out of hiding.

We headed for Hirson on the Belgium border. We turned and entered Belgium. The people here all speak French. They sure are glad to see us. They are all down to the trucks shaking hands. They are kissing the boys.

The Battalion is up a little ways firing our guns (105s). There is supposed to be plenty of Germans still up there. The people are still coming and talking.

A group of four came, the Mayor and a fellow wearing all his medals. They waited all day for Americans to come through their town but we are passing by a couple streets over (by-passing the center of town). They wanted us to parade through the center of town, but we couldn't. They were disappointed. Captain Tooley and some of his men went over later and made a sort of Official visit. They brought back a Jerry who had been left there. We moved off the road to a ravine by a brook. We talked until 11:00 pm and then turned in.


## September 3, 1944
Saut Picquet, Belgium

I had a fair night's sleep. It sprinkled and was very windy. I thought the tent would come down. It was cold when I got up about 9:15 a.m. I washed and about froze doing it. We started to eat breakfast when we got March Order. We finally collected everything together. We moved about five miles to a spot near Saint-Remy. We passed through neat villages. The people have all kinds of colored flags out. They are home made. Some are supposed to be American and have one star others must have sixty.

We ate and then I got the boys to work and cleaned up the back work. It was windy, so I had the tarp set up. We finished all of our work and then got March Order. We passed through Saint-Remy and Chimay. The towns are nice. There are stores with big clean windows. The architecture is a little different; it is more like the Dutch. The church spires are more like one would picture in Bucharest. They are round. As we neared Baileux, which is off the road a bit, the people all came to see us. They had a band playing and everyone was wearing small flags and yelling as we passed. The column had stopped once and I was kissed four times by the girls. They gave us two flags (black-yellow-and red). We stopped for the night, about 9 p.m., near Boussu-en-Fagne.

## September 4, 1944
Boussu-en-Fagne, Belgium

I had a good night's sleep. We were told to be careful that we didn't shoot any French or British paratroopers that were to be dropped nearby during the night.

I got up at 9:30 a.m. to the Mail Call and the sound of some Belgian visitors. They still speak French here. We are to stay here until about 4:30 p.m. and then move all at once. I got an attack of Malaria. I lay down all afternoon in the sun, after taking some Atabrine. The boys all took baths. We had plenty of Belgian visitors.

We moved out at 4:30 p.m. and passed through some nice villages. The homes are nice and look like ones back in the States. There are nice tile squares in front of the houses.

We passed through a fair sized city, Philippeville. We are joining the rest of the Division here. It is a pretty city and the road leading to Dinant is wide. Soldiers are in the cafés drinking and the people are sitting out in front of the stores and houses. They sure are happy. There are many ruined buildings from the 1940 war. The people are giving us apples and flowers. There is a huge Jerry airport here. The planes were camouflaged in the woods.

We bivouacked a little later, and the truck we were on went off for a load of ammunition. I slept in the woods.

Personnel near Dinant, Belgium

## September 5, 1944

Philippeville (on the Dinant road), Belgium

All during the early hours of the morning there were guns firing. Up ahead there was a Jerry machine gun burping and every time he did an American one would answer. It sounded like it was only a few fields away, but I believe the wind was bringing the sound closer. The artillery also fired occasionally, not too far away. They are firing across the Meuse River where the Germans have retreated in an attempt (rumor) to get back behind the Siegfried line, by order of Hitler. There was some small arms fire again, not too far away. Then there were planes over and they sounded like Jerries.

I dozed off. I couldn't figure out the meaning of the machine pistol fire and it was getting closer all the time. I thought maybe some Jerries were trying to get back to their lines. I didn't sleep too well in my spot in the woods.

About 4 a.m. Rusty (the driver), came back from the ammunition dump. The moon was brilliant. Not too long after it began to sprinkle. I

78

got up at 8:45 a.m. and there was a slight drizzle. I had some coffee and crackers and feel a little better today. I think I have enough Atabrine in me to check the malarial attack.

A captain from the Ordnance Company across the street came over and wanted to know if any of us were firing our guns, as the bullets were going across his area and hitting the trucks. We assured him we weren't and it must be a loose Jerry.

Captain Tooley came around and I went back to Division Rear. I collected the money to pay the officers and men. They are located in Trelon, France. It was a long chilly ride and I was shaking and chilled when we got there. I could feel my Malaria acting up again. They are set up in a church school. I went to the Army Post Office and then came back to Finance. Captain Applegate is going to follow us back to Division Artillery. I saw Frank Page as we drove by. We made good time coming back. We went to Battalion to leave off their payroll money and I took ours back to Service Battery.

I came back with Lieutenant Obeldobel and I am in rough shape. The guns are still firing a lot. I went right to bed and slept from 4 p.m. to 6 p.m. I sweated a lot and stayed in bed all evening but did not sleep. During the night we had that machine pistol and small arms fire again. It changes direction as if one party is stalking the other. Vehicles on the road get all excited, roar around, and go back. They figure this is the front and they have come too far forward.

## September 6, 1944
Rosée, Belgium

The machine pistol and small arms fire happened during the night and up until 5:30 a.m. this morning. We still can't figure it out. I feel fair and got up at 9:45 a.m. I ate a little bit but went back to lie down on the cot for an hour. I got up after a while, censored letters and signed a few things.

We heard that Ordnance, after shooting it out, caught a Jerry sergeant with a burp gun who was shooting everything up. He must have been the one causing all the trouble.

We hung around all day and it is cold and miserable. I spent a lot of time in the cot, as I am still a little under the weather. It gets so dark now (9 p.m.) that we all went to bed at 10:30 p.m.

## September 7, 1944
Rosée, Belgium

I slept better; it rained heavily but there wasn't any shooting. I got up at 9:30 a.m. but couldn't eat very well. It is cold, rainy, and miserable.

Tony went on the ammunition truck run last night with Rusty and Brock. They brought in six Jerries this morning that they got near Philippeville. One was a captain in the paratroopers and was dressed in nice green pants and boots, a

Rosée, Belgium. Around the fire.

lieutenant, who spoke very good English, a medic, and three soldiers. They were cold and hadn't eaten for four days. They looked like corpses. The Belgian partisans told our men that there were 500 Jerries around who would only surrender to Americans. The German lieutenant could only find five around to surrender. He told us that he had been in Los Angeles and represented Germany in the field events in the 1934 Olympics. Harry said to him, "It's good it's all over for you as many of your men have been wounded or killed." After saying this, the captain, who hadn't said anything, piped up in perfect English and said, "Many of yours are dead, too." I was mad and told Rusty to take them the Hell back to the POW camp near Rosee.

We hung by the fire all day. When they came back they gave me seven rolls of film they had bought in town. We packed things, as we are to move across the Meuse River tomorrow. I went to bed about 11 p.m.

## September 8, 1944
Rosée, Belgium

I didn't sleep any too well. There wasn't any shooting but I was a little leery, as the tanks across the street have moved out, leaving us the only ones here.

I got up about 6:15 a.m. We packed our bedrolls and had a hot cup of coffee. The first group moved out but we had to wait until a little later. We moved a good distance and came to the Meuse River. We traveled along beside it because the bridges are blown out. It is very pretty here; we came to a resort area and the stores and homes are spic and span. I took some pictures, as it was so attractive. We crossed over on a pontoon bridge at Heer. We moved on and passed two dead G.I.s lying near a burning tank. One was uncovered and was ripped open and

Hastière, Belgium. Along the Muese River

bloody on his legs. I took a picture as we passed. The tank was still smoking.

We pulled off the road near Ciney. Some Belgian girls came over and gave us eggs and margarine. They talked a long time with Skoczylas. They were nice kids. They were clean cut and attractive, about 14 and 16 years old, and were well dressed.

We ate and moved out about 4:30 p.m. and passed through Ciney, which is a big town. The people lined the streets and waved and yelled. There were big crowds and they yelled "Vive les Americains!" I took some pictures. We are traveling through nice country. We pulled into an area on the other side of Ciney. We moved out again in about 17 minutes. We went through small towns and the boys got some sandwiches and apples from the ladies. We pulled into a wooded area to stay for the night. We are getting closer to the German border. I set up a droop tent, and after listening to the news on the radio I went to bed.

## September 9, 1944
Ciney, Belgium

I had a good night's sleep despite the fact it rained a bit heavy. I got up about 9 a.m. and it was clear out. I ate. When the water truck came in I heated some water. I have to take a bath, as it has been 12 days since I have had one. I am dirty and my olive drab uniform is grease stained and dirty.

We moved out of the wooded area about 1:15 p.m. We passed through a few towns and the people line the roads and wave. I took a few pictures. We pulled into an area near Warzee. I sat around and read. There is firing up ahead.

We ate supper here. We had visitors and they brought us jam, cake, lemonade, and onions. There were some planes zooming over low. We watched them and they drew ack-ack fire from over a few fields. They were identified as 21 Jerry planes. We were just watching them figuring they were ours. We moved down the road a bit to a little valley. We listened to the news and then went to bed.

## September 10, 1944
Warzee, Belgium

I slept cold last night. There were many planes over. The rest of the gang felt the cold last night, also. We got up about 8 a.m., as we are to move out about 10 a.m. While waiting there was a roar of an airplane motor away up and then a white parachute blossomed out. The paratrooper drifted through the air far away from us.

We moved out through many nice villages. We passed through Esneux. It is a nice city on the river. There are nice homes, clean (American like), cafes, and stores, with plenty in the windows. The people are well dressed and sporty. We traveled by a sign, Luxemburg 139 KMs. We turned and came to the edge of Sprimont. We sat by a tree. Soon the people came in droves. First a blonde, then a fellow called the Prince, and his pretty fiancé, a red head. We put up the tent and the boys worked. We kidded around with a little girl and her gang, showing pictures. I was given some eggs and we sat around the fire talking French and English. There were men, women, and children.

## September 11, 1944
Sprimont, Belgium

I had a good night's sleep although it was chilly. I got up at 7:50 a.m. We started with breakfast. I cooked myself an egg. I began to shave when my friends the Prince and the redhead showed up. They brought a few things to eat, and I talked with them.

All the people are flocking around us. We are like an exhibit at a fair. The redhead had her cute sister with her. I took pictures of the party and they gave me some pictures.

In the afternoon I went up to Battalion Headquarters to arrange for Sergeant Dougher to go back to Division Headquarters. He is to get discharged as a G.I. to accept an appointment as a second lieutenant.

The Battalion is in a luxurious Chateau. It belonged to a Baron, who was killed by the Germans in 1940 (in Aywaille, have pictures). I played the grand piano, looked at their photo album, and explored the rooms. It has many beds where the Jerries had a billet. The woodwork, furniture, and paintings are wonderful. It is similar to the Royal Palace in Palermo. I got a few photos from there.

Sprimont, Belgium

I came to C-Battery, saw Dougher, and then came back. The people are all over the place, like the hornets of Belgium. The Bebe and her gang and all the rest were here. Janet (from the hill) cut the food for us to eat. We hung around the fire by ourselves tonight. Shortly after we retired the planes came droning over. They dropped flares and bombed in the distance. It sounded close though. They were over all night.

## September 12, 1944
Sprimont, Belgium

I had knocked off my top covers that was why I was so cold.

I got up at 7:45 a.m. I ate and then Dougher came down in a jeep with Sagle. Captain Tooley came around and I got his command car for transportation. I took a C-Battery jeep and went up to Battalion to get some papers. I came back in the command car and brought Corporal Galfo with me to Division Rear. It is in Esneux. We went cross-country to get there. We passed through a few towns beyond Esneux, climbing the heights to a Chateau where they are located. I found them and worked in Finance fixing up his Final Statement and discharge. I had Corporal Galfo complete it, and then I sent the Pay Transfer Accounts.

I pinned the bars on Dougher and he came with me and ate at the

Officer's Mess. We had a good dinner.

I took pictures from the height. We finally got away about 2:30 p.m. I came back and talked with Captain Parrish and Lieutenant Welch at our place.

In the evening the people were around and our men were allowed away from the area for one hour. I walked to the road for a while and then came back.

Taken from castle overlooking Esneux, Belgium. Three other Warrant Officers from Division; Alley, Ott, Whitney.

**September 13, 1944**
Sprimont, Belgium

The planes were over and bombed in the distance. Am ack-ack fired overhead once or twice. Outside of that I slept well.

The people were around early today. We are now all alone (Personnel), as Service Battery left and the Ammunition gang went on a trip. We are now to guard the ammunition, do our own work, and wait for the return of the Ammunition gang. Being the only ones here (twelve of us), there are beaucoup people. They are in our tent, using our typewriters, watching and talking to us. All day I was talking to, Bebe, Mary Jean, and the Prince.

We had Service Battery's leftovers, (pancake batter, and eggs) to eat. Everyone seems to have a girl and some friends. I took a walk by myself before dark, to the top of the villa hill. Near this area a man came up to me and said there were four Jerries in the bois (woods). I explained that we had to guard the ammunition and for him to get the Armée Blanc (former regular Belgium Army). As it got dark, Jack and Harry were still visiting; there was a rally of shots. We all knew what it was all about so we got up and lined along the lane. I told them to use the password (Hoop-Shy-Hoy), whatever it means, so we wouldn't shoot each other. The others and I lay in the dirt drainage ditch on the road, listening for the Jerries. Jack and Harry came and were challenged by Charlie. We laid there in wait for a long while and then went to bed.

## September 14, 1944
Sprimont, Belgium

I slept in my clothes. It rained at night. In the morning, 8:30 a.m., a Belgian uniformed soldier stuck his head in the tent, and asked in good English, if we had seen any Germans go by. We told him that we hadn't but we heard the shooting last night and looked around. He said that they had killed one German and captured three. He said that one of them (Belgians) had also been killed. The rest of the Germans, about eight, had escaped and must have passed by us, to a little fir woods not too far away. They left and about 10 minutes later they returned. There were about 20 Armée Blanc soldiers with a Jerry Luftwaffe sergeant; he had his hands on top of his head. They marched him into town.

Two men from C-Battery and three men from Message Center came by with mail and messages. Mary Jean and Bebe (meaning Baby) came down early. All were around and we talked and gestured all day. We had the little girls sing the Belgium National Anthem (called Brabanconne) but we reneged when they asked us to sing ours, as we knew we couldn't. We, while talking to the little girls, had talked about cheese, and they gasped, saying it was a naughty

Sprimont, Belgium

word. We hastily explained that we meant fromage (French for cheese), and everyone was relieved.

A man came by and said he saw a Jerry, so Skoczylas and George went into the woods. We heard shots later. Sergeant Nix, Delli and Jack went to see. They all came back together. They didn't see anything, so they had fired to see if they could flush anyone out. I sat around with Red (Mary Jean), Joe (with his magazines), and Bebe all afternoon. The boys all went to eat at peoples' houses and they brought back food. In the evening all (the local people) were around as usual.

## September 15, 1944
Sprimont, Belgium

I had a good night's sleep. I had a little to eat for breakfast.

The people came around. Message Center came around and said that Battalion is to go into Germany today. Red (Mary Jean) was around for me to mail a letter to a soldier.

I accepted a man's invitation to dinner and four of us went. We had soup, salad (tomato-onion-lettuce-potatoes), beef, potatoes, cabbage, coffee, and pudding. It was a delicious meal. The nice stove impressed me. It had two ovens, one on each side. They have four for dinner each day.

After dinner (the others went to another home), a man and two fellows with a young woman came. It seems there is a little trouble between the three parties in power here. There is the White Army, called the Armée Blanc (regular army who had surrendered to the Germans), the Communists, and the Liberation Army.

It seems that these people's friend is in jail and they are going to shoot him. I sent George down with this fellow so they could talk them out of shooting him. Jenny, his young, pretty wife, stayed here with us. Her uncle is the priest and is mixed up in this. We all had our pictures taken with her. I took off with her arm in arm. She is lovely. We went to their in-laws' home. The priest managed to get the man released. They gave us wine. George was there and we talked. I am improving in my French. I walked with her to the store to get some meat. I then came back to camp to shave. They are having a supper for me this evening.

I found out from the kids here that the in-laws and the priest had revealed the hiding place of American and other flyers (being worked through the underground back to England) to the Germans. It was a very questionable situation as there were so many contesting for control. I was on my guard on the return trip. We had a good supper of wine, salad, meat, potatoes, and peas. We talked for a while and at 7:30 p.m. we left. Jenny had dressed for dinner and is she nice. They walked us back to camp. Some of the ammunition train came back; they had come from Paris and were all drunk. The couple that came with us left as I half hinted.

We tidied things up and talked and sang with Red and family (Pop and her sister). We finally went to bed.

Sprimont, Belgium. 1944. Left to right. Me, Jenny (whose Uncle was to be hung or shot the next day and I stopped it (who could resist)), Jack Markowitz, then the Jewish couple who hid behind the walls of this building for three years, during the German occupation, the Belgian woman who helped hide them, and Harry Hammer.

## September 16, 1944
Sprimont, Belgium

I had a fair night's sleep. One of the drunks yelled out during the night.

It was raining in the morning. I got up and had a little to eat. We packed up and got ready to move. It cleared up a bit. I rode a bicycle uptown. We had a cold dinner.

All the people came down to see us off. Leo LeBlanc was down right after breakfast. He presented me with a pair of clogs inscribed to me with the writing "9th of September 1944, Day of Liberation of Sprimont, Belgium". Jenny and her husband came down. I talked with them and then we got March Order. The Jewish friends (he and his wife had to hide behind secret walls, for three years during German occupation) brought us soup (Potato Latkes?). It was delicious.

We pulled out. I took a lot of pictures of the people. We were sorry to leave. Many of the people were crying.

Inscribed clogs given to Frank Lovell. Inscription reads (as translated from French to English), "To Frank - In Remembrance of the September 9th, 1944 - Day of Liberty of Sprimont, Leo" On bottom of shoes in French is written Leo Le Blanc - Rue Du Centre - Sprimont (Liege) Belgique.

Sprimont, Belgium.
The Jewish folks who brought us potato soup as we were leaving, so we would have something substantial in our stomach. Note the woman is wearing our insignia. It is a popular idea. Standing: Tony, Shipe, and Jack. Sitting, Harry Hammer.

We went towards Liege, then to Verviers. We passed through some nice towns. There are some beautiful homes. We passed near Spa. There are trolley cars and trains. The people all waved. We neared Germany. It wasn't long before the names began to get German. We passed through towns where the people glared or turned their heads. We went through a former German Garrison. It was flat from our bombs. We camped with Service Battery. We are at the end of the barracks. The fellows hunted souvenirs and then we all slept outside. The camp is known as Camp Elsenborn.

## September 17, 1944

Elsenborn, Germany-Belgium

I slept fair until this morning. It was damp and misty out. In the early morning, small arms, machine pistols, guns, and our machine guns opened up below us. It sounded like they were just over the hill. There were mortar and artillery shells landing just below. It was chilly and cold.

We cooked breakfast on a fire. Morrison and Senn were here (from Message Center).

I decided to go to Division Rear today. It began to rain. I went to Service Battery nearby. They are in huts whose roofs are almost level with the ground. Sergeant Linscott drove and Corporal Staff and Skoczylas came along. We had some fresh meat to eat before we left. We took all the boxes of souvenirs to be mailed home. We traveled back to Sourbrodt. We then went by the roadblock and on into Eupen. There are only a few soldiers here and there. The people in Eupen glare or don't even look. Most of them stay indoors. It was a damp, chilly ride. Division is in the center of Eupen. I accomplished my business (sent a $50.00 bond to new niece, Linda). I let the boys go to Verviers while I did my business. I talked with Frank Page for a long while. We left when they came back.

It started to rain. We were slow coming back as we had to lead Sergeant Campbell to camp. We all went into the barracks for the night. We lit fires, set up office, cooked something to eat, and then went to bed.

Camp Elsenborn, Belgium.
A former German camp.
Frank Lovell

At former German training camp, Camp Elsenborn, Belgium. Charlie Nagy, Eugene Skoczylas, George Neuhardt, Harry Hammer.

A Pay Transfer Account (PTA).

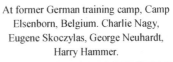

## September 18, 1944

Elsenborn, Germany-Belgium

I had a good night's sleep. It rained heavily during the night but let up in the morning. We ate at the kitchen.

The Ammunition train is going back to Paris for ammunition. I rode up to Battalion who are about three miles into Germany. The people just look, but the kids wave sometimes. I did a few things and then came back. I then left for Rear Echelon (Division Rear) in Eupen about 10:30 a.m., with Lieutenant Dougher. We did a few things, ate dinner there, and then went back to Eupen. He got a blood test at the 10th Lab. The people are coming out more and some speak or nod.

We came back to camp and had supper. It cleared up a bit. About 20 Jerry planes met 25 US planes. Two Focke-Wulf 190s shot down one of our P-47s. We heard it but couldn't see it. The pilot parachuted. He saw the white circles on our equipment so he maneuvered to land nearby. Captain Tooley picked him up and he is okay. We sat in the candlelight and I opened my ration of Scotch and passed it around, as I don't drink it.

## September 19, 1944

Elsenborn, Germany-Belgium

I did not sleep too well and neither did anyone else.

I cleaned up and censored the mail. There were planes overhead and shells landing below us during the night.

In the afternoon we expected to move so we packed everything. It is a swell day. They are not going to pick us up until later on, so I went walking with Warrant Officer Ramsdell into the camp. We prowled through the buildings. I picked up some soldiers' hats and a helmet, also an axe. We went through the chapel. It is shaped like an octagon (Catholic) with a large swastika in the center.

We stopped at the Hotel Elsenborn here, which is open; he had a beer (5 francs), and then rummaged through more buildings. We helped a

G.I. load up his truck with rations from the ration dump here. He took off before we could get a ride to the new location. We had to wait for our ration truck to return and it came after dark. We helped load it and then stopped at the Hotel again. We all had some wine and I played the piano.

We went outside but decided it was too dark (black-out driving) to go on. We tried to get back into the Hotel to stay for the night but they wouldn't open up. We started out and almost went off the road twice. We stopped in Eupen at Division Rear. After wandering around the area in the wee hours of the morning I returned to the truck and slept in the cab. The boys got their blankets and slept inside.

## September 20, 1944
Roetgen, Germany

I rested fairly well until 6 a.m. and it was raining. The two puppies, Rita Cherbourg and Killfrigan, soaking wet, were staring at me through the rear widow of the truck. I went to the building to find the boys but couldn't locate them. A little later I started out again but the dogs began to howl so I waited, they came about 7:15 a.m. Division was just starting to line up for breakfast as we took off.

We found Service Battery in Roetgen, Germany, about 12 miles away. We passed a huge tank trap that is supposed to be part of the Siegfried Line on the way here. We had a late breakfast. I had pancakes.

It was still damp out. I fixed a box to mail the souvenirs.

After dinner I took the command car and Linscott, Staff, Prosnowski, and I went to Eupen. I went to the 10th Medical lab and 128th Evacuation Hospital to complete my business. I saw Colonel Adams, our former Commanding Officer, here.

We came back to Roetgen. There had been a lot of fighting here, as there are two German tanks and a half-track. There is also a Mark VI and an anti-tank gun. The Battery was moving out when we arrived. I stayed behind and then went to Battalion Headquarters in Zweifall to relay a message.

I came back, ate, and then helped Charlie do a rush job. We finished it and Sergeant Major Urban and Captain Tooley came by and picked it up. We moved out about an hour later but only over about one mile from here. I set up my pup tent by the stream and I gave the boys a ½ bottle of Gin (my ration) and then I went to bed.

## September 21, 1944
Rott, Germany

I had a good night's sleep, as I sure was tired. The big guns boomed all around us, and the shells resound through the hills as they go through the air. The setting ring around the shell (especially the big guns, 240mms), separate and whirl through with a screech. They often land not too far away as we are in front of them.

I ate, then Captain Gray came along. We talked for a long while. We put up the pyramidal tent and Major Elliott came. He was hopping mad. He wanted court martial charges on a soldier. Technical Sergeant Nix worked on them and finally got them out about two hours later.

I took a bath and washed my clothes plus the souvenir Jerry hats. I took all afternoon cleaning the paper work. We had stew for supper.

We had a German kid around and we had him saying words. He is still shy. These people thought we were going to kill them so they were afraid. They are beginning to find out that we are just trying to end the war, so they are friendlier now. We sat around and talked in the evening. It gets dark here about 7:45 p.m. I went to bed about 8:30 p.m.

## September 22, 1944
Rott, Germany

I had a good night's sleep even though the guns were booming on all sides of us all night. They are the large ones, the 155 rifles, 8-inch, and 240s. It is terribly noisy as they resound through the hills and valleys. There were some incoming ones over on our flank.

We had breakfast at the kitchen at 8 a.m. I worked all morning on various things. There are a thousand and one things to do. I got a lot of it accomplished. I finished drying my clothes.

After dinner I counted the Pay Transfer Accounts. There was a premature burst from one of the big guns not too far away. I left for Eupen about 3 p.m. with Service Battery's command car. I finished my business at Finance, talked with Frank Page for a while and ate supper there, then returned to our area. We sat around and talked.

I got a couple of letters in the mail. We talked until 8:45 p.m. There is a lot of artillery firing. The sky flares up every now and then as something gets hit. There is a constant rumble of artillery up there and the guns near us are firing.

## September 23, 1944
Rott, Germany

I got up as the breakfast whistle blew. We had hash, cereal, and coffee for breakfast.

I came back and censored mail and then shaved. Lieutenant Brown (Air Operation-Piper Cub Pilot) dropped around about his voucher for travel. I wrote a letter home.

I heard that Lieutenant Hamilton, A-Battery, was killed. He was a new second lieutenant replacement, and I had never seen him.

Captain Tom Gaffney was injured. It seems Tom was with a forward Infantry group, about six of them. Tom was the Liaison Officer. They came to a clearing, as they were moving forward, all of a sudden shells came pouring in on top of them. Tom said he just dropped and clutched the earth. After a few minutes it was all over. He said as the dust began to rise he raised his head a bit, like a turtle, and then got up. He said he was the only one to get up. The others were all dead.

I worked all day on various things and now it is raining. I went into the cottage nearby. It is a miserable afternoon. It hurts to see a nice warm cottage for Service Battery to sleep and play cards in and we have to do office work in the cold tent, without light.

## September 24, 1944
Rott, Germany

I got up about 7:45 a.m. and went to breakfast. It had rained all night and was overcast and drizzly this morning. I shaved after breakfast and then hopped in the water truck.

We went to the church (Sunday) in town (Rott). It is about one and a half miles away. It is a nice little church with one shell hole through it. Father Connors said mass at 9 a.m. and I went to Communion. There were two kids and two ladies plus Father Connors in church. It was drizzling when we came out.

I did some work, most of it in the cottage. We talked with a man and some kids by the fire for a while. It is a miserable day. I hung around all day doing various things.

In the evening I went to the cottage and visited and read. It is nice to be inside in a nice hot place, especially as it was raining out. Personnel should have a place like this to work. Instead, Service Battery got here first and sleeps and plays cards here. It was wet getting to bed in my tent.

## September 25, 1944
Rott, Germany

I got up for breakfast and it has stopped raining. It rained on and off all morning though. I collected various things together and am going to the rear at Eupen this afternoon. I left about 3 p.m.

It is fair out although it looks like rain at times. I stopped at Finance and the Adjutant General. I talked with Frank Page for a while. I ate there and still the command car hadn't returned. They came, as it was getting dark, about 7 p.m. We hurried along; it is wet and muddy out.

We stopped at the 10th Medical Lab to see if Horton, who was visiting his uncle (a Major), was here, but he had left. We got to Roetgen and picked him up on the road. We got to the bomb crater there at the tank trap and they were building a bridge. We had to wait a good while until they fixed something. We made three attempts and finally crossed it. We got back and it was dark. I sat in the cottage until 10 p.m.

## September 26, 1944
Rott, Germany

I got up at 8 a.m. and my tent was cold and wet. It rained all morning.

I signed some things and went to the cottage to sign some more, as some of the men are working here. I took a jeep and driver and went to Division Artillery to deliver a few messages. I came back and I am sure dirty, wet, and discontent. It is miserable to try to work in the cold and rain and to do office work.

As we were eating dinner the sun came out. It was in and out all afternoon but it didn't rain. Around supper it became overcast and sprinkled. It is now cold and wet. I went into the cottage and worked all evening. I cut some true copies, sat around until 9:30 p.m., and then went to bed. It sure is nasty trying to undress and get in under that wet, cold, tent.

## September 27, 1944
Rott, Germany

I had a fair night's sleep. I got up in time for breakfast. It is damp, overcast, and threatening to rain. It had rained during the night. We all gathered around the fire but had to retreat to the big tent when it rained.

The clerks did most of their work in the cottage. Skoczylas did his payroll in the coal bin room. It began to clear, as the sky got blue with the sun out and white clouds around. There were still occasional low flying dark clouds.

I changed clothes, as my olive drabs and jacket are filthy. It is still cold out. The two kids were around and gave us apples, the best we have had yet. I made occasional trips in the cottage to sign papers and to check work.

After supper we gathered around the fire for a good long time and then retired to the cottage. I talked and also cut some true copies of orders. It is smoky and stuffy but I stayed until 10 p.m.

## September 28, 1944
Rott, Germany

In the early hours of the morning I heard a plane go over very low. The big guns boomed heavily in the early hours. They sound like they are firing through my tent. I got up at 7:50 a.m. and it is clear but cold. I had breakfast and then sat around the fire. I signed a few things, censored some mail, and then shaved.

After dinner I sat in the sun writing. I signed some papers, checked some, and worked on the payrolls. We had the kids around and they brought us some apples. I heard a few shells whistling in below us. After dinner we sat around the fire and I did some work there. I went into the cottage and did some more work until 10 p.m. Just after I got in bed a shell or two came whistling in and landed somewhere close. I lay there listening and about one-hour later a few more came in. The boys are moving about. I finally went back to sleep.

## September 29, 1944
Rott, Germany

I slept fairly well after a poor start. It was cold sleeping, which got me up for breakfast. I signed papers by the fire, and checked the payrolls.

After dinner I worked for a while and then washed my olive drabs and jacket. The young German woman, who lives nearby, told the guys in Service Battery that the people who lived in the cottage had buried some liquor in the garden. All the guys in the cottage are out there digging it up, end to end. The German woman and all of us are laughing and jeering them on. We yelled at them, "If you were ordered to do it, you'd all be moaning and groaning."

I sat around the fire and did some work. After supper we hung around the fire. The boys made a couple of batches of French fries. I went in the cottage and wrote a letter and read.

## September 30, 1944
Rott, Germany

It was sprinkling when I got up. After breakfast, we stood around the fire and it began to rain. I did a few things and then shaved.

I sat in the cottage and wrote for a while. It has been a miserable week for weather. We were busy all day on various things. I went to Eupen and sent some Pay Transfer Accounts. I spent the night in the cottage and then went to my tent to bed.

# Chapter five: October 1944

October 1, 1944 to October 31, 1944

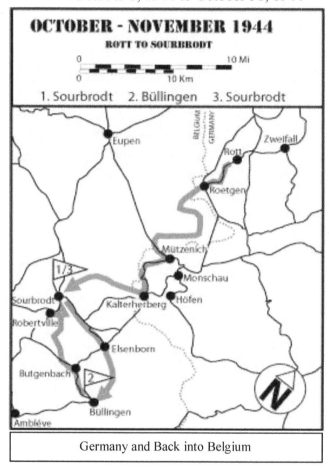

## OCTOBER - NOVEMBER 1944
### ROTT TO SOURBRODT

0            10 Mi

0     10 Km

1. Sourbrodt   2. Büllingen   3. Sourbrodt

Germany and Back into Belgium

October 1944 Historical Overview
Month of October 1944 Corps Assignments: First Army, 12th Army
Group
October 1 to 25, 1944 – VII Corps

October 26 to October 31, 1944 – V Corps

General Overview

Russian troops continued to gain ground moving westward.

The Battle of Aachen ends with Allied victory.

The Allies movement forward is thwarted by lack of fuel and heavy resistance encountered by German forces defending their homeland.

9th Division Overview: The 9th Division is mired in the quagmire known as the Battle of the Hürtgen Forrest, an area south of Aachen, Germany. The same territory is won and lost again, and again. On both sides casualties are enormous.

At the end of October the 9th Division is sent to rest and regroup in Sourbrodt, Belgium.

\*\*\*

*October 1 1944*

Rott Germany

I got up for breakfast, and per usual, it was rainy and cool. We put on raincoats and Delli, Galfo, and I walked up to the town church to Mass, as it is Sunday. We met the civilians on their way back. Father Connors is saying this Mass. I went to Confession and Communion. We walked back. Major Elliott and Captain Tooley were coming to our tent when we arrived. I got some things out of the safe for Major Elliott.

I worked all morning and afternoon on awards. I took a trip back to Battalion at Roetgen. I talked with Captain Pete Thivierge and Major Elliott. They have a nice home to stay in. I came back at dark and it is wet and muddy. I worked all evening on the awards, as the Major wants them all done by tomorrow. The generator quit and the lights went out about 9:30 p.m. We called it off until tomorrow.

**October 2, 1944**

Rott, Germany

I got up for breakfast and hung around the fire for a while. I started in early to work on awards. I handed out most of them to the clerks to type while I rewrote some. We worked all morning on them, ate, and then worked until 2 p.m.

I wrote up two Bronze Stars, one for Delli and one for Jack Markowitz. I have written quite a few for the Battery Commanders. I wrote a posthumous one a few days ago for Corporal Hefter, the colonel's driver (I wrote it for the colonel). Hefter had backed the jeep into a driveway to turn around. He backed over a teller mine, killing himself and Major Hochdoerfer, and injuring Colonel Adams. It was awarded the other day, and the catch is I don't think anyone knows who wrote it. I sent Charlie Nagy up to Battalion with the written awards, and there were 18 in all. I took a break for a while.

After supper I finished a few odds and ends. From 11:30 a.m. to about 1:30 p.m. it was almost like automatic artillery fire. It didn't slacken up. The guns around us fired plenty, there also was plenty of incoming mail with whistles and a sharp crack when they hit. It was a noisy night, as there was small arms and machine gun fire.

## October 3, 1944
Rott, Germany

I got up a little late and made my own breakfast. It was damp and looks like rain.

I feel filthy, as I haven't washed or shaved for three days. I gathered things together and then cleaned up my personal items. After having chow I got my things together and took Skoczylas and Jack with me in a command car. It was muddy, wet, and rainy. We took Rusty's dog Rita Cherbourg with us. I felt that we couldn't cope with a dog anymore. We left her out at Division Rear in Eupen, where we knew she would get a new home.

I signed some things and went to Finance. I had left the Pay Transfer Accounts back in camp and so couldn't send them. We took off for Corp

Headquarters. We passed through Verviers. The movies for the civilians were in full swing. It was nice to see pretty girls and meet people who wave and are happy to see you.

We stopped at Corp Headquarters but couldn't seem to get anything we wanted. We missed Joe Devine as he had left for our Division Headquarters earlier. We left for Liege. It is a big place and very nice. We drove through the city along the canal or Meuse (?). There were boats for ferries as the bridges had all been blown up. We left Linscott off and drove around for a while.

We met a crowd pushing a girl in front of them; they had cut off her hair (she had evidently collaborated with the Germans). I took three pictures as the people cheered (about 50 or 60 of them) and laughed. It was at a busy intersection.

We left Liege after having some ice cream. We came through Verviers and the store windows were lighted up. We got back, it was dark, and so we ate in the cottage. It was nice after we pulled in wet, cold, and muddy, to get into the warm cottage. We had soup, hot cakes, and coffee in the kitchen.

## October 4, 1944
Rott, Germany

I got up in time for breakfast. It was damp, as it had rained for a while during the night. I cleaned up some of the paper work and then wrote some letters. I ate early chow and then went with Lieutenant Freeman to Division Rear at Eupen. We went in an open jeep and it was cold. I finished my business. I sent Pay Transfer Accounts and deposited Soldiers Deposits. I sent $100 home myself (to my mother). Lieutenant Freeman was counting the enlisted men's payroll. I took the jeep, and who should be playing around it but Rita Cherbourg, the puppy. She sniffed me and followed after our jeep barking.

We went to a couple of hospitals looking for the 28$^{th}$ General Hospital. I couldn't locate it so we came back to Division. I met Joe

Devine here; he was down from Corp Headquarters. I bought some perfume from him to send home. I talked with Frank Page for a while, picked up Lieutenant Freeman, and then came back to Service Battery. It was cold. I ate and then spent the night in the cottage until bedtime at 9:30 p.m.

## October 5, 1944
Rott, Germany

I got up for breakfast. The card players had played all night in the cottage, and came right over to breakfast from the game. It was overcast and I did some work during the morning.

After dinner I took some water and put it in the portable Jerry bathtub in the stream. Just then a group of planes came over, about twenty-four of them, and all German. The ack-ack was coming from every direction. My helmet was beside the tub as I was using it as a basin. We watched them as they came directly overhead. A little bit over to one side, one of them exploded in the air. The sky was black with anti-aircraft fire. They dropped a few bombs over a ways. A few of them streaked back our way. They came right over us and even Service Battery fired. I got

Heating the water. Rott, Germany. 1944

Open-air bathroom. Rott, Germany. 1944.

under the trailer for a few minutes to get away from the flak.

I took a nice bath in the stream, and put on clean clothes. Two of the planes came back and every one fired. The ack-ack was so heavy I squatted by the trailer. The sky was black once again. After supper I went to the cottage.

## October 6, 1944
Rott, Germany

I had a good night's sleep. It was clear but cold. I got up for breakfast and it was clear with the sun out.

I gathered up the ballots. I am the Battalion Voting Officer for the upcoming presidential election, and left for Battalion with Captain Tooley. I went to Message Center and then to Headquarters Battery. I completed my business and then came back to Message Center and talked to Rousse and "Bebe" Neuhardt. I also went to S-3 in the building and fixed up allotments and Pay Transfer Accounts. A big air attack started while I was here. The German planes roared over. Our ack-ack opened up evidently prematurely. The bombs were dropping and began to land pretty close. It all died down so I completed things, came back to Message Center and got a ride back to Service Battery in Reed's jeep.

I cleaned up some work. After dinner I couldn't get any vehicles so I washed my clothes and did some work. I got a Motor's jeep at 3:15 p.m. I took Harry Hammer and Delli with me and went to Eupen, to Division Rear. I changed money while they extended figures on the payrolls. I spoke with Frank Page. We rushed back and ate late and then I worked in the cottage.

## October 7, 1944
Rott, Germany

I got up for breakfast and prepared to take a trip. I washed and shaved and got all my papers together.

I met with the Division Voting Officer and talked for a while. We finally left about 11 a.m. as we have been waiting for a command car. There was Prosnowski, Neuhardt, Shipe, and myself. We went to Quarter Master, in Roetgen, to send some personal effects of one of the men killed. Some planes whined overhead. The fellows saw them bomb. I saw two silver ones dive a short way over. Our 50s opened up on them. There were planes all around. I could see some and they looked and seemed marked like our P-47's. They circled, so I got in the doorway of a building while they strafed and our 50s fired nearby. They kept circling and came again, so I went down to the cellar where it was dark but safe. They strafed all around. I came up and watched them in the distance. As I was watching them, something caught my eye over the roof. It was a plane coming in. I dove through the door into the hallways on my knees. I could hear the slugs singing all through the yard behind me. I went down to the cellar as I can see more planes coming the same way, rooftop high firing. They made one more pass and then left.

We left Roetgen and went to Eupen, going the wrong way on a one-way road. We ate here and picked up Frank Page. It was a great day and the sun was out and we had the top down. We made good time to Verviers, turned north, and came to the Liege-Aachen road. We again

turned north and entered Holland. The First Army is still in this sector. There is a difference here. The people all waved and although not as neat in appearance as the Belgians, they are cleaning up everything. We went about 12 miles into Holland, to the fairly large city of Maastricht. It is nice and the store windows are full of appliances, clothes, and equipment. We crossed the river and

Maastricht, Holland. Snipe, Frank Page and George Neuhardt.

then a canal. They have a canal system here. We took some pictures and looked around. I even wrote a letter heading before we left, "Somewhere in Holland."

We crossed the Meuse River again about 3 p.m. and came directly back to Verviers. We made time and cut cross-country by mistake but made out okay. We came to Eupen and left Frank Page off. We turned into the muddy road at Service Battery and slipped off the road into the mud. We walked the rest of the way but arrived in time for supper. I went to the cottage in the evening.

## October 8, 1944
Rott, Germany

I was up early and ate before the rest and it was drizzling out.

We walked up the back way to church (Sunday). It was the 8 o'clock Mass for civilians. The people and soldiers were jammed to the doors. We stood outside the door and listened to the Mass and the singing. We watched the trucks go by, one was a load of German prisoners, and we walked back. We stopped and talked with the crew of the 8-inch gun that fire over our head. Their sergeant came over and reported to me. He said that the gun had blown all the windows out of the house beside it. This is the house where the blue-eyed Fraulein lives. We came back to camp and worked all morning.

In the afternoon, I traded my Beretta, an Italian automatic pistol, for a pair of Jerry binoculars. I gave the G.I. $10 to boot. I got a ride and went forward to Division Artillery at Zweifall. I then went to the Battalion and did my business in both places. I returned for supper.

After supper I worked in the kitchen, counting money. We had $100.00 dollars too much but it turned out to be a mistake. Harry had his figures mixed up. We had coffee and some swell doughnuts they had made. I went to bed about 11 p.m.

## October 9, 1944

Rott, Germany

I got up and had breakfast and worked on Pay Transfer Accounts and Soldier's Deposits all morning. I didn't shave or clean up today. I tried to get transportation (but didn't) for Sergeant Nix to go to the rear.

We worked all afternoon on various things. I got a telephone call from Captain Thivierge, so I got some things together for him. I wrote a recommendation for the Bronze Star for Nagy, at the request of Major Elliott. It was stuffy and smoky in the cottage so I went to bed early.

## October 10, 1944

Rott, Germany

It was raining all morning. I poked my head out and the flap of my tent was thrown back and the bed was wet. I got up and went to chow.

I sent Sergeant Nix to Division. I cleaned up and did some work in the cottage. After dinner I worked all afternoon. Second Lieutenant Planting made first lieutenant and First Lieutenant Wilson made captain. I sent a note via Corporal Staaf to Division to try to find out why Lieutenant Wilson's promotion came through and Lieutenant Pritchard's didn't.

It was miserable all day. It is getting muddier than ever. In the evening I stayed in the cottage for a while and then went to bed early.

## October 11, 1944

Rott, Germany

I feel a lot better as it has cleared up. I ate breakfast and then took my tent down and hung it in the sun. I cleared and aired my things and did my paper work all morning. A little later it clouded up, so I put my tent back up. It turned into a nice day later on.

Today the Americans gave the German command in Aachen until 10:50 a.m. to give up or else (Aachen isn't too far away, just over the hills). They didn't surrender so our planes started coming over. The fighters first, then the medium bombers, and our big guns fired often.

I got notice that my good friend Tattnal Pritchard made captain and Captain Williams made major.

I worked on some recommendations for the Bronze Stars for B-Battery men. We sure are rushed for things. I wrote the Sergeant Burns case also, his battlefield promotion as second lieutenant.

In the evening I went to the cottage and talked and worked. The generator went off. They finally got it going again but I went back to my tent early.

## October 12, 1944
Rott, Germany

I got up, had breakfast, and feel good as the sun is out. I started early to work, as there is a lot of work to do.

I got a call from Captain Pete Thivierge that Sergeant Crabbe's (B-Battery) Teletype Transmission (TWX) came through as a second lieutenant. I made plans for him to come down. I started Harry Hammer on the papers. Sergeant Crabbe came down after dinner. I took the discharge papers and went up to Battalion (with Sergeant Jones as driver). It sure is muddy through the woods. The ack-ack opened up on two planes overhead as we were in the Battalion area. I edged in the woods as I still talked with Sergeant Major Urban and everyone else got into foxholes. I spoke to Major Elliott and Major Williams and got Sergeant Crabbe's discharge signed. I came back to Service Battery area and took all the records. Harry Hammer, Sergeant Crabbe, and I went back to Eupen. It was muddy. I got him discharged and did a few other things. It was late so we ate there. I saw Frank Page at the Adjutant General's.

We left just as it was getting dark. As we came along we could see Aachen being bombed (by Jerry?). We crawled up to the top of the hill and could look down on Aachen. The sky was red from burning buildings. The flares came down out of the clouds. The bombs seem to be white phosphorus. There was a lot of ack-ack going up. We watched it for a few minutes but it was getting dangerous. It was real dark now, flak would be coming down, and a plane from the Roetgen area came directly overhead, diving in. We came back to the Service Battery area and I stayed for a while in the cottage.

## October 13, 1944
### Rott, Germany

I was restless in the early hours of the morning. The guns all around us were firing frequently. I got up for breakfast and hung around Service Battery Orderly room until Captain Thivierge came along from Battalion.

I had Sergeant Crabbe's papers fixed up and he had Harry complete it. He, Sergeant Nix, and I went to Battalion. I stopped off at Message Center. I got a jeep from the Liaison section and Sargent Nickerson as driver. I took Crabbe and we went through Zweifall toward Monschau to the 60th Infantry Regimental Command Post. I met with Major Elliott, and Crabbe was then sworn in as a second lieutenant. I stayed around for a short while and then came back to Battalion Headquarters.

I got a ride to Service Battery. I had chow, which was saved for me. I had to write three recommendations for the Croix-de-Guerre (Major Williams, Staff Sergeant Dalrymple, and Sergeant Rousse) for the colonel. It took me three hours and even then I was late. I even typed it myself. I ate a late supper and took my personnel work to the cottage to complete. Sergeant Nix had taken Lieutenant Crabbe to Division Rear to complete everything.

## October 14, 1944
### Rott, Germany

I got up for breakfast, washed, and shaved. Worked all morning on papers and reports. We had to do more work on the Croix-de-Guerres, and I typed one of them.

Before dinner I went to Roetgen, to the Division Artillery Air Observation Post. I left some film to be developed. I talked with pilot Lieutenant Tom Hall. He said Captain Severson was shot down in one of the piper Cubs. He is missing in action (MIA). The lieutenant (observer) with him was killed.

I worked all afternoon, as I had so much work to do. Jack and Delli went up to Battalion, as they had shot six deer and are going to have venison for supper.

I went to the cottage in the evening. A Jerry plane dropped some personnel bombs near-by. All in the cottage recognized the sound and stampeded. I was almost trampled on. I went to bed about 10 p.m. Shortly after Jerry came over and dropped flares and bombed. I didn't get up although it was close, but many were up. He roamed around up there for a good long while.

## October 15, 1944

Rott, Germany

About 2 a.m. the German planes were around low and bombed over toward Aachen way. I was ready to get out of bed, but didn't. The planes were over once again and then it began to rain. They come over once again about 5 a.m.

I got up for breakfast, as the weather is clear. It turned out nice and the sun came out. I heated some water and filled up the portable tub and took a bath. I started to wash clothes but it clouded over and began to rain. Some German shells came whistling over but landed a good distance away. A tank must have broken through.

It rained all afternoon. Some of the fellows went to Battalion to a show. I had to hang out my wet clothes in the rain. I sat in the cottage after supper for a while and did some work.

## October 16, 1944
Rott, Germany

There were planes over during the early hours of the morning even though it was raining. They bombed with personnel bombs a short way over.

It is raining off and on. I moved my tent and things to under the shed roof. They had been making a shed and it had a door, window, roof, and side built. It is dry under here.

The fellows worked in the cottage throughout the day. We have quite a bit of work to do. Service Battery is building a road here and it is quite a job. Battalion Motors is building a bridge.

In the evening I sat in the cottage as it was raining out. I wrote recommendations for Service Battery men for Captain Tooley. I have to think up sweet words and deeds for fellows that are beside me snoring or playing cards. It is some world. I work my fingers to the bone while they sleep.

## October 17, 1944
Rott, Germany

I had a good night's sleep under the shed roof, although when two Jerry planes circled around low, I sat up. I was ready to go to the brook and get below the ground level. They dropped their bombs over quite away, toward Aachen.

I got up for breakfast and heard a rumor that we are to stay here for the winter. All are building better shelters and roads. They have Service Battery working for the first time and they let everyone know about it.

I had George start typing recommendations for awards. The rest of my gang is fixing up a shack next to mine. In the afternoon some of the Service Battery guys told Tony Wisniewski that Sergeant LaMontagne wanted Personnel to get out of the cottage. He said that everyone dirtied it up and no one cleaned it up. I didn't say anything to him. I told George and the guys to stop working. The ironic thing about it is that George was typing a recommendation for a Bronze Star for LaMontagne that I had written up. So he is cutting his own throat. I refused to continue to work on it. I told Tony Tooley at supper about it. I also told him I am going to move into town. He wants me to build a place down here.

After supper all Personnel sat around our fire then sat in the pyramidal tent. I went to bed at 10 p.m. The sky was red and there was a lot of noise from Aachen.

## October 18, 1944
Rott, Germany

I had a good night's sleep and got up for breakfast.

I told Captain Tooley that I am looking for a house. He suggested getting one of those portable ones. I cleaned up. Then about seven of the clerks went, with a truck, in search of lumber.

I went with Harry Hammer in search of a house to work in. We stopped at Raymond's house, he is one of the boys that bring us apples, but it was filled with people. The next one had an old lady in it. She spoke French and German mixed. We looked over the place but it was too crowded. We felt like German soldiers looking for a place to take over. But we couldn't force anyone from his or her home, as it isn't bred in us.

We left with Raymond and went to the home with large windows. The house was filled up with people on one side. The other side the old man said "No" to us. We should have forced him to show us but couldn't.

We went across the street to a little red brick house with a slate roof that was being built. It needs a floor, doors, and a window. We think we will take this. We came back and ate dinner. The whole gang went up to look at it after dinner. They came back after a short rain burst. They said they found a place in a furnished home. I had to be a bit forceful, as I wanted to move this afternoon, wherever. It was a rainy miserable afternoon. We got a truck later in the day and loaded it up with all the equipment and some of the bedrolls and the guys went up with it.

After eating dinner I walked up to the new furnished house. It is nice but not roomy enough. It has a large former bedroom on the second floor and an attic with a small bedroom. I have a nice white bed to sleep on. We sat around and talked by candlelight. We all went to bed about 9 p.m. It sure is nice to sleep in a soft bed. Their beds have a wedge section, which props the head section of the mattress up. The windows rattle every time the big guns fire.

## October 19, 1944

Rott, Germany

I was comfortable in bed but did not sleep too well. I got up at 7:30 a.m. for breakfast.

It is muddy and damp. I talked at Service Battery Orderly room for a while. Everyone in Personnel was busy arguing and rearranging the desks. One does one thing and the other one yells at him. They are yelling so I laid down the law, a little more than I used to, through necessity. Some of them are working in the kitchen. Tony Wisniewski is going to sleep in the kitchen on a couch. The lady cleans the steps with a cloth and water.

I did a little work before noon. I went to Service Battery to try and get a generator or power.

After dinner I shuffled around doing odds and ends. We went down for supper and went back to our house and sat down. We all ended up in the kitchen. The old German lady is downstairs. We had a little snack. I brought out the half bottle of Scotch and they finished it. The lady came up about 9 p.m., and we left, some of them talked with her for a while. There were two German planes that dropped personnel bombs nearby. Later the ack-ack opened up on something. I sat up and looked out the window.

114

**October 20, 1944**

Rott, Germany

I got up at 7:30 a.m. after a good night's sleep. I hurried down to breakfast, talked with Captain Tooley at Service Battery and then called Captain Gray.

The boys (back at the house) are all hopping mad with each other over trivialities. I let them burn themselves out. I cleaned up with some hot water from the kitchen and then changed into a clean uniform. The fellows built a latrine outside and a place to heat water. They put in a telephone for us.

I started typing awards and then went to dinner. I then walked up to the church and back and it is still muddy out. I sat around, read, and signed papers. I was almost late for supper because I was typing awards. I cleaned up the mail and left it at Service Battery and then came back to the house. They are giving three-day passes to a few of the men to go to Liege and Verviers, starting tomorrow.

**October 21, 1944**

Rott, Germany

I slept good and warm. There were a lot of incoming shells in the early hours. They weren't landing any too far away.

I got up at 7:35 a.m. and hurried down to breakfast. I came back and did a few odds and ends of work. I took my clothes out of my pack and hung them up to air them out. The guys built a fire right beside them so I took them down.

I jumped in Corporal King's jeep and rode up to the Battalion. We veered off the road, as it is still muddy, and hit a pack of mud. It splattered all over me. I talked with Captain Pete Thivierge in the morning and we fixed up different things. He is going to have the Batteries send me their voting officers so we can clean up this national election voting.

I came back and rode right down to chow. I walked over to look at the shacks they had built. The sun is out now.

I went to the 84th Field Artillery Battalion Personnel section in town. I borrowed some papers for voting from them. As I came back to the house, there were incoming shells whistling over and landing a fair distance away. I did some work and then went to supper. I checked with Service Battery but nobody wanted to vote. I worked and read after supper by candlelight and lamplight.

## October 22, 1944
Rott, Germany

I got up and went to breakfast, came back, and cleaned up.

I went to Battalion to clear up the voting, but there wasn't anyone at Battalion as there was supposed to be. I got a jeep (Dixon's Liaison Section) and went up to the 60th Infantry Regimental Headquarters to see Major Elliot. I talked with him for a while and had him sign a paper.

I came back to Battalion and ate at Headquarters Battery. There are some 28th Infantry Division officers around. I got our mail and then came back to our house. I cleaned up some work.

After supper I started to write a letter and also read a little. The light is too poor as we only have an oil lamp.

## October 23, 1944
Rott, Germany

About 4 a.m. I heard shells whistling over. They sound very close. I rose up on my elbow and looked out of the window. I couldn't see anything. The shells seem to whistle over in pairs. There isn't any time between the whistle and the ca-whoom, which shows they are very close. There was a response from the guns below but Jerry whistled a few more low ones in. The last one I heard was about 4:50 a.m. A few of the shells seemed to have a smothered sound as if they exploded in the dirt. They sure sounded like they landed right near here. I was sort of uneasy but no one else seemed to be awake. I got up and went to breakfast. Some of the fellows said the ack-ack group said one of the shells landed on the other side of the road. There is a fresh dirt spot there. I started a fire and heated some water. I did some work but when the water was heated I took a bath.

I talked with Lieutenant Crabbe. There was a captain from the 28th Division here; they are evidently going to take over this sector. I worked all afternoon. I got a chill suddenly and it is a good one and I know its Malaria again. I got dressed for chow but changed my mind. I undressed and went to bed and I took some Quinine. I feel miserable. I was cold for a few hours and then began to sweat. All the boys want to do something for me. I tossed and sweated all evening. The fellows wrote letters until 10 p.m.

## October 24, 1944
Rott, Germany

About 1 a.m. Jerry started shelling around. They were whistling in low and the exploding of them landing nearby is causing the house to shake and the windows to rattle. They are coming three at a time, then two. I was sweating them out. I don't know where they are landing but they sure sound close.

In the morning I felt better, but when I sat up I could feel the Malaria in my head. I lay down. The fellows said the shells came in at 4 a.m. too. They were sweating them out. The ack-ack fellows said some burst short and over away. Some of them were high bursts. Their other Battery, over the hill, was in foxholes last night from 4 a.m. until 12 noon.

I sweated in bed all morning. I took Quinine and about noon I threw up. I felt better for an hour after that. About 3 p.m. Lieutenant (Doctor) Garre was here to see me. I had another spell shortly after he left. In the evening I felt better and had some chicken soup they had heated. I felt better after that.

117

## October 25, 1944
Rott, Germany

I rested although I didn't sleep too well. I did not get up for breakfast. Instead the fellows drummed up a little one from the 10-in-1 rations. I stayed in bed until about 11 a.m. I got up but was wobbly. Malaria sure saps your strength.

I signed some things and then walked to chow. I couldn't eat much. After dinner I walked up to town and back. I was fixing things up when we got March Order over the phone. We started hustling. I changed into my old (clean) clothes that Raymond's mother had washed.

All the boys were stuffing the comforters in their rolls. We took the equipment out and have to wait for a truck. "Hilka" began running around counting the comforters (there's none left to count). She was running to the neighbors. So to prevent trouble from the Military Police, I had them put them back. We had the English-speaking woman here about it; she is sly. Our trucks came late. We loaded the stuff. To get even with "Hilka," (the maid), the fellows told some of the 28th Division boys they could have our place. They are taking it over, as we are moving out.

We went to the outskirts of Roetgen, pulled up a side road, and parked for the night. I ate a little supper in the dark, threw my stuff in a little half-built house. I moved from here to the house below with my Personnel gang. There are three old women here, one 85, a mother and two daughters, one 50 and one 48. The 48 year old one smokes, she says she learned from the Americans. We all stretched out on the floor. It is warm and we sat around for a while and talked. I had only my bedroll and that floor is hard.

## October 26, 1944
Rott, Germany

I had a fair night's sleep and got up at 5:30 a.m. We ate at 6 a.m. and got ready to move at 7 a.m.

We had a little difficulty getting around the first sharp corner (because of the trailer). We traveled the same way back to Eupen. We are passing the 28th Division who are coming to our sector and we, in turn, are going to theirs. We are going near Elsenborn. A buzz bomb passed over while we were on the road.

We arrived at Sourbrodt. The boys are complaining and yelling and Captain Tooley was "browned off." He wanted us to go into a stinking stable and latrine. They were in a nice warm house drinking coffee. We, an office, are supposed to go into a stable while all they have to do is flop down or play cards. The boys were all streaming into a house across the way. Captain Tooley showed us the laundry section of their house to use. He finally agreed to let us go to the other house. We set up an office in the kid's playroom. The kids were cute and running in and out. The boys sleep in the attic. There are five families here (no men).

After dinner we moved to a Hotel Schmidt, with the Battalion Command Post. We are to be all together. We are to be in a room by the bar. I have a nice bedroom with electric lights. Sergeant Sortino, of Headquarters Battery is to be here also in the Command Post (actually the bar). I sat in there all night, with the rest, reading, writing, and listening to the radio until 2:30 a.m.

## October 27, 1944
Sourbrodt, Germany-Belgium

I had a fair night's sleep although the bed was a bit short. The girl, who was outside yesterday and used to sleep here, was trying to get in and get some of her things, but they wouldn't let her in.

I heard a buzz bomb go over about 5 a.m. I went to chow in the Service Battery area and the setup for chow is nice. It's in a nice home. They said that there were many buzz bombs over yesterday morning.

I returned to the hotel and got the electric stove working in the kitchen. I heated some water and shaved. I went into the office area and they are all working. I did a few things there.

119

The rest of the Battalion is arriving. I worked on the payrolls all morning. About 10 a.m. a robot (buzz) bomb came over. You could see this one. It was really hustling along. It is an eerie feeling that there is no one in this "propulsion of destruction."

After dinner we all worked. I type out a Bronze Star recommendation to help Corporal Nagy out. We have to get them in today. Major Elliott came back today from the Infantry.

We all listened to our Division Band playing outside and a lot of the civilians were listening also. After supper I did some work then I listened to the radio and talked in the Command Post with the bunch.

## October 28, 1944
Sourbrodt, Germany-Belgium

I had a good night's sleep and got up at 7:15 a.m. It sure is cold today.

I worked all morning. I got the ration report for Corporal Childs (his father was the one time Mayor of Newton, Massachusetts). I got the figures together myself. I am almost cleared up.

I stopped off at the Medics, which is across the hall from the mess hall. I got a slip to get a blood smear (about Malaria). I waited for my result and it was negative. I met Marston here. He has Malaria. I came back and it sure is cold out. I worked the rest of the day.

After supper I did a little work and then went into the Command Post. I wrote and listened to the radio until 10:45 p.m. I had some sweet cider and German black bread.

## October 29, 1944
Sourbrodt, Germany-Belgium

I heard a buzz bomb going over about 5 a.m. I got up about 7:20 a.m. I went outside the building and there was a buzz bomb tearing across. The flames were coming out the rear. It was over a little ways. When I got to Headquarters another one was racing across. This one was headed northwest while the first one was headed west.

I came back and then went to the 8:45 a.m. Mass in the church, up about a mile. It is a nice church. Father Connors said the Mass. I came back and shaved. After dinner, I hung around the office. I had to go the Signal Company about soldier's voting. I worked and chewed the fat the rest of the afternoon.

After supper I sat around and read, wrote, and listened to the radio.

## October 30, 1944
Sourbrodt, Germany-Belgium

I walked down to breakfast with Major Elliott. I came back and shaved.

I worked all morning on various things. Tony Tooley talked to me about getting into Adjunct General Office in Machine Records Unit work (he had worked for IBM prior to going in the service). Everyone is getting ready for the presentation parade.

In the afternoon I worked and then walked up to the Headquarters to get some coffee and doughnuts from the Red Cross Mobile Unit.

After supper I sat around and read, and listened to the radio.

## October 31, 1944
Sourbrodt, Germany-Belgium

I got up and hurried to chow and came back and went to a meeting at Adjunct General, in Camp Elsenborn, by the V Corp. We are now in V Corp. There were some speakers on the methods they will use. A buzz bomb went over and it sure was low.

I took a bath afterwards. It was a nice place but I couldn't coordinate the shower and the hot and cold water. I worked the rest of the morning. It seems the Battery Commanders went to Finance but the rolls weren't ready. It was a mistake.

Lieutenant Freeman paid me and it is about $80.00 for the month.

After dinner I did some work. A Warrant Officer and some clerks from the Inspector General were here and checked our records. We had a few discussions. After supper I listened to the radio and read.

121

# Chapter six: November 1944

November 1, 1944 to November 3O, 1944

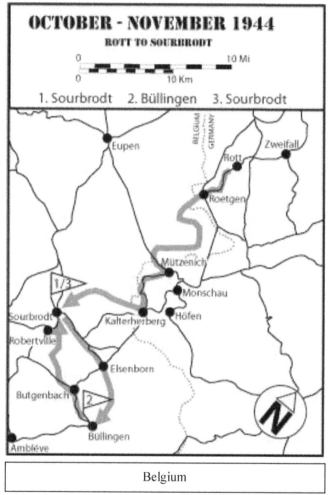

**OCTOBER - NOVEMBER 1944**

**ROTT TO SOURBRODT**

1. Sourbrodt  2. Büllingen  3. Sourbrodt

Belgium

Historical Overview
Month of November 1944 Corps Assignments:
First Army, 12th Army Group
November 1 to 31, 1944 V Corps

122

General Overview

The Allied advance is hampered by fuel shortages.

The Allies liberate Greece.

Allied forces advance from southern Italy pushing German forces north.

9th Division Overview: After sustaining heavy casualties in the battle of the Hürtgen Forrest, the 9th Division is sent to rest and regroup in Sourbrodt, Belgium

\*\*\*

*November 1, 1944*

Sourbrodt, Germany-Belgium

I went to breakfast, came back, and shaved. General Craig (General Louis Craig is the Division Commander) was in the area.

I worked all morning on a soldier's case. I tackled the lieutenant reclassification case and finished it up after dinner. I am quite busy as there is much to do.

The Battery Commanders still could not draw the money because when they got there, Finance was too busy taking returns. I worked all afternoon on various things.

In the evening I read a little. There is no radio as it was loaned to B-Battery. I prowled and probed through all the books, cans, and boxes in the kitchen.

**November 2, 1944**

Sourbrodt, Germany-Belgium

I was late for breakfast. I worked most of the morning on the Table of Organization. There are so many little things to do. I shaved in the kitchen. In the afternoon I worked on various things. The Doctor went to the Hospital feeling sick this morning. He thinks he has appendicitis. The other day the Doctor and I went over Article 230-105 on the

123

reclassification case.

The men got paid today, $10.28 in Belgium Francs and the rest in Marks. Tony Wisniewski and I went to Division Rear to straighten out the Table of Organization and other things. We bumped into Joe Devine, who was here from VII Corps. He introduced me to his boss, Captain Bergman, from Braintree, Massachusetts. We came back to the Battalion feeling determined to try and do something about getting back into VII Corp. It will be a long cold winter and VII Corp is always administratively conscious and aware of our setup. I walked over to the Personnel boys' house and talked. I then returned to the Hotel.

**November 3, 1944**
Sourbrodt, Germany-Belgium

I went to breakfast and all they had was a little cereal, coffee, a slice of pork sausage, and bread. I will starve at this rate.

I did some work and then went to Division. I fixed up a few things there and then came back. After dinner I worked, as there is quite a bit to do. I decided to clear up all the work as we expect to move soon. There are quite a few buzz bombs going over. They make plenty of noise.

I happened to see a list of the recommendations for the Bronze Star Medal and lo and behold there was my name.

**November 4, 1944**
Sourbrodt, Germany

I got up and had breakfast and then did some work. I am cleaning up everything as we expect to move tomorrow.

I went to Camp Elsenborn and had a swell bath and shower. It sure is swell to climb into a steaming hot tub of water and then rinse with a hot shower. There are quite a few robots (buzz bombs) going over. Two of them went off a few miles down the road. We could hear their motors stop and the explosion. I watched a close one and it seems to wobble, rise, and nose down as it goes along.

I bought a pair of combat pants at the Post Exchange here, $8.00. I worked all afternoon until 3 p.m. I drove with Smitty, Nagy, and Evans to the 4th Infantry Division Sector. We went to the Quarter Master section and saw Captain Richardson. He used to be a clerk in Service Battery and Personnel. We talked for a while.

It is raining out as we started back (16 miles). The roads are slippery and we went sideways as well as forward. It was cold and dark by the time we arrived back.

We had a snack for a supper.

**November 5, 1944**
Sourbrodt, Germany-Belgium

I could hear the fellows getting up early, as they are to leave about 9:30 a.m. I went over and ate at the regular time. The gang at the Hotel is all loaded up. I did some work and then talked with the colonel. I am to check the building and see that everything is okay after they leave. They left at 9:45 a.m. I was supposed to go with Captain Tooley to get a place but didn't, as he is just going to find the location. I went through the rooms and found equipment and writing material. I took the radio that was in the attic and returned it downstairs. I cleaned up a bit but one of the women here said she would clean up, so I left.

The soldiers from the 84th Field Artillery Battalion, who were stranded here on their return from Paris, are still here.

I ate dinner with Service Battery and then went with Lieutenant Obeldobel to the new area. I picked out a home for our section. It is two small homes attached to a barn. There are five beds, a kitchen, and a living room. I came back via Malmedy. We had a flat tire and it was cold. I came back to the Hotel and will stay for the night.

**November 6, 1944**
Sourbrodt, Germany-Belgium

I had a fair night's sleep on the couch. I was afraid that the strong wind, which was blowing, would keep the front open and let the hall light stream out. But no one stopped or said anything.

I got up at 7:30 a.m. I packed up but did not have any breakfast; however, I did have some coffee in the kitchen. The radio is playing. I checked the rooms and took care of the equipment and papers. The 84th gang is still here.

It is raining out. The two and a half ton truck came. I got in front with Rusty the driver. Corporal Shipe and Tony Wisniewski were in the back. It was real wet and the roads slippery. It took us about one hour. We are in Büllingen. We unloaded the stuff and unhitched the trailer. About one-half hour later the rest of the gang came along. I had them draw straws for the five beds. We set up the office and cleaned up around a bit. I did a bit of work as the lights work. We had some trouble later with fuses and lights. We all read or worked until the lights finally went out about 8:30 p.m. We used lamps and then went to bed about 10:30 p.m.

## November 7, 1944
Büllingen, Germany-Belgium

I heard Charlie Nagy talking in his sleep, laughing, and sometimes talking in Hungarian. The old man, who owns the house, alarm went off about 5 a.m. I rolled over and slept until 7:50 a.m. I got up and went to breakfast. I have a slight headache.

I did a few odd things around. I read about the reports I have to make, as this is Election Day (Presidential) back in the states. I signed a few things. I ate dinner in a room with Captain Tooley, Lieutenant Planting, and Lieutenant Obeldobel. Warrant Officer Bob Ramsdell came in with the liquor ration. It is one quart of Cognac, two quarts of Brandy, two quarts of Champagne, and one quart of Benedictine. This is the ration that cost us $16.00. I was supposed to get another bottle but they say some were broken in a truck accident.

I worked in the afternoon. The lights were out most of the time. A robot bomb came tearing over and turned and nosed straight down. It landed a few miles up and I took a picture of the black smoke rising in the air. There were about three explosions from it. After dinner I came back to the house and opened a bottle of Champagne and some Cognac for the guys.

## November 8, 1944
Büllingen, Germany-Belgium

I got up this morning and went to chow. I worked all morning, mostly counting money for Pay Transfer Accounts and Soldier's Deposits. I had $10,035 in all. I sent $100 home myself.

After dinner, about 1 p.m., I left with Corporal Staaf, Harry Hammer, and an ack-ack (376 AAA) soldier as driver. We make good time to Camp Elsenborn, as the roads are dry. At Finance I sent the money and then stopped in at the Adjutant Generals. Harry and I went to a movie here, while the other two took a joy ride. I then took a nice hot bath and shower.

We started back at 5 p.m. It is sprinkling and cold. I went up for chow, which they had saved. It is now snowing. I came back and caught up on the work and wrote. While we were gone a robot landed on the other hill.

## November 9, 1944
Büllingen, Germany-Belgium

It is still snowing out and it is a few inches deep. I was busy working on an excess personnel report. I also checked and signed various things. I paid off Gelders and Dewbury on a supplemental payroll. I worked all afternoon. It has stopped snowing but still looks like more.

There are rumors of us moving to the place we just left (Sourbrodt). There were a couple of robot bombs over during the day. In the evening I wrote and also had some milk that the old man had brought in from his cows. I brought out a bottle of Cognac and I dished it out to the boys, then I wrote a letter.

**November 10, 1944**

Büllingen, Germany-Belgium

It is hard to get out of a nice bed and go to chow. I came back and did some work. It is snowing off and on. I worked on the mail, the morning reports, and some correspondence.

After dinner, Captain Tony Tooley came back with me while Captain Thivierge checked their quarters. He checked the circulars and memos. Captain Thivierge dropped in and checked our quarters and then left the reports to be made out. I got a new holster for my gun (Remington 45).

After supper I went to the other side of the house and talked with the boys. I came back to the office and brought out the remains of the Cognac. I had some nice fresh milk from the old man with G.I. butter and bread. We get the fresh milk from the old man every night now.

There was one robot over today.

**November 11, 1944**

Büllingen, Germany-Belgium

About 4:15 a.m., while rolling restlessly I heard a robot bomb coming. It was sputtering and coughing (there wasn't any more robot sound). I saw a flash of light in the room and then a resounding crash. The windows rattled and the house vibrated and shuddered. It couldn't have landed any too far away.

I got up for breakfast and was busy all morning checking and signing papers. The stories are flying fast about our moving. The 99th Infantry Division, fresh from the States, is taking over here. Some of our units have moved back to the Elsenborn area already.

I took a walk up to the main road and back. I worked all afternoon on various things and wrote a letter to straighten out my allotment. There were a few robot bombs over today. I brought out a bottle of Champagne for the boys. I had a glass myself and then later had some fresh milk and bread.

**November 12, 1944**
Büllingen, Germany-Belgium

I had a fair night's sleep. Charlie was yelling in his sleep again.

After breakfast I went to work and there isn't much to do. After dinner Captain Pete Thivierge was down talking to us. There are all kinds of wild rumors going around.

A captain from the 99th Infantry Division is around looking at the area. They are going to relieve us.

Shortly after supper the lights went out so we are using lamps. There were a few buzz bombs (robot) bombs over. One was directly overhead and low. We just sat them out. We had toast and fresh milk from the farmer for a snack. I did some figuring just for the fun of it and I figured, with the help of the others, that we have had 70 officers in the Battalion since landing overseas. The Table of Organization calls for 35.

**November 13, 1944**
Büllingen, Germany-Belgium

I got up for breakfast and it is snowing off and on. I worked on various things. It is wonderful and warm in this room.

After dinner I came back and the 99th Division Personnel section was in the house. I met the Chief Warrant Officer, Personnel Adjutant. They are like us, i.e., in a Field Artillery Battalion and traveling with Service Battery. I gave them a few points and they are to move in as soon as we leave. The whole of their section showed up and talked for a while. We worked all afternoon and sort of cleaned things up. The rumors have turned into combat ones and so are lessening.

I brought out the bottle of Champagne I had in my bedroll and we all drank it. We talked until 10:15 pm about insurance.

**November 14, 1944**
Büllingen, Germany-Belgium

129

I got up and had breakfast. We are to move this afternoon. We came back to the house and loaded the trailer. We had to scrape the snow off, and the camouflage net was a problem. We hung around and then went over to dinner. We got a 99th Division truck to move us. We moved about 1:30 p.m., by ourselves. I showed them the way.

We unloaded the trailer in the yard of the Schmidt Hotel. We set up the office in the same room. We had to walk down to Service Battery to eat. I looked through the Café International for names on the doors of the bedroom, but there weren't any, so I decided to sleep in the Hotel Schmidt. We hung around the Personnel Office in the evening.

## November 15, 1944
Sourbrodt, Germany-Belgium

I had a fair night's sleep but it was a little chilly. I walked down to Service Battery for breakfast them came back and cleaned up. I signed a few things and then took off in the jeep with Eddie Rousse to the Battalion at Hünningen. It was a cold ride in an open jeep. I talked with Captain Thivierge at the Message Center and then went with him to the Command Post. The 99th Division has moved in on them and everything is crowded. Major Elliott, Major Williams, Captain Waters (60th Infantry), and Lieutenant Graham were there. I sat around for a while and then went to chow at Headquarters Battery with Lieutenant Gene Welsh. I came back to Headquarters and sat around again. I came back to the Hotel in Major Elliott's command car. I rode down to Division in a jeep a little later, did some business, came back, and ate. I did some work, played the piano, and wrote.

## November 16, 1944
Sourbrodt, Germany-Belgium

I had a pretty good night's sleep but I didn't get up for breakfast.

Captain Tooley came around looking at the set up. He had to arrange accommodations for men as they are going to set up a rest camp. I was still in bed. I got up and made a cup of coffee. I have a lot of work to do. I kept pretty busy fixing up different papers. I hung around all day trying to catch up on everything.

The kitchen is in the bar, in the Hotel, across the way. It is a good set up. Service Battery cleaned the Hotel for tomorrow. The men will arrive about breakfast time.

After supper I hung around the office. We talked until 11 p.m.

## November 17, 1944
Sourbrodt, Germany-Belgium

I had a good night's sleep in the new room and went to breakfast. The mob, one comes from each Battery for two days rest leave, tramped in. We put up signs and are keeping to ourselves. They are complaining and what not. Actually the place isn't really ready. It should have been planned a little better.

I've got Sandy Burns here to take care of. I have to discharge him as a G.I. and make him a second lieutenant. Delli got the papers ready and I did some of it. Meanwhile Colonel Beets and Captain Thivierge dropped around. They stayed at the Café International overnight.

A Military Policeman came in to us to ask about the radio that is missing from here. He had a report that we, Nuptial, our code name, Sergeant Nix, by name, were here and therefore responsible. I made out a certificate that when we had left the area the radio was still here.

I went down with Sandy Burns to Elsenborn and took a shower. We ate dinner and then went to Camp Elsenborn to Division Rear. I got him all fixed up as a second lieutenant. When we came back it was raining. I finished up some work.

After supper I went over to the Café International and listened to Lieutenant Wilensky, 60th Field Artillery (Dorchester, Massachusetts), play the piano. He was a professional piano player. I had a few glasses of wine. I talked with the girls there. There is a cute one named Marie. We sang and talked. We went to the movies in the mess hall and it was pretty good. I came back to the Hotel Schmidt and talked for a while.

Lieutenant Bernard Wilensky, Dorchester, Massachusetts. He was later Killed in Action on March 12, 1945.

## November 18, 1944
Sourbrodt, Germany-Belgium

I had a good night's sleep, got up for breakfast, and worked all morning. I got the payrolls ready and after dinner I rode down to Elsenborn to Division Rear. I stopped at Finance, the Adjutant Generals, and then at the Judge Advocate General. We then went to Battalion, who are now in the woods about two miles from Elsenborn. We got stuck in the mud near C-Battery, when Linscott, going too fast as usual, slipped off the road into the ditch. We got out of it and went up the street and found Battalion Headquarters. They are in tents and just sitting around.

I got back at 4:20 p.m. After supper I went to the Café International and listened to Bernie Wilensky play the piano. There were quite a few people there, Colonel Beets, Major Elliott, Captains Thivierge, Wilson, and Monson, and many of the rest of our gang. I left and went to the movies but it wasn't too good.

## November 19, 1944
Sourbrodt, Germany-Belgium

A buzz bomb landed up a ways and knocked out part of my broken window. I got up for breakfast and walked up to church. It was muddy and I had to dodge vehicles. It was the 9 o'clock Mass. I rode back with Father Connors. I did some work.

The new gang has arrived here for a rest. I stood outside for a while in the sun. In the afternoon I did some work and then hung around. I then went over to the Café International and talked. After supper I went back to the Café and talked, sang, played the radio, and fooled around. I talked with Mary, the cute German girl there. I came back to the Hotel for the 8 o'clock movie. The light was on making it bright outside. I had it put out, and the Military Police are investigating it. Some of the guys brought over two of the sisters to the show (Mary and her sister). It is the same movie I had seen earlier.

**November 20, 1944**
Sourbrodt, Germany-Belgium

I got up to eat, came back to the office, and worked all morning. It is raining out, and the snow, which fell during the night, disappeared. I initialed A-Battery records.

After dinner, I worked all afternoon. Major Elliott, Captain Thivierge, and Colonel Beets were around all afternoon. They had the C.I.C. (Civilian Investigative Corp) investigating the civilians. A couple of them were seen giving the Nazi salute.

I went to Division Rear at Camp Elsenborn with Warrant Officer Bob Ramsdell. We went to the shower to see Captain Tooley and then went to the Post Exchange, but did not buy anything.

In the evening I went over to the Café International and talked, sang, and had a good time. I listened to the radio, and talked with Mary and her sister in English and French. I went to the 8:30 p.m. show in the Hotel.

**November 21, 1944**
Sourbrodt, Germany-Belgium

I had a good night's sleep and then got up for breakfast and worked all morning.

The new gang came in today for a rest (this means that they can get out of the woods, tents, and dirt. They can sleep in a Hotel room, have hot showers, good food, movies, while the situation is quiet). I worked pretty steadily. The Battery commanders came down for a rest also.

In the afternoon I rode down to Division Rear at Elsenborn to take a shower and turn in work. I had to wait in line at the shower. It was nice to soak in the hot water. I came back and did some more work.

In the evening I went to the Café International. There were quite a few of the officers (60th Field Artillery). They were drinking and singing. I hung around for a while and then came back to the Hotel Schmidt. I went to the 8:30 p.m. movie. It is the same picture as last night but it is something to do.

## November 22, 1944
Sourbrodt, Germany-Belgium

I was awakened intermittently by Buzz Bombs at 2 a.m., 3 a.m., 4 a.m., 5 a.m., 6 a.m., 6:10 a.m., and 6:20 a.m. They are really sending them over. They are averaging three an hour. One exploded up a little ways. I got up and had breakfast; it is raining and miserable out. It snowed for a while.

I worked all morning in the office and I washed out a few things. The Buzz Bombs are still coming over frequently. I worked all afternoon and talked with my old gang, A-Battery boys, down for a rest, and had a drink of Cognac with them. In the evening I dropped over to the Café International. I listened to the radio and then went to the movie there. I came back to the Hotel Schmidt. We heard a lot of the Buzz Bombs going over last night and today. They are landing in Liege.

## November 23, 1944
Sourbrodt, Germany-Belgium

Thanksgiving Day

There were a few Buzz Bombs over during the night.

I got up, had breakfast, and came back to do some work. The lights were out and it was dark as it is raining. We got a couple of lamps going. I was supposed to be at a meeting at 9:30 a.m. I remembered it at 9:20 a.m.; I called Service Battery and waited for transportation, which did not come.

The new gang came in for a rest. We had a swell dinner and there were quite a few there. We had turkey, stuffing, and potatoes with gravy, coffee, and pie.

I worked for a while in the afternoon and then we drove down to Division Rear where I did a few things. I didn't eat very much for supper. I went to the Café International and the movie there. I returned, had a turkey sandwich, and then went to bed.

## November 24, 1944

Sourbrodt, Germany-Belgium

I got up, had breakfast, and worked all morning on various things. I made arrangements to go to Liege with Service Battery. It is raining and we went in the command car. Sergeant Brush, Linscott, and Prosnowski went along. We made fairly good time. I stopped in Trooz and checked with the 509th Military Police on a private. The sergeant referred me to the Liege or Eupen detachment. I went to Liege as the rest of the gang is going there anyway.

We parked the car in the center of the town parking area. We had some problems getting there, as a lot of the streets are only piles of rubble. The Buzz Bombs are coming in like mad here and knocking everything down. I walked uptown with Linscott; we stopped in an ice cream parlor. We had firsts and seconds, as they are nice sundaes. We talked with some girls. I paid for their sundaes. The sundaes were actually delicious and are the nearest thing to anything in the States.

The sirens started to wail, which means a Buzz Bomb is coming, then its motor died, which means it is gliding in to crash. The women all rushed out of the room going somewhere near, especially as this place has a glass roof. Linscott and I put on our helmets and crawled under the table, only to find, as we looked up at the roof, the table had a glass top. The bomb crashed over a bit and everything shook.

We left here and drove over to the Military Police. I went upstairs, and a captain tried to get me some information on the private. I was here an hour and during this time a couple of bombs came over, sirens wailed, and they landed over a little ways.

Linscott and I separated and both went to various sections of Liege. He had some things to do and he bought some Cognac.

I heard an alarm, heard the Buzz Bomb, heard the motor die, and saw it glide in to the city and crash over a little ways. The people, when hearing the siren, all run for the buildings and evidently get in the cellar.

We went to the 28$^{th}$ General Hospital where I did some business. We gave a Doctor a ride to town, then drove around and picked up the rest of the guys. We left about 5:30 p.m. and it was dark and raining. We stopped off in Verviers where they bought some Cognac. We got back about 7:45 p.m. I had a piece of steak the gang had fried for me. I went to the movie here and the picture was good.

It was rumored that at least fifty Buzz Bombs landed in Liege today.

## November 25, 1944
Sourbrodt, Germany-Belgium

I had a good night's sleep and got up for breakfast.

I rode up with Captain Tooley, in the two and a half-ton truck, to church. There was supposed to be a Mass but evidently it was a mistake as no one showed up.

I worked all morning, signing documents as Power of Attorney. After dinner I went to the showers at Elsenborn and had a good hot bath. I met quite a few people I knew there, Lieutenant Potts, 60$^{th}$ Infantry, and a lieutenant colonel, who was just a first lieutenant coming over on the ship from Sicily. He is now a battalion commander in the 60th Infantry (he is Lieutenant Colonel Keane Wilson ("Slick Wilson") who went from first lieutenant to lieutenant colonel in 77 days). He did some boxing while at Mississippi State. He has been wounded four or five times already, and survived to get these combat promotions.

I worked in the office all afternoon. After supper I went to the Café International and sat around talking. I went to the 8:30 p.m. movie at the Hotel Schmidt. I came back to the Café International. There were some doughboy officers here (Shuttleworth, Voller, and Brown), sitting with Captain Wilson, Captain Monson, and Lieutenant Van Leuven, of the 60th Field Artillery. They were pretty high and singing. I went into the next room and then came back to the Hotel Schmidt.

Lieutenant Colonel Keane Wilson, 60th Infantry. From first lieutenant to lieutenant colonel in 77 days.

**November 26, 1944**
Sourbrodt, Germany-Belgium

I got up at 8 am, ate and went to the 9 'o clock Mass at Sourbrodt. I got a ride down and back.

The gang told me that an Officer I knew had killed himself at the Café International last night, about 12:30 a.m. I had spoken to him at 10:30 p.m. They said he sat in the corner and put a pistol to his head. He did a good job. He slumped and then slipped to the floor in a pool of blood.

This Officer was a quiet fellow who seemed kind of morose. He had a different philosophy of life and read odd books and poems. He was always shy and quiet. He had threatened to take his life before.

In Africa, he had been one of the most fearless officers. He refused to retreat and stayed in his foxhole calling fire missions against the advancing Africa Corp. A shell landed right in his foxhole and blew the radio parts into him. He was sent back to hospitals, eventually ending up in England. He dated one of the girls from the Bank of England, who used to be at the Gables, and married her. She was one of the gang we used to take to the White Hart Hotel lobby and have Scotches in front of the flaming fireplace. I can still taste the desert from there, gooseberry tarts with sour cream.

He was still very shaken up after returning to us. I can remember, when he returned to us, we shared the same foxhole in France, June 10, 1944. We were under a heavy attack and he hung on my shoulders in the mud shivering and shaking. He was more scared than I. I often said to myself, "Why are they sending this man back into this? He has had too much. The best thing they could ever do would be to send him home." The colonel seemed to think he was doing him a favor, making him an Officer, and thereby a Liaison Officer with the Infantry. He always said he would be killed before it was over.

Before he shot himself, he said to Red (Captain Wilson), "Say goodbye to Wally" and pulled the trigger. Wally Wade was the son of the Tennessee football coach, Wallace Wade, himself a lieutenant colonel in the Army and an occasional visitor.

He had contemplated this before. Everyone is talking about it and the Military Police are investigating. I talked with Captain Thivierge and Doctor Copleman about it.

I worked in the afternoon, and in the evening I went to the Café International and saw a movie.

## November 27, 1944
Sourbrodt, Germany-Belgium

There were Buzz Bombs over during the night and at 4 a.m. one exploded not too far away, shaking the building.

I had breakfast and then went to work. Major Elliott was here getting statements from some witnesses so we had to clear the Personnel room. I stayed and did some work. I ate dinner and then did some work. Major

Elliott cleared the room again for another witness.

I took some money to Finance to exchange. I brought over $1000 in French Francs for the men going to Paris. I was delayed waiting in line and so had a late supper.

I went over to the Café International and sat around and listened to the officers singing. I went to the 8:00 p.m. movie here, by myself. A Buzz Bomb landed close by during the show. This has happened the last three nights during the show. I went back to the Hotel Schmidt afterwards.

## November 28, 1944
Sourbrodt, Germany-Belgium

There were plenty of Buzz Bombs over during the early morning. One landed just short of here and gave the building a good shake.

I got up for breakfast and came back to the office and cleaned up some work. The gang didn't get up, so I had some one wake them at 9 a.m.

Major Elliott had Lieutenant George Obeldobel in for a statement on the Officer's suicide. I stayed there and did some work and answered the phone. Later I went to the Medics and got a typhus shot. We all worked until noon. We are busy fixing up letters to families of the men awarded medals by the General.

I worked after dinner and then went to Division Rear with Lieutenant George Obeldobel. It sure is cold and sharp out. I came back and saw Chaplain Lorenz, Colonel Beets, and Captain Thivierge, at the Medics. They are visiting Doctor Copleman, who is leaving for an assignment in a General Hospital. Doc came to us from the Infantry. It seems that the Germans had captured a lot of men and they had Doctor Copleman caring for the wounded. We put on another drive and overran the Germans and recaptured Doc and the men. He was then sent to us to get a little rest. The new Doctor will be Doctor McFadyen.

## November 29, 1944
Sourbrodt, Germany-Belgium

I got up for breakfast and went to work. It was crowded here this morning. Major Elliott is here working on the Officer's suicide case with Corporal Charlie Nagy. I have quite a lot of work to do and it is hard to get started on it. I inventoried some of the Officer's personal effects. He collected poems and evidently wrote them. He had written for the *New Yorker* Magazine (he graduated from Cornell University). We all were very busy all day.

I went to the Café in the evening and had a good time. I listened to Bernie Wilensky play the piano. Lieutenant Sagle had a beaut of a haircut; he had "Hedy," one of the German girls cut it. She must have used a bowl.

We all went to the second show at the Hotel and sat on the table in the rear. After the show we returned to the Café. I played a little Ping-Pong and listened to Bernie play the piano. We had coffee and toast and sat around and talked (there was Major Elliott, Doc McFadyen, Captain Wilson, and others). I came back to Hotel Schmitz about 12 am.

## November 30, 1944
Sourbrodt, Germany-Belgium

I got up for breakfast and I have plenty of work to do. Off and on all morning we thought we would have to move out of here. The 47th Infantry are to move here but finally they said we could stay as they found a temporary setup.

Charlie Nagy is very busy on the Officer's suicide case. We lost the Café International to the 47th Infantry already. After dinner I found out that we are alerted and the Battalion is to move tomorrow.

I got my pay ($80.45) for the month. The men all got paid also. Everyone is coming in today making it a very busy day. I ran up to Camp Elsenborn with Pete Thivierge and took a bath. I came back and worked all afternoon. In the evening I walked up to Service Battery. I picked up my ration, a bottle of Scotch.

I have that Malarial feeling again.

We talked about living a full life and doing what we really want to do when we get back to civilian life. Something exploded over a ways and a lot of windows clattered.

I went to the second show and sat beside "Marie" and "Ilka." The show was just fair. I came back to the office and talked for a while.

# Chapter seven: December 1944

December 1, 1944 to December 31, 1944

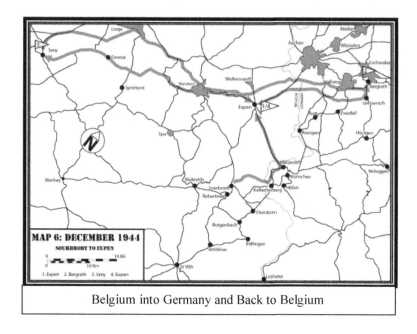

Belgium into Germany and Back to Belgium

December 1944 Historical Overview
Month of December 1944 Corps Assignments:
First Army, 12th Army Group
December 1 to 5, 1945 – V Corps
December 6 to 17, 1945 – VII Corps
December 18 to 19, 1945 – V Corps
December 20 to 31, 1945 – attached, with the entire First Army to the
British 21st Army group

142

General Overview

The Battle of the Bulge, also referred to as the German Ardennes Counteroffensive, began the night of December 16$^{th}$ – 17$^{th}$, 1944. During this battle the Germans broke through American lines in in attempt retake territory and gain access to the port of Antwerp in Belgium. The battle raged on until January 28, 1945. The casualties were the highest of any campaign during WW2.

9$^{th}$ Division Overview: At the beginning of December, the 9$^{th}$ Division after a well needed rest in Belgium, goes forward into combat in Germany.

As the 9$^{th}$ prepared to cross the Roer River and progress into Germany they were halted and forced to retreat due to the German breakthrough (Battle of the Bulge).

Knowing the 9$^{th}$ Division was a veteran Army unit the German Command planned to bypass them and launch their assault to the rear of the Division, where there were new untried troops. During this initial German troop movement, the night December 16$^{th}$ – 17$^{th}$, 1944, the 9$^{th}$ was pinned down, by bombing and artillery fire.

*\*\**

*December 1, 1944*
Sourbrodt, Germany-Belgium

A Buzz Bomb landed not too far away and shook the building. I didn't get up for breakfast.

The rest camp boys have already left, returning to the Battalion. The Battalion convoy moved out at 9 a.m. They are moving to the Monschau area. I did some work and washed clothes.

After dinner Father Connors said Mass. Service Battery moved out except Battalion Motors, Battalion Supply, a few Ammunition boys, and us.

We had a 10-in-1-ration for supper.

I checked the Officer (who committed suicide), clothes and papers. He was no doubt a writer, but I believe under a pen name. He is also a philosopher and I believe he taught it. He read extensively on life and death. He had books by T.S. Elliott, Schopenhauer, Mann, and Spangler.

I ate 10-in-1. They got meat at the market and it was delicious.

## December 2, 1944
Sourbrodt, Germany-Belgium

I got up about 8 a.m. I came down to the kitchen and had some coffee and bread with jelly.

We got everything ready to move. The 47th Infantry officers were around and waiting to move in. The truck came for us and is an empty one for a change. We loaded it up and took off. We are going via Eupen.

We followed some 240-mm guns for a while. They sure are huge and travel in two pieces, pulled by two trucks. We turned off in Eupen and took the Monschau road. We arrived at lunchtime and we are in the middle of the woods (it is known as the Eupen State Forest). We ate and then unhitched the trailer. We set up the pyramidal tent. We put it up after putting up our pup tents and built a fire. We stood around it and then had supper at 4 p.m. as it began to get dark. Some wandered off to bed at 5:30 p.m. and we made fun of them, but we followed at 6 p.m.

A few Buzz Bombs passed over and one exploded over a ways. I heard the Royal Air Force (R.A.F.) overheard. One can tell the British planes by the radial ring to their motors.

## December 3, 1944
Eupen State Forest, Germany-Belgium

It was cold and it rained in the early morning. I could hear the guys' mess kits clanging but I waited for the whistle to blow. I didn't hear it so I stayed in bed. I could hear the guys standing around the fire. I got up at 12 p.m., which gave me 18 hours of rest. I ate dinner and I am crummy, not having washed or shaved since yesterday.

We hung around the fire. It is cold and would be practically impossible to do any work. It seems foolish to have us move out here in the woods and have the Battalion look again for another rest area, especially when the rest of the Division are at Elsenborn. We are supposed to do office work in the woods, in a tent, sans heat and light.

I am going tomorrow to look for a stove and light fixtures. I got a phone call at the Service Battery Orderly Room, so I stayed and listened to the radio and talked. I came back to our tent and sat in the dark and talked.

**December 4, 1944**
Eupen State Forest, Germany-Belgium
I got up for breakfast this morning. It is cold and damp. We hung around the fire all morning and then put up two tents to work in.

After dinner I got the three-fourth ton truck with the help of Jack. Then Delli and Charlie came with me and we dropped Jack off at Battalion. We went toward Kalterherburg and then took the Camp Elsenborn road that is under enemy observation. We stopped at a vacant house that was still under construction. We rummaged through it and got some light fixtures, a stove, and a bed spring. We hustled through this, as this is a dangerous area; you can look across the flat area to the hills where the Germans are. We returned via Battalion, picked up Jack, and came back to camp. The stove wasn't very good so we left it by the Service Battery kitchen.

After supper we all hung around the tent. I went to bed at 9:30 p.m. The Buzz Bombs and Royal Air Force came over during the night.

**December 5, 1944**
Eupen State Forest, Germany-Belgium
I got up for breakfast and then hung around the fire. It snowed or rather hailed for a while until the ground was all white.

We had dinner, struck the two tents, and hauled them to the road. We

145

got the old stove, fixed it a bit, and set it up in the pyramidal tent. We all sat around the stove in the evening. We got some mail.

They called up about 10:30 p.m. and wanted a report on rotation. I made it out with the beat-up typewriter by lamplight. It was cold, too. Someone forgetting at Battalion must have caused this late work.

We have just about everything loaded as we expect to move out tomorrow. I went to bed at 11:15 p.m.

## December 6, 1944
Eupen State Forest, Germany-Belgium

The whistle sounded at 7 a.m. and it was raining. I got up; it is dark so I had to eat breakfast in the dark and cold. I came back and rolled up my bedroll and the boys all got their things together. We loaded the trailer, fell the tent, and loaded the truck. We were slow and just made it as we pulled out at 9:45 a.m. We pulled out by the road and waited for Battalion. We waited for an hour or so. The messenger that was supposed to come at 7:30 a.m. came just as we were moving out.

It is sprinkling and cold. We passed by the sawmill, Eupen, and there sure is plenty of traffic on the road. There must be a big push to come. We went toward Aachen, cut off and passed through Walheim, some Dragon Teeth, and then Gressenich. The towns here are all beat up. We passed a factory, which is Division Headquarters, and pulled in a short way up. This is on the edge of Eschweiler. We waited for Service Battery, 32$^{nd}$ Field Artillery Battalion, and 1$^{st}$ Infantry Division, to pull out. We moved into the house that they were in and it has shell holes through it, as do all the houses in the area. We are in the town of Bergrath. We cleaned up the side of the house we are to be in. Supply section is in the other half. We have light from the Service Battery's generator. We talked until 10:45 p.m. and I then went to bed.

Morrison, from Message Center, awakened me. He had a message for me.

## December 7, 1944
Bergrath, Germany

I got up for breakfast. I had a sneaking suspicion, but no word, that the men for rotation would be in today. Sure enough about 10 a.m. they came in prepared to go. I had the clerks get the records ready. The men were supposed to have been at Division Rear, Camp Elsenborn, about 10:30 a.m. I sent Sergeant Nix to Battalion for the men's clothing records. The men ate dinner here and left about 12:30 p.m., the lucky stiffs. They are to go to the third Replacement Depot, and then to the nearest Replacement Station at home in the U.S. They will have 30 days at home.

It is cozy here and the stove is hot. The nearby large guns make the house shake and the windows rattle. Late in the afternoon another man was picked to go home (his mother is ill). It is Technician Fifth Grade Peters, B Battery, and we went right to work on his records.

It is sprinkling out. I wrote a couple letters in the evening. They brought Peters here and we gave him his records and he left. I washed my feet and went to bed.

## December 8, 1944
Bergrath, Germany

I got up for a breakfast of French toast, "Gut, ya." I came back and shaved. It is nice and warm with the kitchen stove going.

I went to Service Battery next door and played the piano upstairs. I then went to the Orderly Room in the cellar and telephoned to Battalion. I came upstairs and played the piano again. It was a nice day, so I took some pictures. There is a machine gun fire sounding off all day and not too far away. There is also mortar and artillery fire. The big guns keep the house shaking when they fire. The planes were away up and left streams of vapor trailing like minnows in the pond.

I took a walk to the railroad station at Nothberg, up the road, and poked around in a few homes. I worked until supper, writing citations for awards. After supper I wrote letters.

## December 9, 1944
Bergrath, Germany

I got up for breakfast. It is misty and chilly. I came back and signed papers.

I looked at some German Art books. I did a lot of odd little jobs. It began to snow a bit around dinner. I stayed in all day, reading, looking at German books, and writing. The artillery has been firing all day. Machine gun fire still comes from up Eschweiler way and over by the hill. Jerry is throwing in plenty of shells below.

Tomorrow is supposed to start the big push, Duren to the Rhine River. I read and wrote in the evening.

## December 10, 1944
Bergrath, Germany

I got up for breakfast, censored mail, and signed a few things. We had a telephone put in. It sure is hard to wash in this water, as it is so hard and heavy with chlorine. The Batteries have been drawing ammunition all morning as the drive is still on.

The sky is clearing. After dinner I went on top of the huge pile of coal dust. It must be 60-feet high. There was a crowd from Service Battery here. We watched the Artillery mark the targets and then the medium bombers bomb. They sent up pillars of smoke and dirt. The P-47s dive-bombed, coming down vertically. You can see Jerry's shells landing in the town up ahead every once in a while. It was chilly so I came down.

I walked up to Division Artillery a little while later (it's about 500 yards from us). It is getting monotonous here. The boys were out scavenging again. I sent a jeep out later to pick up some mimeograph paper and a radio. The radio needs some adjustments. At 8 p.m. there was ack-ack fire all around us.

148

**December 11, 1944**

Bergrath, Germany

I got up for breakfast, cleaned up, and started counting Pay Transfer Accounts. It is quite a job as there are Marks, Belgian Francs, and French Francs. Something came whistling over. It was a little different than a shell, and another one came over. It is like a rocket, it can't be a V-2, as they are invisible.

After dinner I walked to Division Forward who are now about one hundred yards down the road. I wanted to take a shower but it was too small and there were too many there. A flying Fortress came over very low with two motors gone and the wing damaged. It was headed for enemy lines, losing altitude, with one wing much lower than the other. We climbed to the top of the coal pile to watch. There are a lot of fighters also flying over. We watched as the Fortress approached the German lines and they opened up with everything on it. The aerial display reminded me of the finale of a theatrical display on a Fourth of July. It might have lost direction, or been so damaged it was going down in the midst of the enemy with its bomb load, like the great sacrifice. Then again, the crew may have set it on automatic pilot, with its bomb load, so it would be shot down in the middle of the enemy. Our hearts went with it. Were there American G.I.s in it dead, or wounded, who couldn't bail out? It's a very emotional feeling.

We have another radio the boys found and they got it going. I wrote and talked in the evening. Some shells came in nearby just after I went to bed.

**December 12, 1944**

Bergrath, Germany

I got up for breakfast and it is sprinkling out.

They have the radio in the other room playing. I signed some papers and worked at the desk for a while. Sergeant Nix took the Pay Transfer

Accounts to Division Rear. They are located in Stolberg.

In the afternoon I worked compiling a list of the awards in the Battalion. I also fixed my records of casualties. The boys brought back two more radios. One is a real good one. I sat around read, talked, and listened.

### December 13, 1944
Bergrath, Germany

I got up for breakfast.

Chase of C-Battery was killed last night and three more were wounded. I worked in the morning and we have the radio going. Chaplain Orville Lorenz dropped around.

After dinner I went to Division Rear at Stolberg. The buildings are all damaged and the fields are littered with dead cows, horses, and full of shell holes. There are civilians in Stolberg. We saw some nice looking girls. The town itself isn't damaged too badly. I didn't stay too long as we had a lot of trouble locating Division. My foot is numb. I have a feeling I have a touch of Trench Foot.

I came back and did some work and then had supper. I typed a paper on awards, wrote, read, and listened to the radio.

### December 14, 1944
Bergrath, Germany

There was beaucoup incoming mail in the early hours. There were concentrations and I could hear them whistling in. They seemed to be landing on the other side of the coal pile.

I got up for breakfast and worked all morning writing correspondence and reading. It is a pleasure to listen to the radio all day.

In the afternoon I worked on a few things. I went out and climbed to the top of the coal pile. It was too hazy to see far. I came down and talked with Rusty and Mangun who are on extra duty fixing the drainage on the street. I played the piano upstairs in Service Battery. I worked some more and listened to the radio.

Some of Jerry's shells came in on the other side of the coal pile. The Battalion is also having trouble, as the shells are landing in their area. I was busy working on my income tax and writing, reading, and listening to the radio.

## December 15, 1944
Bergrath, Germany

I got up for breakfast, did a few things, and then got a jeep. I took George and Charlie with me and we went to Division Rear at Stolberg. We did a few things and I sent home a $100 Pay Transfer Account. We hung around the Red Cross Club mobile, had coffee, and then decided to leave. We headed for Aachen.

We passed through long rows of Dragon Teeth defenses. We passed civilians fixing the road under G.Is with guns. We entered the outskirts of town, and then came to a wide road and then into town. The buildings are a mass of rubble, and there are many civilians still here. We finally located VII Corps Headquarters. They are in the former Gestapo Headquarters building. We talked with Joe Devine. I got a VII Corps Christmas card and insignia from Captain Bergman.

We hurried back to Bergrath and worked all afternoon. In the evening Corporal Galfo and Technical Sargent Nix had an argument. Galfo told Nix, "He's just an enlisted man, and who is he to tell him what to do." Galfo is raving about. Nix wants to Court Martial him and is writing up charges. I'm quiet and I hope it quiets down and is forgotten.

## December 16, 1944
Bergrath, Germany

I didn't sleep too well as Jerry was bombing, flaring, and harassing all around. He landed many close by. The whole area was lighted up most of the time. He didn't leave until 7:15 a.m. I was peeking out of the window from my bed most of the time. We had some searchlights working on them.

I got up, ate breakfast, signed papers, and censored letters. The flare-up between Galfo and Nix got worse. Nix still wants to Court Martial him and he has the grounds and the witnesses all written down. I don't want any part of it. It means a lot of unnecessary work and bothering the Battalion at a time like this. I had to do something, so I called Captain Parrish and arranged to send Galfo back to him (Battery C). He sent me Corporal Lawrence, the Orderly Room clerk. Galfo was mad and when he left, he shook hands with me saying, "You were a good fellow, too bad you let that guy lead you." He didn't even look at Nix. I felt pretty bad as he was an excellent worker and he will have to go back to the Battery at a rough time. He has been a changed man since his best friend, back in the States, eloped with his fiancé and took the joint bank account.

Jerry started early dropping flares and bombs.

## December 17, 1944
Bergrath, Germany

It was a hectic night. Up until 7:30 a.m. this morning Jerry planes have been bombing and strafing all around. Our 90 millimeters are bursting overhead. Jerry had hung flares all over the place and dropped both personnel and regular bombs. I stayed in bed but was awake almost all of the time. I saw them hit a Jerry plane and he came down in a ball of fire. Jerry dropped flares over the church and they floated over the factory. He has hung quite a few flares below us, on the other side of the coal pile.

Sergeant Burrows (Service Battery) came in and said that the Germans were dropping an airborne unit. I got up and yelled down to Nix and then started up the stairs. The 90 mms were breaking overhead and lighting up the stairs as I climbed. I alerted them upstairs.

About 7:35 a.m. the agent came in from Battalion and Sergeant Nix got him what he wanted. The feeling between the other clerks remains unchanged. They are acting like school kids. They evidently blame me; curse Nix and cold-shoulder Charlie and Tony. I don't like to think that they have changed their attitude toward me.

About 11:30 a.m. there was the sound of many planes and diving motors and then machine guns. I ran out and saw a plane smoking. There were about 30 P-47s in the sky. The smoking plane had three P-47s on his tail and they were shooting at it. It banked and dove and then came straight down. I thought it would come down on top of us, but it edged over and crashed by the church just across the field. It sure looked like a P-51 Mustang. The pilot had bailed out and the strong wind carried him toward the enemy lines. He was tugging at the shroud lines and swaying. The ack-ack boys said he was a German ME (German Messerschmitt).

The planes are evidently protecting the movement of troops. The enemy has broken through our lines, and of all places around Büllingen, all the way to Luxemburg. Only one

Looking from our house in Eschweiler at Nothberg. We watched them shoot down a German ME 109 here one day. It fell near the church.

month ago we were in Büllingen and now Jerry is back there. I worked on the payrolls and the boys went to a movie.

After supper we had trouble with the lights. We finally put in a straight line to the generator. Every half hour Jerry drops flares and the 90s fire at him. He bombs and runs.

## December 18, 1944
Bergrath, Germany

It was noisy until 7:15 a.m. and the 90s broke overhead constantly. Planes are passing over and diving. They are dropping flares, bombs, and personnel bombs. I got up at 8:15 a.m. but did not go to breakfast. I cleaned up, but before I could finish about 12 German Messerschmitts went over. All hell broke loose. Our ack-ack ran to their guns but they were too late.

I counted Pay Transfer Accounts and signed papers. All morning Jerry planes were over in strength. The ack-ack was fierce but didn't bring anything down. There must have been 30-50 in all. There was a big dogfight beyond the factory. The sky was full of smoke trails and diving planes. You can see their guns flashing. Jerry had dropped Paratroopers around last night. A Junkers JU 88 passed over after dinner and they all fired. He wasn't bothered. Spent bullets are landing all over the place. About six of the 50 Calibers landed all around us. One hit the house over our head and sprayed us with pebbles from the shingles.

Eschweiler, Germany. We watched some wonderful dog fights over this factory. Jerry had up as many as 200 planes. We saw 60 at one time. Some fun. 1944.

I went to Division Rear at Stolberg and did a few things. I took a hot bath at the Stadt Bad. It's a former bathhouse and they also have a damaged swimming pool, which they are going to fix up. We stopped at the Quarter Master and then came back via Eschweiler. There are patrols here looking through houses for Paratroopers. Early in the evening they started firing the 90s as Jerry was dropping flares.

I received a 2-pound box of chocolates in the mail from my sister in law, Eleanor.

## December 19, 1944
Bergrath, Germany

There weren't so many planes over in the wee hours of the morning. I heard some anti-aircraft fire, flares, and personnel bombs. They dropped bombs nearby. One has a false sense of security in a house, but I had a good night's sleep, got up, and had breakfast. I worked on various papers in the morning.

There weren't very many planes out and the clouds were too low to see them. It was a quiet day. We (60th Field Artillery and 60th Infantry Regiment) are attached to the 104th Infantry Division, as the rest of our Division is down south to stop the German breakthrough. The Germans are supposedly in Büllingen, where we were not so long ago. Everyone is kidding about the Germans taking Sourbrodt and cutting off the hair of the girls for fraternizing with the Americans.

I washed my clothes in the afternoon. The paper says that the Germans employed about 450 planes yesterday.

## December 20, 1944
Bergrath, Germany

I got up for breakfast this morning and was the only one of my gang at that. I came back, built a fire, swept the floor, and then washed. It is foggy out and quiet, as it had been last night. I did some work checking personal effects of men killed or evacuated. After dinner I typed a few things, namely letters concerning footlockers. We don't have any lights as the generator burned out. I wrote and read in the evening by lamplight.

There is all kind of rumors about the German breakthrough. They are supposed to have over run the 99th Division, Headquarters and all. They are reportedly in Malmedy. We all wonder if they captured or killed the Personnel gang that took our place in Büllingen.

## December 21, 1944
Bergrath, Germany

Up for breakfast, after a quiet night and did some work afterwards.

I went to Division Rear at Stolberg and did a few things and came back.

After dinner I hung around the office and Lieutenant Cole, B-Battery, came by. I took some information, talked with him, and initialed records while he was there waiting for his driver. He left about 3 p.m.

About 3:30 pm Sergeant Burrows walked in and said "March Order." We are to move about midnight. We that are here (the rest are at the show), started to get our things together. We packed things, as we want to beat the darkness. We went to chow at 4 p.m. and then started to load the trailer. The two-and one-half ton truck is overloaded with ammunition. All the bedrolls went on top, but there is still stuff left over on the ground. Where to put it? It is raining too. We sat in the room in the lamplight. Later we find out that they aren't moving out until morning. We got our bedrolls off the truck and I slept in the kitchen.

## December 22, 1944
Bergrath, Germany

I got up at 5:50 a.m. and they fed us at 6 a.m. It is dark, raining, and miserable. We had to load up on any truck with room and the men did the same thing. They are all riding up on top of the loads in the open.

We moved about 7:30 a.m. We are supposed to go down and help out the Second Armored Division. We traveled slowly to Stolberg. We stopped on the other side and are to wait until 4 p.m. We all went into an empty house there. We built a fire. An armored unit had left here in a hurry leaving lots of things behind.

We ate dinner. I heated some water and shaved. We ate supper at 3:30 p.m. and then moved out at 4 p.m. We stopped at almost every town along the way. We went through Verviers to Liege.

We stopped on the road when the Luftwaffe dropped flares. They hung clusters of them on one side of the road and some on the other. They don't seem to see our convoy. They bombed and strafed anyway and our ack-ack is firing. We went into a bicycle shop and went down into the cellar. They dropped a lot of bombs around; we were lucky as all our trucks are overloaded with ammunition. We continued on again. There is a convoy of tanks on the road also. We went through Esneux but by-passed Sprimont. We stop now and then and we nod off. It is terribly cold and we just sit and bear it. The gangs on top of the trucks are taking a beating. We went over rough roads and many vehicles are on the side of the road. There are accidents.

## December 23, 1944

In Convoy, Belgium

All during the wee hours, until 8:30 a.m., we stopped and started. It was good blackout driving however because the moon was out. We nodded off once and the convoy started to pull out. They had to come from behind and tell us. Another time the fellows in front fell asleep and we had to wake them. There are trucks in the ditch and accidents.

We finally came to the town of Seny (it is now daylight) only to find out we aren't needed and are to return to Eupen. We pulled into the woods to eat. Our truck got stuck and it is cold and miserable. We ate and then had to push the trailer out. The truck had to be winched from tree to tree to get out. We left about 12:30 p.m. It was better returning, as we could see.

157

We stopped in a town as Jerry planes were firing on it. We moved along and got hot coffee (ersatz) from the kindly natives. They gave us pork sandwiches with bread and butter. We also got waffles. It is a long, cold, and tiresome ride.

We passed through Liege and it sure is beaten up from buzz bombs. We even saw some going over. I talked a little French with a girl. We passed through Verviers and it is now getting dark. As we came to the next town, the truck in front got a flat tire. We stopped to give them our spare and we sat in a café. The girl and woman gave us two loaves of bread and a glass of beer each. We had some cheese. We left here and Sergeant Thomas said he knew where we are to go. We passed through Eupen and traveled the Monschau road. Jerry has Monschau I believe. We passed by the old Battalion area. The guns are firing all around here.

We found out that Service Battery is back in Eupen. We unhitched the trailer so we could turn around. C-Battery passed us headed in, on their way to their position. We went back through Eupen and were flagged down by the Military Police and had to give the password. We found Service Battery on the outskirts of town. We parked, ate, and Harry and I found a little room in the basement of the Public Utility Building. It is steam heated and lighted and has a nice washroom. We cleaned up and went to bed.

**December 24, 1944**
Eupen, Germany-Belgium

I had a great night's sleep. In the morning there were women's voices in the next room. There was a kitten running along the wire fence and then jumping on top of me. I rested and slept until 11:35 a.m. I got up, shaved, and then went to dinner. There was fresh meat and the Third Section record player was playing records.

It is cold out but the sun is nice. There are enemy planes overhead and there is a lot of ack-ack. They have been over off and on during the day. Our bombers are out also. They are way up and look like minnows with their little streams of vapor behind them. A few Jerry planes were shot down.

The Third Section moved upstairs in this building. It is Christmas Eve so I let the boys take it easy. I sat in the room in the basement, reading and writing. There were some more men who moved in downstairs, in the laundry. They were drinking. I had some cognac myself that Windy Frued had given me. I went to bed about 9:30 p.m.

## December 25, 1944
Eupen, Germany-Belgium

I had a good night's sleep and got up at 9:30 a.m., as I want to go to Mass. Instead of going to the G.I. Mass, Skoczylas, Wisniewski, and I went to the Cathedral. It has two large, green spires and was built in 1774. We walked around town and then went to church. We stood in the back. The priest was speaking in German. It was a high Mass and there were about 10 altar boys. The choir sang and there was an organ and violin. The songs are the same as in our churches. The violin solo was Ave Maria. At Communion, American soldiers, Belgian soldiers, and the German and Belgian civilians went to the altar rail together. It was a nice ceremony and an impressive altar.

We walked back. We had a nice turkey dinner and I let the boys have the day off, as it is Christmas Day. Everyone else is working and it is a great day. There were enemy planes over and they bombed the other road, about one-half mile over. They also knocked out the electric light system.

In the evening we talked in the upstairs room and also downstairs. I went to bed after reading by flashlight for a while.

## December 26, 1944
Eupen, Germany-Belgium

I got up for breakfast and came back to the room. The lights are still out and you have to grope your way about.

I had the boys set up the office in the cellar where Archie Dougan and Murray sleep. It is the house beside the kitchen and the tile factory. We did a few things. I came back to my room and lay down for a while.

In the afternoon I hung around the office doing a few things. Jerry bombed the lines again and the lights are still out.

Every time the civilian workers climbed the poles the Military Police would call them down and frisk them. After seven times, they had to post Military Police there to stop undue delay.

In the evening we sat in the office and talked. The young woman "Alice," from upstairs came down for a while with the old man (her father in law?) and talked. I went to bed about 11 p.m.

### December 27, 1944
Eupen, Germany-Belgium

Jerry bombed in the wee hours and the old German janitor came running in. The civilians were also jabbering away. I didn't get up for breakfast but got up at 8:40 a.m. I came to the office in the cellar. The lights aren't on as yet, so it isn't very light. We all talked and had coffee, toast, and cake. I signed a few things and then went to dinner.

I went in a jeep with Rusty and some of the guys from Headquarters Battery. We went looking for a shower but didn't find any. We came back to Eupen and had one at the Victor Bath. It was crowded but we got a shower. I came back and signed all the morning reports.

I went to supper, came back, watched them sort the mail, and the lights came on. Jerry dropped a couple of bombs a few minutes later that shook the building. The lights went off for a while and then came back on.

### December 28, 1944
Eupen, Germany-Belgium

I had a good night's sleep but didn't get up for breakfast. I got up at 8:45 a.m. and had coffee at the office.

I did various things, such as censor the mail and sign reports. Many people drop in to both Personnel and Headquarters Supply in the cellar here. I read, talked, and worked all afternoon. We all sweat the mail out. It was quiet out as the weather held the Luftwaffe away.

I talked with Lieutenant Harry Link (one of his high school class mates was Marilyn Maxwell, the actress). He is an Artillery Observer in the cub planes. He said a German Messerschmitt shot their cub up, with a 20 mm hole right through the fuselage and some 50-caliber holes. He had an exciting 35 minutes.

In the evening I sat around, wrote and we talked about our travels and experiences until 12:05 a.m.

## December 29, 1944
Eupen, Germany-Belgium

I had a good night's sleep and got up at 8:45 a.m. I had coffee at the office.

I signed papers and censored mail. People come and go; it is busy here. Captain Parrish dropped in and then Captain Thivierge came by. I wrote and read in the afternoon. Most of the clerks are somewhere else; some are at the showers, others in their rooms. I wrote and read in the evening.

## December 30, 1944
Eupen, Germany-Belgium

I didn't get up for breakfast but got up at 8:50 a.m. I came to work and had some coffee. I did a few things and then got a jeep. I went to Division Rear in Stolberg. We passed through Aachen and it sure is in ruins. It was brutally cold.

I completed my business and talked with a few fellows. I met Chief Warrant Officer Phil Moyer here. I picked up a casual man from B-Battery, who was returning to us from the hospital. It was even colder on the way back. I really was cold, not in the body so much as the face, from the sharp wind.

I worked in the afternoon. In the evening I wrote, read, and we talked.

## December 31, 1944
Eupen, Germany-Belgium

I heard some of the men and civilians running down the stairs. A plane dropped bombs nearby. The 90 mms were cracking away overhead. It lasted for a little while.

I didn't get up until 9:30 a.m. I came to the office in the cellar, shaved, and then went to the 10 o'clock Mass at the big Cathedral. We were a little late, I came back and did some work.

In the afternoon I worked and washed some clothes. We sorted the mail.

After supper I read and wrote and did some work. We walked with "Alice," over to the woman's house across the street. We are to fix the Victrola. We had some wine, talked, listened to the records, sang, and listened to the radio. The woman, her young daughter, and some others were there. She said her husband was in the German marines or navy. Alice says her husband is in the German Army in Hungary. It is interesting to see them sway their heads when the Straus Waltzes are played. It's like the movies filmed in old Vienna. We sat and talked and ushered in the New Year. We came back to the cellar and talked until 12:30 a.m.

# Chapter eight: January 1945

January 1, 1945 to January 31, 1945

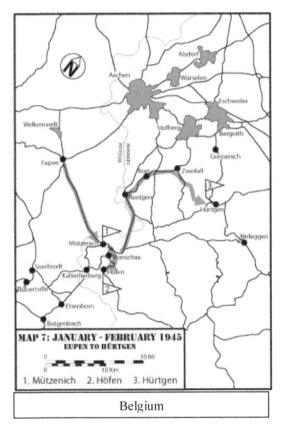

MAP 7: JANUARY - FEBRUARY 1945
EUPEN TO HÜRTGEN

1. Mützenich    2. Höfen    3. Hürtgen

Belgium

January 1945 Historical Overview
Month of January 1945 Corps Assignments:
First Army, 12th Army Group
January 1 to 17, 1945 - Attached with the entire First Army to the
British 21st Army Group
January 18 to January 31, 1945 - V Corps, First Army, 12th Army
Group

General Overview

The Battle of the Bulge, also (called the German Ardennes Counteroffensive), continues to stall any forward Allied movement. As January proceeds, this German offensive fails. The official ending of the battle is considered to be on January 28, 1945, when German troops begin their withdrawal from the Ardennes Forest.

On January 27, 1945, Soviet troop liberate Auschwitz and Birkenau Concentration Camps.

The Campaign to eliminate the Colmar Pocket is begun. The Colmar Pocket refers to an area around Alsace, France. It is the last area of German occupation in France.

9th Division Overview: The 9th Division is stalled in moving forward by the German Offensive.

During the month of January 1945, the 9th Infantry Division held defensive positions in the area of eastern Belgium.

***

### *January 1, 1945*
Eupen, Germany-Belgium

Got up at 9:30 a.m. (New Year's Day). German planes were over early this morning and the lights went out. Either Jerry's bombs or our ack-ack knocked them out. I went to the office, washed, and shaved.

The men were paid today and I did a little work. We can't work without the lights, as it is too dark in the cellar. The Personnel gang (that's us) is hard to find these days. Some stay in their room across the street and the others group upstairs in the office building.

In the afternoon I did a little work and talked with the usual collection of fellows. There were a few officers who dropped in. The mail came in and we watched the sorting.

After supper we sat in the lamplight. We read and had a discussion. I went across the street to bed about 11:30 p.m.

**January 2, 1945**

Eupen, Germany-Belgium

I got up at 9:30 a.m. and went to the cellar to work. I signed a few things and talked to some folks.

A request for my status, as well as 34 others came in. It is advance notice of an award.

After dinner I took a long walk through Eupen looking in the windows. The electric lights came on. I watched Carter sort mail.

In the evening we had a snack of chicken, corn, toast, fruitcake, and coffee. We read and wrote.

**January 3, 1945**

Eupen, Germany-Belgium

Got up at 9:30 a.m. and worked all morning on various things. The men are working on Pay Transfer Accounts.

After dinner I walked down to the Hotel Bosten and found some of 9th Division Finance. I changed some Marks to Francs. I came back to the house and looked at the tile paintings the man upstairs sells. Afterward I sorted the mail out.

After supper I wrote, read, and talked. The drain in the cellar is clogged and it stinks. We had a snack of salami, with mustard, toast, and coffee.

**January 4, 1945**

Eupen, Germany-Belgium

Got up at 9:30 a.m. and it is snowing. I went to the office in the cellar. The cellar drain is flooded and the pipes are clogged.

I went down looking for a bath. I dropped in at the old V Corps shower but it was crowded. I came back and made preparations to take a bath in a washtub in my room.

I went over and spent a while looking at the tile paintings of the fellow upstairs. After dinner I heated water on the stove and took it to my room and took a bath. I went back to the office and finished up the work.

After supper I read, wrote, and talked. Later we had a snack of tuna fish, toast, and coffee. We all got together and jointly composed a letter to a couple of girls who are friends of Freddie Murray's sister.

## January 5, 1945
Eupen, Germany-Belgium

Got up at 9:30 a.m. and Father Connors was in the area. He had Confession and Communion. I didn't get up to go. I signed papers and reports.

Sargent Nix went to Sourbrodt. I sat around, worked, and talked. I checked regulations on the wearing of awards for Service Battery. Major Elliott dropped in. I stayed, worked, and talked. There is a crowd down here. I had quite a session with the washer-woman (Putzfrau) over the language, soap, clothes, and money.

After supper I hung around the cellar, read, and had coffee and cake.

## January 6, 1945
Eupen, Germany-Belgium

Got up at 9:30 a.m. and had coffee and toast at the office. I did a few things and we are pretty well caught up.

After dinner I took a good long hike around town. I dropped in at Finance on the corner street at the Hotel Bosten. I came back and did some work.

After supper we all talked, and later had a snack of salami, mustard, and toast avec coffee. We talked until two o'clock in the morning, as it was Saturday.

## January 7, 1945

Eupen, Germany-Belgium

Got up and had coffee and then went to the Cathedral to the 10 o'clock Mass. Mass is sung but only one priest said it. Charlie Fabre (Brooklyn, New York) and Skoczylas were there. We watched the people file out. There were Belgian soldiers in their English uniforms, girls, women, a few children, old men, and a young man here and there. I came back to the office, fixed the fire, and cleaned up. I signed a few things then sat around talking.

After dinner I sat around, worked, read, and talked until supper. We did the same thing after supper. I worked later on a list of men of the Battalion, killed in action, and missing in action. I will give it to Sergeant Burrows, who will give it to Colonel Adams who has been evacuated to the States. I checked both Sergeant Burrows' and Embry's records as they are going back to the States. I got through about 12:30 a.m.

## January 8, 1945

Eupen, Germany-Belgium

Got up at 9:20 a.m. and went to the office. Burrows and Embry left this morning for a rest in the States.

I hiked all around town looking for the Quarter Master sales store at the Hotel Duriport on Gospertstraße. It was slippery walking, but nice out even though it was snowing a bit. I just looked around enjoying the walk. I got to the other side of town without noticing any sign of the store. On my way back I inquired. I found it just below the Cathedral and bought some woolen underwear for $1.50, and then I came back and ate dinner.

In the afternoon I worked and talked. After supper I read and talked. Later on we had a snack of cheese, onions, toast, coffee, nuts, and candy. I fixed up a report for Lieutenant Obeldobel. Harry and I went back to our bedroom. We talked for a while about sports, chiseling, and music.

167

## January 9, 1945
Eupen, Germany-Belgium

Got up at 9:25 a.m. and went to the cellar to work. I had coffee and toast, signed papers and talked.

Tom Gaffney (Danvers, Massachusetts - former Harvard football player) dropped by with two lieutenant friends (a Lieutenant Bloom and another lieutenant). He is checking up on some of his stuff. We fixed up some papers for him. I took the three of them to chow and fed them. Tom then went on to Battalion. I hung around in the afternoon. Tom returned and picked up some more papers we had prepared. I worked, read, and talked.

After supper I read, talked, and wrote until 11:30 p.m.

## January 10, 1945
Eupen, Germany-Belgium

Got up at 9:30 a.m. and went to work, it is slow so we talked.

In the afternoon I tried to fix some skis. I took some pictures outside in the snow. We worked and talked until supper. Dougan and Murray

Eupen, Belgium.1945.Harry Hammer (on right) and I.

went to Verviers in the afternoon. We talked and argued in the evening. The discussion was bowling candlepins (Boston) verses ten pins (New York). We had a snack, read, and then went to bed at 12 a.m.

## January 11, 1945
Eupen, Germany-Belgium

Tony Tooley came and woke me about 8:15 a.m. to make out his marriage papers to an Army Nurse. He wants to take them with him at 9 a.m. I went to the office and typed it up myself, as he doesn't want every Tom, Dick, and Harry to know. I had coffee and heated an egg omelet that the boys brought back from breakfast. I did a little work and talked.

After dinner I tried to get transportation to Verviers to take a shower and look around. I can't get anything until tomorrow afternoon. I did a little work on the skis and then did some paper work and talked until supper. After supper we all talked, wrote, and read. We had a little quiz program from a magazine. We had fun. I went to bed about 12 a.m.

## January 12, 1945
Eupen, Germany-Belgium

I was awakened by Sargent Nix to fix up some more papers for Tony Tooley's marriage. I went to the cellar at 8:30 a.m. and started working on it. Service Battery was having a meeting at the same time on fraternization. I finished Tony's papers and did other odds and ends, then had coffee and toast.

I ate an early dinner and took the command car to Verviers. Linscott drove. I tried to change Marks to Francs there, but no luck. I tried to find a nice place to take a bath. There was only one, a public bath, and it was overcrowded. I window-shopped and had an ice cream sundae, also an encore. I walked through the stores. There was one huge department store just like in the United States, but the stock was sad. We came back

169

to Eupen at 3 p.m. and I worked until supper.

After supper we read, talked, and had a snack. I opened up my Scotch ration and passed it around.

## January 13, 1945
Eupen, Germany-Belgium

Got up at 9:30 a.m. and worked in the cellar all morning. After dinner I took a walk around town. It was very cold out. In the evening we sat around and talked, read, and wrote.

Me, Freddy Murray (from Wilmington, Massachusetts) and Harry Hammer (from Brooklyn, New York). Eupen, Belgium. 1945.

## January 14, 1945
Eupen, Germany-Belgium

Up at 9:30 a.m., went to work and had coffee and toast.

We decided to go the 11 o'clock Mass at the church on Aachen road. Charlie Fabre, Fred Murray and I went and stood in the rear. The people sing and say prayers aloud throughout Mass. After Mass we watched

170

the passing parade of churchgoers. We then walked around town, up the hill and down past the concentration camp for Nazi collaborators. People were passing in baskets of food to the people. We came back to a chicken dinner.

I took a good walk in the afternoon, all by myself. I went to the heights of the hill overlooking Eupen. It is a great day and there is plenty of snow. I took some pictures and wrote a poem. I came back to town and walked up to the coasting hill. I watched the G.I.s and the civilians coasting (kids, girls, and G.I.s). The soldiers, riding with the kids and the girls, all had a good time. I continued down the road where others were coasting and then came back to the office. I came outside and met "Alice" and her girlfriend. I took their picture and the guys in the kitchen snapped me with them. After supper I read, wrote, and talked.

---

Winter Town

(Eupen)

Nestled in a blanket of snow below,

Slowly breathing the sounds of earth

Like reports of children employed at play

And the resounding bark of dogs.

Smothered under the heavy snow

Lies the beating heart of the town and

Street cars screeching wheels and whistles

And the distant blare of automobile horns.

The faraway noise of a village street

Rises melodious to the lofty heights.

A tune too descriptive for musicians to express

And a picture too diminutive to paint.

Frank Lovell

Eupen, Belgium-Germany

## January 15, 1945

Eupen, Germany-Belgium

Got up at 9:15 a.m. and went to work. I shaved, cleaned up, and signed papers.

After dinner I got Service Battery's command car and went to Division Rear at Stolberg, Germany. It was snowing. I took Fabre, who was looking for his dog, Mac, and also Harry Hammer who is looking for his brother in the 8th Infantry Division. The 8th is all over Stolberg. I made a few official calls at Division. I dropped in and saw Frank Page and went to his room. I weighed myself; I weighed 71 1/2 something or other, which is approximately 157 lbs. I went back to the command car at 3 p.m. Harry wasn't there. Charlie Fabre said that Harry had found out his brother had been killed a few weeks ago. A trip wire was kicked and four of them got it. Harry had hopped a ride to Zweifall to see his brother's Commanding Officer. We came back without him. It was a miserable ride as there was a half rain, half sleet deluge. It stuck on the windshield and we had to stop every now and them and scrape it off. We even put on alcohol (Cognac) but it didn't help much.

After supper I read, wrote, and talked.

## January 16, 1945

Eupen, Germany-Belgium

I was just going to get up when I heard that Major General Craig, The Division Commander was in the area checking around. I got up in a hurry and went to the cellar, shaved, and had coffee. The General passed by outside and went into the kitchen. He then left the area. Everyone down here was jabbering about what they were going to say if he asked them anything. I did a few things.

After dinner I walked up town and met Skoczylas on the way. I went to the hill, half way up town and watched them coast. Rusty (Raymond Rust, Beverly, MA), Mangum, Childs, and Smitty had their toboggan made from skis. They were the center of attraction. The rest of the people have wooden sleds.

I came back and got a jeep and tried to find the Notary Personnel Section. I took the Herbesthaler Straße road instead of the Aachen road. It was almost suppertime and cold so I gave up and came back.

After supper I read, talked, and went to the show at the 9th Medics. Came back at 9 p.m. and had coffee and a snack. We talked and read until 12 a.m.

## January 17, 1945

Eupen, Germany-Belgium

Got up at 9:25 a.m., had coffee and toast at the cellar and did some work. I went to the Service Battery Orderly Room and found out they want me to take the Council Books to the Inspector General. I had to get a ride on a two and one-half ton truck, as the rest of the vehicles were being used. The truck is going on a coal detail to Eschweiler so they will drop George Neuhardt and me off. George is going to be dropped off in Aachen to see Joe Devine at VII Corps. The Military Police stopped us at a checkpoint. I had to show my Adjunct General Card as they are looking for a Lieutenant Richardson who is a Jerry.

George got off at Aachen and I got off at Stolberg. I walked around Division, left the Council Books, and completed a few odd jobs.

I met George here. He came from Aachen. The VII Corps has moved to Dinant and the 9th Army is now in their place.

I waited by the road for the truck; George got a ride back with some Military Policemen. There are a lot of girls and others walking by. There is beau coup G.I.s around, the 8th, 78th, 9th, and 104th Infantry Divisions. They take showers at the Stadtbad. An Engineer Officer talked with me for a while; he has a brother in the 39th Infantry.

Five Jerry prisoners came in on the back of a truck. The civilians all stared and called each other's attention to them. They (the civilians) were apparently embarrassed or mad. My truck came along and we came back.

173

After supper I read, wrote, and talked. Pop and "Alice" came down with some white (Bordeaux) wine. It is Pop's 40th wedding anniversary. We toasted him, talked, and had a good time.

## January 18, 1945
Eupen, Germany-Belgium

Got up at 9:25 a.m. and it is windy and snowy. I had coffee and toast at the cellar. I signed papers and censored mail all morning.

In the afternoon I did the same. I did get the command car, had George drive it, and we went to the Second Evacuation Hospital. We went to check up on Lieutenant Brown, Air Observation, and Pilot of one of the Cub planes. I got the information and we came back to Eupen. George dropped off his radio after supper. I read, wrote, and talked until 11:30 p.m.

## January 19, 1945
Eupen, Germany- Belgium

Got up at 9:25 a.m. and it is windy and snowy again. I had toast and coffee. I wrote some recommendations for awards. I read the paper until dinner.

After dinner I rewrote awards until supper.

After supper I read, wrote, and talked.

## January 20, 1945
Eupen, Germany-Belgium

Got up at 9:25 a.m. and had coffee and toast at the cellar. I sat around and worked and talked until dinner.

After dinner I wrote recommendations for awards (tri-monthly period for Bronze Stars for Meritorious Service). I took a walk around Eupen in the afternoon. I watched the kids, soldiers, and girls coast.

I read, wrote, and talked after supper. Some men and Captain Gray are going on pass to Paris tomorrow.

## January 21, 1945
Eupen, Germany-Belgium

Got up at 10:15 a.m. and went to the cellar and had coffee.

Murray and I took Charlie Nagy to Mass (he's a Protestant). We were late and it was crowded as usual. We were able to squeeze in the door. We were there for about 15 minutes. We came back to Service Battery and I went to the cellar and did a few odd things until dinner.

Coasting at Eupen, Belgium.

After dinner, I took a walk around Eupen and back. I went to the office and wrote some recommendations for awards.

After supper we went to the show at the 9th Medics. We had to wait about one hour. I met Captain Turnipseed and Lieutenant Paterson there. I came back instead of waiting any longer. Dougan, Murray, and First Sergeant Stoll were with me also. We had a snack, read, and wrote, until bedtime.

## January 22, 1945
Eupen, Germany-Belgium

Got up about 9:25 am, had coffee and toast and did some work.

After dinner I met Lieutenant Sagle, A-Battery, outside the dentists. I suggested going to Verviers. We got his three-fourth ton truck and took off. It is a chilly but nice day. We walked around town a bit and ended up in an ice cream parlor. We went upstairs; there were two nurses (U.S.) ahead of us. There were a lot of girls, kids, and some G.I.s there. We had three sundaes each and then some Belgian girls came in. They were in uniform (civilian auxiliary workers, they help the evacuees). We had a time talking with them in broken English, French, and German.

175

One of them was a cute 19-year-old blond. We had a sundae with them. I had four in all and Lieutenant Sagle had five. He paid for our three each. I paid for all the rest, girls included. It must have cost us about 200 francs, or over four dollars. We had a good time with them. We came back to the truck and returned to Service Battery.

After supper we read, wrote, and talked in the cellar. I collected my liquor ration. It was two bottles of Champagne and one of Cognac. I got the Post Exchange rations also (candy). I gave the cognac to the Section in the building. I gave the majority of my Scotch, received the other day, to the boys upstairs in "Alice's." I brought a

Bennie Guanciale from Pennsylvania and Robert Tate from Illinois.

one-half bottle of gin to the cellar. Bennie Guanciale mixed a few drinks. We read and talked.

## January 23, 1945
Eupen, Germany-Belgium

Got up at 9:25 a.m., had coffee and toast, shaved, and then worked. I wrote some recommendations for awards.

After dinner I worked for a while and then got a ride to the Post Office in Eupen. I tried to get a money order for one of the officers to a girl in England. The Post Office clerk said he couldn't do it.

I came back and then took a walk with Murray. We watched the gang coasting and skiing. Some of Service Battery was there with the toboggan. Skoczylas and Charlie were there also. Charlie was with a girl coasting.

After supper I went to my room and got a bottle of Champagne. I brought it back to the cellar. We all had a snack of coffee and toast. Later I opened the Champagne. It was pretty good. "Alice" dropped down and talked for a while. Charlie got her going; he said he was

Hungarian (he's American of Hungarian parents), who joined the U.S. Army. He said the Russians were big and hard fighters and that they were cutting the Germans down like hay. She said, "You mean my husband is dead?" and she broke down crying and ran to the wall, crying like a kid. Archie Dougan soothed her and she snapped out of it.

We went to bed about 12 a.m.

## January 24, 1945
Eupen, Germany-Belgium

Got up at 9:35 a.m. and went to the cellar. Archie had a bottle of Champagne he got from "Alice." We had Champagne for breakfast, with coffee and toast.

I wrote a few things about awards until dinner. In the afternoon I talked, wrote, and read.

After supper I read, wrote, and talked. We had a snack of tea, toast, and cookies.

## January 25, 1945
Eupen, Germany-Belgium

I got up at 9:15 a.m., had coffee and toast, and washed. I worked on awards, Morning Report, and mail.

After dinner I walked around town, up to the top of the hill, near the Hospital, and down the hill. I went past the place where the kids are coasting and past the concentration camp. I came back to the cellar, read, and did a few things.

After supper I walked to Nutmeg (60th Infantry) Service Company with Dougan. We saw a movie, it was a good picture but the sound (acoustics) wasn't any good. It was cold out, a still cold. A Buzz Bomb streaked across the sky in the distance.

We got back at 9 p.m. We read, wrote, ate, and talked. I got a call that Lezon of Medical Detachment, was going home. He lives in Ipswich, Massachusetts. He is leaving tomorrow so I had George get some of his records ready.

## January 26, 1945
Eupen, Germany-Belgium

Got up at 9:35 a.m. and went to the office, had toast and coffee. I shaved and washed there.

I checked the records going out and censored the mail. Teddy Lezon came in toward noon for his records. He is going home via a Hospital ship as a nurse. He will have 10 days at home. I checked his records and gave them to him.

After dinner I stayed around doing a few things. I went to Captain Thivierge's room, talked for a while, and did a few things, read, and talked until about 12 a.m.

## January 27, 1945
Eupen, Germany-Belgium

Got up about 9:40 a.m., went to the office and made coffee and toast. I did a few things. I tried to check on the recommendations for awards, but the telephone lines were busy. I wrote one or two more awards.

This place is the same every day, i.e., Skoczylas kidding Archie about "Alice," going or gone to Aachen, big friendly arguments over who throws the most bull, tending to the little stove, the stink of the cellar especially when the drain backs up, sit and reminisce or foretell or rumor, snow, Old Pop from upstairs coming for water, bowing, taking his hat off and laughing, the kids of workers coming in, speak and think German but claim to be Dutch, Headquarters men down to try and get supplies and equipment from Archie, who is Headquarters Battery Supply Sargent.

After dinner I went to Captain Thivierge's room and we talked over the new Table of Organization. He had spoken and arranged for a Technician Fourth Grade for Charlie Nagy. Now the new Table of Organization only calls for a Technician Fifth Grade, which he already is. I brought the Table of Organization back to the office and had Tony Wisniewski go to work on it. He is supposed to be a Technician Fourth

Grade under it and Jack Markowitz a private.

I started to get malarial chills about 4 p.m. I hugged the stove. Murray thought I was kidding but then said my eyes were bloodshot. I went back to my room and went to bed. I took two Atabrine tablets. I became violently ill soon after. Harry brought me juice later. I then started to sweat and the water was streaming down my legs, arms, and face. I threw up. Nubby Collins (nicknamed Nubby as he is missing a couple of fingers), one of the medics, took my temperature. It was 101. Harry, Tony, and Nix dropped in.

## January 28, 1945
Eupen, Germany-Belgium

It was a pretty restless sticky night and into the early morning hours. The Malarial sweat has gone. I got a couple hours sleep, until 6 a.m. At least now I feel a little bit comfortable. I got up at 7 a.m. and emptied my helmet out, as this is what I used to throw up in. I went back to bed. Harry brought me some tea and toast about 10:30 a.m.

It is Sunday, I had forgotten. Sergeant Nix dropped in to see how I was. Nubby Collins the medic dropped in. Windy said, "Hello." I am feeling okay but not normal and I am weak. I had taken one Atabrine and one Quinine tablet with a little grapefruit juice. Harry brought me some coffee and toast for dinner. He and Jack went to services (Jewish service). Skoczylas had been in earlier and borrowed my pistol. He had to have sidearm, and a pistol is easier to carry.

I got up and dressed about 1:15 p.m., but I am pretty weak, although I feel fairly good. I went back to bed, as I only feel fair. Different people dropped in and I went to sleep.

Harry brought me supper; it was chicken, potato, cocoa, and chocolate cake. I ate a little of it. I lay down and rested all evening, as I didn't feel any too well. I had another attack but am doped up enough to shake most of it off. I took two Atabrine and one Quinine before 11 p.m. I got up once later on.

179

## January 29, 1945
Eupen, Germany-Belgium

I had a poor night's sleep. I had some chills and a sweat but I am doped up enough to overcome the worst part of it. My stomach was not well and I was restless.

Harry brought me breakfast. I could hardly touch it. Captain Tony Tooley dropped in but I was asleep. Numerous people dropped in, Nix, Tony Wisniewski, Delli, Archie, Windy, Charlie Nagy, Charlie Fabre, and George.

I sat up about 11 a.m. and read. Harry and Windy came in at noon, and I talked to them for about 20 minutes. Jack Markowitz came later in the afternoon with hot soup. They all have been extra good and want to do something for me. Archie brought in a couple of oranges. Skoczylas brought in Mike Maher my good friend, a clerk in the 34th Field Artillery, who is here to see the dentist. We talked for a while. He has the same twist in the 34th as we do in the 60th but in a worse environment. Personnel are dead weight, undeserving of anything, useless work with no relief or outlet, last in consideration for passes, relief, benefits, and credit.

I got up and dressed about 3 p.m. I only took one Atabrine tablet today. I went over to the office and saw the boys. I feel weak but well. I signed the morning reports and talked. I went to supper but didn't eat much. Lieutenant "Doc" Graham and Captain D.C. France were there. Tony Tooley said we might move tomorrow. The doughs are supposed to jump off.

After supper I spent some time in the cellar reading and talking until 11:30 p.m.

## January 30, 1945
Eupen, Germany-Belgium

I felt tired and weak this morning so I didn't get up. It seems to affect my back, making it weak. I rested until 11:30 a.m.; I got up, dressed, and went to the office. I did a few things and talked until dinner.

I didn't eat much for dinner. After dinner I sat around the office and arranged a trip to Stolberg for Steponik, Headquarters Battery. I sent Jack along with him to help find the information he needed. It was too cold for me to go, as I would be back in bed with this Malaria.

Harry had arranged hot water for me in Fabre's room downstairs, in this building, where Harry and I sleep. I went there and it is a good setup. There is a large hot water heater. A faucet runs from the bottom and it has a coal fire. I filled the washtub and cooled it with the cold-water faucet overhead. The tub sets on a drain and the room is warm, so it is ideal. I soaked for a good while. I was all alone, as the wire section was out. They came in as I was almost through but I had a good bath.

I talked with Walter Quigley, Windy, and Powers, all of A Battery, in their room. I showed them some pictures of Africa and Sicily.

After supper I brought my Val Pack inside to dry. I read and then went to the show at Service Battery (very good). We talked until 12:10 a.m.

## January 31, 1945
Eupen, Germany-Belgium

I rested all morning, as I feel listless and lazy; Malaria sure saps your strength for a long while. I didn't get up until 11:20 a.m. I went to the office and signed the morning reports and a few letters.

After dinner I sat around for a while. We are to move tomorrow to the town of, Mützenich Germany. It is the town that the Liaison parties just left. We cleaned up a few things and I arranged my equipment. The boys put their desks upstairs. After supper I read and we had a snack. "Alice" came down from upstairs to say goodbye and she brought some red wine and a cherry pie. We all talked and joked and she went back upstairs. I opened a bottle of Champagne that I had. Archie took my blouse and jacket upstairs. He gave me a new green one. He had the women sew on the Division Insignia. I also had overseas bars sewed on my blouse. I washed a few things and dried them out. I went across the street about 12 a.m.

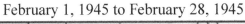

# Chapter nine: February 1945

February 1, 1945 to February 28, 1945

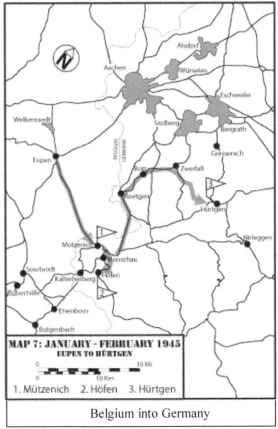

Belgium into Germany

February 1945 Historical Overview
Month of February 1945 Corps Assignments:
First Army, 12th Army Group
February 1 to February 16, 1945 - V Corps
February 17 to February 28, 1945 – III Corps

General Overview

With the defeat of the German Ardennes Offensive (Battle of the Bulge), the Allies once again proceed to travel east through Belgium and again into Germany.

The Allies, carry out massive bombing campaigns on German Cities. One of the most controversial is the bombing of Dresden, Germany.

The Colmar Pocket is eliminated. The Colmar Pocket refers to an area around Alsace, France. It was the last area of German occupation in France.

9th Division Overview: The 9th Division finds itself again in the Hürtgen Forrest. This was territory fought for over and over again by many divisions, including the 9th, during the fall and winter of 1944. For the final time this area is secured and the 9th continues eastward.

On February 22, 1945 the 9th is part of the Allied offensive to sweep eastwards into Germany from the Roer River to the Rhine River. They capture the dams of Schwammenauel and Uft.

*** 

*February 1, 1945*
Eupen, Germany-Belgium

Got up at 7:30 a.m. but didn't go for breakfast.

I packed my things and walked over to the office. I checked it out and then came back and loaded my stuff on a truck. We pulled out about 9:30 a.m., for Mützenich. It is an uphill grade all the way and slow going. We got there at about 10 a.m. It is the town we were in once when we were scouting for a stove, at the time we were bivouacked in the woods.

We unloaded our stuff at the schoolhouse. Our room was on the top floor and is littered with debris. The boys threw the junk out in the hall; I had them throw it out the window into the yard. It was a dusty job and the wind outside didn't help.

We set up about five of the double school desks for a mess table. We got the room cleaned and mopped, and then we had a good dinner.

After dinner we unloaded the equipment from the trailer. We set up Archie's stove. Archie, in his truck, got stuck in the front yard because of the slippery snow and has been winching himself all over the place. He even pulled the flagpole down when he winched on to it.

We got a good coke fire going. We had a good supper and the school benches sure came in handy to sit on while we ate. There was a movie at 7 p.m.; it was a musical comedy and good. Afterwards we read and I fixed up the records of Lieutenant Link (from Indiana), and Captain Templeton (from North Carolina), who are going home on leave. Planes and Buzz Bombs were going over.

## February 2, 1945
Mützenich, Germany

Sure sweated out the planes in the wee hours. They were circling the area low. They let go a load of bombs just below here. A Buzz Bomb came roaring over and it was low and sounded like it would hit the hill here. More planes came over later and they came one after the other, circling around. One plane let a bomb go fairly close and I could hear the bomb whistle faintly as it came down. Later one really came close. This plane was low and I could hear the bomb as it left the bomb bay. It came screaming down and sounded like it would hit us. It landed somewhere close with a crash. The building shook and the plaster came down off the ceiling.

I didn't sleep well at all so I didn't get up for breakfast. I got up about 9:30 a.m., washed and shaved. I had coffee and toast. The boys hitched up the lights to the generator. We had a radio set up and the telephone was put in. I wrote some reports.

In the afternoon I took a walk up by the church and back. I wrote a letter and read. I listened to the radio and lay down.

After supper I went to the show again and it was the same picture.

Mützenich, Germany. Enemy territory in the distant left background.

## February 3, 1945
Mützenich, Germany

I didn't sleep very well all night as the boys are pulling guard and have to awaken each other for relief. About 6 a.m. a couple of strange soldiers came in and set some things down. They went to the window near my bed and rolled up the blackout and set up a Battery Commander's Scope. They are trying to lay guns or observe. I found out later they are trying to check the registration of their guns (200 Field Artillery Battalion, 155 Howitzers). All the fellows were commenting that it is the first time we have had an Observation Post in Personnel.

About 7 a.m. I began to get stomach cramps and already about five of the boys are dashing to the toilet. When it started, I came back and took a dose of salts. I made frequent trips and three times threw up at the same time. It has really knocked me out. I used the great outdoors but it is damp and cold. I lay down all morning. The observers are still here.

Sergeant Nix left with Master Sargent Urban (he's the Battalion Sargent Major) for Battalion. Nix will take his place while Sargent Urban is on furlough to the States. I laid down most of the afternoon. I got up for a spell and signed papers and addressed correspondence. The Observation Party left as they registered on a high burst.

I lay down all early evening. Charlie heated up some chicken soup and I had bread with it. I got up for a while and read and finished some work. I didn't go to the show.

## February 4, 1945
Mützenich, Germany

I feel better although empty, so I dallied in bed until 9:30 a.m. Sargent Urban came by and shook hands all around, as he will be gone for 30 days. He doesn't intend to come back. I got up about 10 a.m., after sitting up for a half hour. I had a cup of coffee and toast.

I signed and checked papers. A little later I ate some dinner. I hung around all afternoon signing and mailing papers, reading, looking out the window, talking, and listening to the radio. We have a swell view from the window. We command a high spot overlooking the Monschau Valley. We can see Elsenborn, Kalterherburg, Höfen, and other villages. Monschau, the town itself, is in a ravine, so can't be seen. I was watching the guns in Höfen firing; you can see the flash and the smoke. The guns behind are firing over us and make quite a noise. They shake the building.

After supper, I didn't eat much. I went to the show. It wasn't very good. My stomach is growling. I read, had a snack, and listened to the radio.

## February 5, 1945
Mützenich, Germany

Got up at 9:30 a.m. and everyone was up, so I made myself a cup of coffee with toast. It is raining and miserable out. I counted Pay Roll returns, Pay Transfer Accounts, and Soldiers' Deposits.

Sargent Nix came down from Battalion and expected me to go to Eupen. He wanted me to change Belgian francs into French francs for the men going on pass. I wasn't moving for anyone today. First of all I had plans for the afternoon, which was to take a bath, as I am well enough to take one. Second of all, I am not well enough to get soaking wet.

After dinner I continued checking money then went into the cellar and drew a nice hot tub full of water and soaked in it. I took a shower also and then worked signing papers and listened to the radio. After supper I read and went to the show. The place was crowded but I squeezed in. The picture stunk so I came back. Some of the men going to Paris came in. We listened to the radio and read. Lights went out at 11:05 p.m. Sergeant Rousse and gang came in from Battalion and are all wet. They slept in here with us for the night.

## February 6, 1945
Mützenich, Germany

I didn't get up for breakfast. Everyone is talking. There is Rousse, Anderson, Gleason, and Carter, from Battalion, who are going to Paris. I got up at 9 a.m. I was issued a nice sleeping bag. I had coffee and toast, checked the Pay Transfer Accounts, and washed my underclothes. It is nice as there is hot water, a tub, and soap downstairs. I put them on the radiator to dry and they are almost dry one hour later.

Corporal Galfo dropped in from Battalion. It is really wonderful here as we have everything right here in the building, heat, hot water, a radio, and light.

After dinner I got transportation, a jeep, and went to Monschau to Division Rear. It is a twisting road and Monschau is in the bottom of the ravine, located by a river. In peacetime it is the Niagara Falls for this part of Germany. The streets of the town are very narrow. I saw Frank

Page and stopped and talked, he had just come in from somewhere. We looked for Finance and the Adjunct General, but didn't see them. Everything is one way, and we made a circle of five miles to get back again. We didn't see it the second time either, but learned that they were just arriving here, so we came back home.

I had the boys load the trailer, as we are to move tomorrow. I met Captain Fritchman; he used to be in the 60th but left us to become a Glider Pilot. He flew a Cub plane from England to Liege, so he dropped around to see everybody (i.e., us, the Battalion guys), and then went to the front lines. He is going back now, 3 p.m., and can have supper in England, if he catches a C-47 out of Liege. He is a rough looking boy and had a real tough time as a Glider Pilot on D Day.

We are all loaded up now. After supper I read and listened to the radio. Sergeant Marston, Goodman, and some B-Battery men, are spending the night here. We had quite a talk session.

## February 7, 1945
Mützenich, Germany

The whistle blew about 5:30 a.m.; I just lied in bed until 6 a.m. I got up and packed my stuff and loaded it on a C-Battery truck. It is sprinkling and dark and we had to tie the camouflage nets on. We finally left about 7:30 a.m.

We went through Monschau and into Höfen. We turned up a side road, we have a house and the dentist is supposed to be with us. There is a big shell hole right through the house upstairs. The woods all around here are just tall trunks. It looks like a forest of flagpoles. This is a result of our new artillery shells. This new shell, instead of hitting and exploding upward, explodes overhead when it comes close to a solid object. It splatters down on top of everything.

There is debris all over the yard and house. One room in the house is crammed with furniture. The floors are wet, as the snow comes in and melts. We started throwing things out. The dentist decided to take a room in another house. We worked all morning cleaning up. We had fun throwing dishes against the house and breaking furniture to get it out of the house. We cleaned around and set up a kitchen stove. Harry and I found a new friend, a big horse, outback. We tried to push it into the kitchen to surprise the guys, but he balked and wouldn't go in. We took pictures and fixed the windows with glass. We put in odd shaped windows and then mopped the floor. The hand pump for water works. George fixed up the electric lights and radio.

Harry Hammer, Charlie Nagy, and Mac (the horse).

After dinner we set up a little stove in the office room. Jack and Delli sleep in the kitchen; Tony, Skoczylas, and Charlie sleep with Dougan up the street. The rest sleep in the other two rooms here. It rained and the water pours in the room with the hole in it. We took clothes and furniture upstairs to block it out.

After supper we went to the show at the kitchen house. It was pretty good and afterwards we read and talked. They all went to bed and I set up my cot in the office, as it is dry there.

## February 8, 1945
Höfen, Germany

I had a good night's sleep in the new sleeping bag. I did not get up for breakfast but lay in bed until 9:10 a.m. I got up and put my bedroll in the wet room, shaved, and had a little toast to eat. I did a few things at the desk, sorting and signing papers. I walked over to Service Battery Orderly Room, talked, and listened to the radio.

After dinner I made arrangements to go to Division Rear at Monschau. We left about 2:30 p.m. and it is a slow, rough ride. There is mud, holes, traffic, and sharp turns. I walked from the Clearing Company (where Bob Ramsdell is going). I went up the hill in search of the Adjunct General and Finance. I came back and went across the footbridge. It is rather pretty here. Monschau is on the riverbed and the sheer cliffs rise overhead. The buildings are old and typical, "Olde German;" plastered, with crooked boards across it. I met Frank Page along the road and we talked for a while. I had just before seen a girl signaling a G.I. She nodded and pointed; he was standing a little over and using undercover signals. It is dangerous to fraternize and costly.

I went to Finance and turned in the payrolls. It took quite some time to check them. I read some material and talked. Bob Ramsdell came in looking for me. I turned in Pay Transfer Accounts. I got through about 4:45 p.m. It was slow going back because of the traffic. The Battalion was on the road, moving to a new position. I came back in time for chow. We are not moving.

After supper I wrote.

## February 9, 1945
Höfen, Germany

Slept pretty well and didn't get up until 10 a.m. and just had a piece of toast, as there isn't any coffee. I took all the papers on the desk, checked them, and then signed them.

Sergeant Nix dropped down from Battalion. After dinner I wrote a couple of recommendations for awards. I signed other papers.

After supper I stayed in and read and wrote, as the rest went to the show. We listened to the radio and I wrote until 11 p.m.

## February 10, 1945
Höfen, Germany

Got up at 9:15 a.m., had tomato juice, coffee, and toast. I cleaned up and shaved. I worked on signing reports and papers.

191

After dinner I took pictures in the back yard. I found what looks like a semi-precious stone, probably an aquamarine, in a setting. It must have been blown out of the house when the shell hit it.

I had George drive the command car and had Harry come along. We went to Division at Monschau (German Niagara Falls) and I took some pictures. I stayed about two hours at Finance and the Adjunct General. It sure was a rough ride getting there. We passed that S curve and it was so bumpy my helmet jumped off my head and hit me on the nose. We got back at 4 p.m.

Monschau, Germany. George Neuhardt and I

After supper we got mail. I got my pictures from the censor. I went to the show at 6 p.m., and afterwards I wrote and read.

**February 11, 1945**
Höfen, Germany

Got up about 9:15 a.m., had tomato juice and toast. I spent all morning on the day's work, checking and signing papers.

After dinner I showed my pictures to Rusty and the boys. I got the command car, George drove and Skoczylas and Charlie rode in back. We went to Division at Monschau. It still is rough going before you cross the river. We saw Sergeant Nix there. I visited Finance, Adjutant General's

Monschau, Germany. George Neuhardt and Harry Hammer.

Office, Judge Advocate General's Office, and the Post Office. I talked and did my business. I heard (overheard) that Frank Page went to the hospital. It is snowing out. Skoczylas, Charlie, and I walked across the river and investigated the Corp shower. It was crowded. We came back as church was just getting out. We left about 3:45 p.m. It seemed like a much shorter ride back.

After supper Father Connors came by, said the Rosary, gave General Absolution and Communion (I received). Tomorrow there will be Confession. I came back to our house and read. Tony Tooley dropped in and I made out a will for him. I made one out for myself while I was about it (I am a Notary Public).

## February 12, 1945
Höfen, Germany

I awoke about 9:30 a.m. and lay in bed. Sergeant Brightman, from the Air Observation Patrol, dropped in. I talked to him while still in bed, until 11 a.m. I got up and dressed, had coffee, toast, and an orange that Jack had brought back from breakfast. They had fresh eggs and oranges for breakfast.

I came back after dinner and worked on different things. I went to Mass in the kitchen room at 3:30 p.m. During Mass the fellows downstairs were cursing so much that, I being nearest the door, went down and told them to take it easy.

I went to the show at 6 p.m. It was a good show about the Navy and the men aboard a tanker. Afterwards I came back and wrote letters until the lights went out at 11 p.m.

## February 13, 1945
Höfen, Germany

I just lay in bed for about one-half hour talking and finally got up at 10 a.m., cleaned up, shaved, and had coffee and toast. Sergeant Nix came down with some papers and I read some of them. I started on the dead files, started throwing away some, and got part way through.

I went to dinner at 12:30 p.m. Captain Thivierge is here, also

Lieutenant Healey. After dinner I talked with Pete Thivierge about the efficiency reports on officers that he is filling out. I completed the dead files and sure threw away plenty of paper.

After supper I read. Delli got his pictures back, of which I get one set. I went over to the show, but there wasn't any as the Special Services is moving. I came back and read and wrote.

## February 14, 1945
Höfen, Germany

I felt rough this morning, as my nose and throat are raw. I got up about 9:30 a.m. and had a little coffee and toast. I read, signed a few papers, and went to the Stations of the Cross that Father Connors had in the kitchen room. We received ashes, as today is Ash Wednesday. I decided to refrain from candy and gum, so gave away all that I had.

After dinner, I went with Tony Tooley to Division; I met Sergeant Krunas that used to be in the 60th Field Artillery Battalion, A Battery, a long time ago. Some of A-Battery guys were talking to him. We chewed the fat for a while and then I went into the Adjunct Generals. I came out and walked up to Frank Page's and we talked for a while. I met Lieutenant Cominsky, 15th Engineers, on the way. I came back to the Adjunct General and we came back to camp. It was a beautiful day out. It is rather pretty here; especially on a high spot overlooking the river as it winds among the pine wooded hills. When I got back, Sergeant Nix was here and my gang came in. They had been to Monschau taking a shower.

After supper I read, wrote, and listened to the radio.

## February 15, 1945
Höfen, Germany

I got up at 9:30 a.m. as we are to be presented our awards today. It is a wonderful day and we opened the windows and doors of the house. I aired some of my clothes as well. The sun is actually hot; the air is cool, though. I got out my overcoat and sewed on the Division insignia. I cleaned my gun, shaved, and washed.

We (Charlie Nagy, Jack Markowitz, Delli and me) ate early chow. Warrant Officer Bob Ramsdell, Lieutenant George Obeldobel and some more of Service Battery men did also. We left at 12 noon in a two and one-half ton truck and are going forward toward Dreiborn. At various cross roads there is damaged equipment, dead cows and horses. We cut off and went winding through the valleys and hills. We got to the 34$^{th}$ Field Artillery Battalion and went to the Command Post. I talked with Tom Collins and Matt Wall. We went down the hill and walked up the side of a hill to an open space. We sat around waiting. Captain Jim Edmonds, Lieutenant Tom Hall, and others were here for various awards, (i.e., Air Medal, Bronze, and Silver Star). Nuptial was late. Between 2 p.m. and 2:30 p.m. they lined us up. General Craig came at 3 p.m. He walked down the columns, about three columns of 100 each. He asked me what I did, pinned on the Bronze Star ribbon (you get the medal later), and shook my hand. He was followed by General Howell (our Division Artillery Commander), and then came Colonel Westmoreland. Everyone was tired when it was over. Father Connors got a Bronze Star.

We came back through the valley and high hills. There were captured guns, dead cows, and horses. It is a nice view and we could see a shell landing on Jerry's positions, as it is so open. Some of our 105s fired over our truck as we passed by. We passed Dreiborn and some of the infantry is billeted there.

In the evening I read and wrote.

## February 16, 1945
Höfen, Germany

Got up at 9 a.m., as there are too many people around and I couldn't sleep.

It was a great day, so I arranged for transportation to Monschau. I collected things together, got the command car, took off the front side curtains, and had George Neuhardt as a driver. We left before 10 a.m. and went to Division. I conducted my business and was through a few minutes after 11 a.m.

I decided to go to Verviers because I was through so early. We had to go to Höfen and go back around the rough loop. I figured that we would go via Bütgenbach, rather than Aachen, as the Mützenich road is closed. We went to Kalterherberg. It is muddy and the ruts are a foot deep. We went through Elsenborn but can't go right through the camp. We continued on to Bütgenbach. We had to detour here. It is muddy and rough and we had to head toward Malmedy, from here. The road is brutal for miles and the ruts are a foot deep. The road crews are out working. We got to a fork and have to turn right but traffic is all tied up. We were here for over an hour and couldn't turn around. The road was almost impassable from here to Robertsville. We snaked along and had to stop when two huge semi-trailers got stuck side by side. We had a grind and finally got to Robertsville. We then had to go into Malmedy. We saw the destruction made by the U.S planes by mistake, in the breakthrough. We headed for Eupen to come back, but were turned off toward Verviers. We cut over and back to Eupen. It was now 5 p.m. We headed for Roetgen then to Lammersdorf, to Monschau, and back to Höfen by 7 p.m. This was the worst ride I ever took for pleasure. The house was not blacked out as the gang was at the show. I ate something and went to bed.

**February 17, 1945**
Höfen, Germany

Got up at 9 a.m. as everyone is around here again and I can't sleep. I had some toast with butter. There is plenty of work to do. I signed various reports, and started checking and signing the payrolls. I worked steadily until dinner at 12:30 p.m.

Captain Crandall and Major Williams were here for dinner. After dinner I was busy on the payrolls and other things. Captain Healey [my former first sergeant, A-Battery (battlefield promotion)] was around. He is going to Brussels along with three enlisted men. I personally cut two stencils for the pass form.

I went to supper and afterwards I worked on the passes and details. I went to the show at 6 p.m. and it was a comedy, light and good. I dropped in at Service Battery and talked with Bob Ramsdell and Captain Ted Healey. I picked up my liquor ration and it consisted of one quart of Scotch and one quart of Champagne. I came back to our house and passed around the bottle of Scotch. First Sergeant Ferguson was here from A-Battery. He is going home tomorrow. I went back to Service Battery with the passes. I left a roll of film with Bob Ramsdell to be developed. I talked with Ted Healey and the rest of the gang there. I came back to our place and passed around the Scotch again and I had a snack of Vienna sausage, pickles, and mustard with toast.

## February 18, 1945
Höfen, Germany

Everyone was around shortly after 8 a.m. and Sergeant Ferguson was coming and going, but I just lay in bed until 9 a.m. I got up and signed Sergeant Ferguson's records so he could start on his trip to the States. I cleaned up and had some Wheaties, after I borrowed some milk from the kitchen. I worked steadily all morning and gave a final check to the payrolls. I signed correspondence, checked some award recommendations, censored mail, and then went to dinner.

The ack-ack (attached) is with us again, they have been on the move since 4 a.m. and are soaking wet. I worked most of the afternoon checking and signing papers.

After dinner I hustled over to the show. It is a good picture and everyone went over a half hour or more early so they could get in. After the show I read, wrote a letter, talked, had a snack, and opened a bottle of Champagne. We got notice to have early breakfast (7 a.m.), as we are moving out in the morning.

**February 19, 1945**
Höfen, Germany

The whistle blew and we got up at 7 a.m., and had fresh eggs for breakfast. I had three. We packed our things and loaded the trailer. There wasn't room for all of us. I went as well as Tony Wisniewski, Skoczylas, George, Harry, and Lawrence. We left the area about 10 a.m.

We went through Roetgen and then to Rott. The 78th Infantry Division and the 82nd Airborne Division are all around here. We stopped just outside of Rott on the road, to wait until they got a spot for us. We were hungry so we heated C-ration hash. It is a swell day and the sun is out strong. We moved out through Zweifall, then about five miles further, and we turned into the forest. We have a couple of log cabins we will use. I hauled my stuff up a ways, then we had coffee and a sandwich.

I went with Lieutenant Francesconi of the ack-ack to Battalion Headquarters. It is a fairly rough road, there are blown out tanks. We stopped on the way as two fellows dragged a lineman out of the ditch. The fellow in the middle had his foot blown off from the mine. All that showed was the bone sticking out of the flesh. He was still conscious. We continued on and had to stop again to cover the windshield and put the top down as this road is under enemy observation. Battalion is beyond the Infantry Command Posts.

My home (with tent flap thrown back) in the Hürtgen Forrest, Germany.

The town of Hürtgen is all beat up and there were plenty of our own tanks destroyed. There are plenty of both sides dead in the field below. This town and forest was the scene of some very heavy fighting.

I got back to our place in time to eat. I set up my pup tent on top of a log foundation that was here. We have the pyramidal tent to put up tomorrow. We sat in the hut until bedtime.

## February 20, 1945
Hürtgen Forest, near Hürtgen, Germany

I didn't get up for breakfast but got up at 9:30 a.m., after a good night's sleep. We put up the pyramidal tent, set up the stove, put in electric lights, and built a fire.

After dinner we chopped wood, sat around the stove, read, and talked. It is raining and miserable out.

After supper we sat around the stove and read. Childs and Slim came in from the Supply section and said that they didn't have any place to sleep. They said that the Supply guys wouldn't let them sleep with them. We said that that they could sleep in our tent. They brought over a pound of butter, cream, and bread. We had a good snack and went to bed at 10:45 p.m.

## February 21, 1945
Hürtgen Forest, Hürtgen, Germany

I had a good night's sleep and got up about 9:15 a.m., had coffee and toast with butter. I chopped wood and helped keep the fire going. The fellows went down and hauled the trailer up. George Obeldobel gave them a little trouble about ripping up his road.

After dinner I walked around, talked, hung around the fire, and washed some gloves, and a pair of pants. The fellows going to Paris were around. Captain Thivierge is going. Sargent Nix, Sargent Dalrymple, and a few others were around.

After supper we stood by the road watching the traffic. I talked with

Pete Thivierge and am having him buy me some perfume, for 1500 Belgian Francs. The gang coming in from leave, in Brussels, came around looking for someplace to sleep. We put them up in our tent as well as a couple going to Paris plus the two from Supply.

**February 22, 1945**
Hürtgen Forest, near Hürtgen, Germany

I got up at 9:15 a.m. and Tony Wisniewski had brought back coffee, bread, butter, and eggs, so I had a nice breakfast. I fixed some papers and signed correspondence. I sat by the fire and talked. I walked around the area, and after dinner I fixed up papers to go to Division.

George drove the command car and Charlie and I went to Division. We passed through Zweifall and took some pictures of blown-out pillboxes. We went towards Rott and half way there used a cut off. We parked near Finance and I took care of the Soldier's Deposits and Pay Transfer Accounts. I walked up to the Adjunct General, did my business and talked. I met Frank Page and Doc Stern (15th Medics) and a few others there. We walked them back to Finance and then came back.

There is plenty of stuff moving on the road, such as Tank Destroyers and pontoons, for this Roer River to Rhine River drive. Back in camp I put on the new pants (paratroopers) I had bought and they fit well. I watched a lot of Tank Destroyers go by on the road. Tomorrow is evidently the day.

Just as supper was over, some Jerry planes were nearby. There was lots of ack-ack. Four P-47s passed right by one Jerry plane and didn't seem to bother it. A spent bullet came singing in by our group and it almost hit Dougan. Captain Tooley and the rest got behind the truck. There were a few more similar incidents up until 7:30 p.m. We sat in the tent around the stove, read, wrote and talked.

**February 23, 1945**
Hürtgen Forest, near Hürtgen, Germany

Got up at 9:30 a.m. and had coffee, butter, and toast. It is a great day so I walked around outside, and then chopped wood.

After dinner I threw the axe at the trees for a while. I sent Harry to Division and I went to Battalion in the water truck with Jake Piekowski. It was a rough ride up as the road is all filled in and ruts. I stopped in at Message Center and talked there. Then I had a talk with Doctor McFadyen. I walked down to Headquarters Battery and talked with Captain Gray. Captain Tooley is here checking on the Cocoa Cola bottles.

I came back and it is slow going and our guns are firing. There are all kinds of guns around here firing. We had to put the windshield down again, as we did coming up, as we pass the area that is under enemy observation. We can look out and see the smoke shells hit in Jerry territory. At a roadblock there are two dead horses and a wagon. I noticed a decomposed Jerry lying in the gutter. This is a busy road, mostly the 9th Infantry Division and the 1st Infantry Division.

Zweifall, Germany Blown out Pill Box.

I got back too late for chow. They had saved it however and I ate plenty. I came back to the tent and had my second coke, which is my allowance. I read, wrote, talked, ate, and listened to the radio. For snacks we can get milk, butter, and bread from Childs.

Bergstein, Germany.
Battalion area.

## February 24, 1945
Hürtgen Forest,
Hürtgen, Germany

Got up at 9:30 a.m. and it is a nice day. I had coffee and toast with butter. In the morning I checked and signed papers. I then went around the area cleaning up the junk. Some Medical Officer had been around yesterday and said the junk should be cleaned up, to prevent disease, I guess. I collected all the cans and garbage. I burned the boxes and buried the junk in the foxhole.

After dinner I spent part of the afternoon cleaning up more junk and cardboard containers. We threw the axe at the tree and wasted the better part of the afternoon. I was lucky to sink four but Skoczylas got 50, consecutively and quit. After supper we read, wrote, did some work, ate, and listened to the radio.

Jack invited 10 of the new recruits from the States, into the tent. They are ack-ack trained, then converted to rifle men in the Infantry, but then lucky enough to be sent to us in the Artillery.

## February 25, 1945
Hürtgen Forest, near Hürtgen Germany

I got up at 9:30 a.m. had coffee, toast, and butter. I spent the morning checking, signing, and sending out the business. It is cold out today.

In the afternoon I finished up a few things. I rode down to Division Rear, near Rott, with Bob Ramsdell and a couple of Service boys. One was Tory from Northampton, Massachusetts. I went to the Adjutant General and did a few things. Major Materavitz called me in to talk me into giving Bennie Guanciale a star for Normandy. I quoted part of the circular and he checked it and found that he was wrong. I came out and got a ride to the crossroads. I walked to the shower but didn't take one, as I wasn't in the mood. We waited here for Bob for a while and then walked back to the crossroads and he came along after a while.

After supper we all sat in the tent, reading, writing, and talking. We had coffee, toast, and butter, and I had some beef I heated that I had brought back from supper. I typed a request for leave for Captain Tooley so he could get married. I did it over again as there was an error in it.

## February 26, 1945
Hürtgen Forest, near Hürtgen, Germany

Didn't get up until 10:05 a.m. and it is sprinkling out, I had coffee and toast with butter. I checked, signed, and mailed all the outgoing business. It sprinkled all morning.

After dinner I finished a few odds and ends and shaved in the rain. Father Connors came around and said Mass in the office tent.

After supper I read, wrote, talked and listened to the radio. Then I had a snack.

## February 27, 1945
Hürtgen Forest, near Hürtgen, Germany

The boys called me at 7:50 a.m.; it was sprinkling so I didn't get up. I got up at 10 a.m., went to the tent, but no one was there. They had all gone for a shower or are still in bed. I had coffee, butter and toast and then cleaned up the business on my desk. Cohen came in from B-Battery. He has some court-martials to make out so I gave him a few points. The gang came in from the shower just as the dinner whistle blew.

After dinner I did some work and walked around outside a bit. Chaplain Lorenz came around for a visit. I got the command car and ran down to Division Rear near Rott. I dropped in at the Adjunct General and then went back to the crossroads to the shower. There weren't any clothes or exchange so I just took a shower. We were late for chow but they had saved it.

After supper I read, wrote, and talked. We listened to the radio and had coffee, toast, butter, and salami.

## February 28, 1945
Hürtgen Forest, near Hürtgen, Germany

I got up when they called me at 7:50 a.m. and ate breakfast. We had dry and hot cereal. I had the dry. We had eggs, bacon, bread, oranges, and coffee. I went back and washed and shaved.

I left in the back of a jeep with Tony Tooley. We stopped in Hürtgen and met other officers who are to pick up money. Colonel Hargy, Finance, came in and gave us the money.

I went to Battalion and it was a rough ride in the back of the jeep. I counted the money in the Medical Detachment tent. I gave Doc McFadyen his detachments. I ate at Headquarters Command Post tent and I paid the colonel and major. I gave Captain Gray Headquarters Battery's pay. I walked to A-Battery and paid them and then got a ride back to Battalion. I walked down to B-Battery and paid them. I had plenty of walking as I walked to C-Battery and paid the officers. I got a ride back to our place in the back of a three-fourth ton and ate supper.

After supper I read, wrote, and talked until 11 p.m. I had a snack of coffee, toast, and butter.

# Chapter ten: March 1945

## March 1, 1945 to March 31, 1945

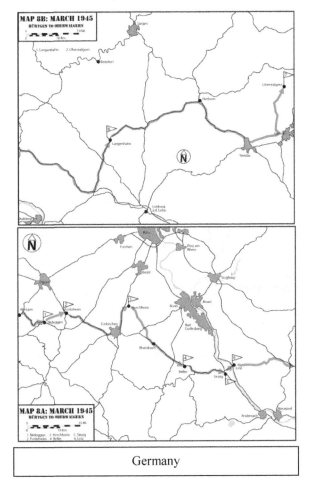

Germany

March 1945 Historical Overview
Month of March 1945 Corps Assignments:
First Army, 12th Army Group
March 1 to March 30, 1945 - III Corps
March 31 - VII Corps

General Overview

Even with the German Army retreating into an ever-shrinking German held interior, enemy opposition resulted in many Allied casualties. The Allies meet stiff resistance with fierce fighting.

Congesting the streets are traveling refugees, consisting of German civilians and forced laborers.

On March 7, 1945 the Ludendorff Bridge, crossing the Rhine River, at Remagen, Germany was crossed by the US 9th Armored Division. Soon after the 47th Regiment of the 9th Infantry Division was attached to the 9th Armored Division. Their objective was to secure the Ludendorff Bridge and Remagen bridgehead. Bloody fighting continued for many days in efforts to secure the Bridge. On March 8, 1945, the 47th Regiment was the first Allied Infantry unit to cross the Rhine River.

The Ludendorff Bridge was attacked by; German Artillery and Infantry Units, Jet planes (first time jet planes were seen and used), and German frogmen attempting to plant explosives, all in an effort to destroy it. The Ludendorff Bridge unexpectedly collapsed March 17, 1945 due to the structural damage it had sustained.

After the Remagen beachhead was secured *The Ruhr Pocket* Objective was begun. The Ruhr Pocket campaign took place March 1945 and April 1945. Allied troops participated in an encircling maneuver surrounding the industrial rich Ruhr area.

9th Division Overview: The Roer River to Rhine River drive continues with the 9th Division continuing its forward eastward movement through Germany, capturing all the towns in its path.

On March 8, 1944 the 47th Regiment of the 9th Infantry Division was attached to the 9th Armored Division to secure the Ludendorff Bridge and Remagen bridgehead. They were the first Allied Infantry troops to cross the Rhine in WW 2.

On March 8, 1945 the 60<sup>th</sup> Combat Team (includes the 60<sup>th</sup> Infantry and the 60<sup>th</sup> Field Artillery Unit) participated in the fighting at the Ludendorff Bridge and Remagen Beachhead. Opposition was fierce and there were many casualties.

After securing the Remagen beachhead the 9<sup>th</sup> moved eastward driving further into Germany

***

### *March 1, 1945*

Hürtgen Forest, near Hürtgen, Germany

Charlie called me to get up, as Captain Thivierge wants to see me at Service Battery, Orderly Room. I got up about 8:45 a.m. and went over, he had a bottle of perfume for me that he got in Paris. It was not a popular brand but almost as good as Chanel. It was Labelle #5 and cost 340 French francs or $7.00. I paid for it but held off on another, as there is some kind of mistake. I came back and had cereal, coffee, oranges, and toast with butter. I signed a few papers and censored mail.

Sergeant Nix came in from Battalion: they had moved this morning. They can see Cologne in the distance. When the first Echelon was moving yesterday the doughboys were taking a hill right beside them. It is raining and miserable today. The ack-ack is back with us once again.

After dinner I sat around and signed things. Lieutenant Dougher dropped in and paid some of my gang. I took the turn backs as I will be going back one of these days. We were told that we are moving out at 6 a.m. tomorrow morning and we will eat at 5:45 a.m. We loaded the trailer and everyone got his things collected.

After supper some of the fellows brought their things in the pyramidal tent and so did I. We sat around the fire drying clothes and tents as well as eating, reading, and talking.


### March 2, 1945

Hürtgen Forest, near Hürtgen, Germany

We got up at 4:45 a.m., it has stopped raining and it is fairly light out from the moon. I ate breakfast and then we all came back and gathered things together. We were supposed to be loaded before eating at 5:15 a.m. The truck didn't arrive until 5:30 a.m. We started loading; I got on the truck and moved ammunition boxes around. I packed the bedrolls on and then I put my own stuff on. We had trouble with the trailer, as it is extremely heavy. The convoy, with the exception of a truck or two, pulled out. We finally pulled out at 6:30 a.m., one half hour late. We know that they are near Nideggen. The road doesn't seem so rough in a two and one-half ton overloaded.

We crossed the Roer River. The railroad station before the river was beat up and the tracks are all twisted like pretzels. A dead person lay against the bank. We found Service Battery staying temporarily in a field outside town. There were many German prisoners at the 9th Division Prisoner of War enclosure nearby. I would guess about 400 and mostly young. There was a dead German paratrooper captain in the field, lying against a bank. He was shot through the groin. I took two pictures.

We moved across the street to another field and set up our stuff. Our Battalion is just across the street, up a ways, not having moved yet. The guns would fire every now and then. I talked with a few fellows from Headquarters Battery. There is a dead Jerry by the road.

We put up the pyramidal tent, and I made coffee by making a fire in one of the trenches. It snowed and then the sun would come out. It was cold. We put the stove in the tent. Skoczylas, Charlie, Dougan, and I walked around the Battalion area. I took a picture of a dead Jerry, with his head blown off, and oddly his face seems to be lying beside his head. There is a Jerry graveyard nearby. This is very high ground and a grand view below; you can see Düren and Zülpich.

Nideggen, Germany.
Jerry paratrooper
captain.

**March 3, 1945**

Nideggen, Germany

I had a good night's sleep and laid in bed talking, as did Morrison, who stayed with us overnight. We had oranges, cereal, coffee, and toast with butter. I signed morning reports. I shaved outside. It was cold and windy. I walked around the area until dinner.

After dinner Shipe, Jack, and I took a walk toward town. It is on a hill, like a Sicilian town. There are the usual sights; destroyed homes, rubble, dead horses, and one dead Jerry in a yard. We walked through the stone towers and entrance to the walled city. We picked up post cards in a ruined shop. We took pictures of the castle from holes in the wall. We walked toward it but missed the road and got through by climbing over walls and fences. We went through a cemetery where bombs had fallen and had caused some of the remains to be brought to the surface. A skull lay nearby.

Nideggen, Germany.
Nideggen Castle.

We went to the castle. It is on a pinnacle, ruined by a Self-Propelled 155, as the Germans used it for observation. I found a German tactical map, showing the whole picture of the valley below. We met a few Service Company, 60th Infantry, doughs here. They showed us the entrance to the castle through the ruins. We rummaged through the things; chinaware, photos, and clothes. We went up the narrow winding stairs to another room. There were oil paintings, statues, swords, and maps. I took a sword for a walking stick. I tried to roll an oil painting of a Dutch scene but it chipped off.

Nideggen, Germany. Overlooking the Roer River and the damage done by our airplanes. Counts and Countesses of Jülich once enjoyed this scene.

We wandered out into the courtyard. There is an empty

209

well, which is about 60-feet deep. Then we went outside to below the house and the natural observation point. We went over to the wall, and could look down on the Roer valley. It is a natural observation point and we took pictures. We could see trucks, winding roads, the ruined Railroad Station, the town, zigzag trenches, craters, the river, hills, and Bergstein, in the distant view below. There are some trees here with Nazi swastikas hewn in the trunks and a cemetery with fresh Jerry bodies in crates on the ground. We came back later and moved to a six-room house in Froitzheim.

## March 4, 1945
Froitzheim, Germany

I didn't sleep so well all night, even though I was tired. The big guns boomed and shook the house; the passing convoys of tanks did likewise. Then there were two guards just outside the house talking all the time. I am still thankful to have a room and a warm bed. I got up at 9 a.m., as they want me at Battalion, to pay the rest of the officers, and a few other things. I had Lawrence drive me up. Hartley of Service Battery went with us; he is going to the Medics.

Germany. Captain Douglas C. France, Jr. and Sergeant William Ferguson.

We followed a couple of Headquarters and A-Battery jeeps. The Battalion is in Bürvenich, only about four miles away, up the road. They have a nice setup. I talked with all and paid Captain France, Captain Prince, and some of the Battery officers. I took Pay Transfer Accounts and gave out information. I left there about 11:45 a.m. and stopped at C-Battery, as Lawrence wanted to get something. We left about 12 p.m. and Hartley came back with us, he had trench foot and is going to the Hospital from Service Battery.

A colonel stopped me at the end of the muddy road. He was from the 9th Armored Division. He

210

wanted to know the names of the towns and if he could get through the muddy road with his assault guns. I was pretty vague on the towns, as I hadn't looked closely at a map. I said he could travel the road safely (the assault guns are very heavy). He moved on.

I ate dinner, counted money, and signed reports and papers. I went to Division Artillery Headquarters at Eschweiler-über Feld. I got some information, gave some out, and returned. It was muddy. The mud was thick on the windshield. The 240 mm guns blasted just as we passed. I read, worked, and ate a snack later in the evening.

## March 5, 1945
Froitzheim, Germany

I didn't sleep too well so I lied in bed until 9:30 a.m. I finally got up as people were coming and going. I made a cup of coffee, soluble as usual, crackers, butter, and jelly. I checked the Service Record and allied papers of Bryant, Service Battery and L. Owens, C-Battery. They are here and are returning to the U.S. for compassionate reasons. I checked and signed the papers.

I walked down to the Orderly Room and met Lynn Freeman, George Obeldobel, and Tony Tooley there. We came back to my office and I paid Freeman and Obeldobel and did a few other small jobs.

Father Connors came in and wanted to say Mass, so I told him to have it here. I took my bunk away and he used the washing table for an altar. The Motor section and Personnel were about all that were there, eight in all.

I took a sponge bath and had just finished when the G.I. from across the street left. I took his heated water and used the tub there to wash all my clothes. They must have left in a hurry as he left the stove going and a little puppy. I set up a clothesline and used the back of the chairs to dry the clothes, as the room is so hot. We are to move tomorrow at 7 a.m., and are to get up at 5:45 a.m. I kept dropping in next door to check my clothes. I fed the puppy and the clothes were all dry, except for a few spots, by 10 o'clock.

## March 6, 1945
Froitzheim, Germany

I didn't sleep all night. The gang started getting up at 5:30 a.m. and they all went to breakfast at 5:45 a.m. I just lay in bed and they returned, so I got up at 6:45 a.m. We got all our equipment together and waited. Rusty showed up with his truck overloaded with ammunition and all their personal stuff. There were stoves, pipes, bags, and bedsprings. We were able to put on only a few odds and ends. The supply truck backed up and will take some things. We loaded more on Rusty's truck. They even had a radio on the front seat and no room for me. I sat on top of it and they took it off. It is sprinkling out. We went to Weller and waited by a haystack. We are waiting for Captain Tooley to return from up forward, where he is scouting our new location. We are going to move in where the Battalion has been.

I ate a ham sandwich. We moved on through Niederberg and past 60th Infantry Service Company and the Service Batteries, for the 26th, 34th, and 84th Field Artillery (all 9th Division). We passed Nudge Red and White Command posts. We even passed by our own gun batteries, and turned off at the Battalion Command Post. We waited until they moved out and then we moved right in.

We had a lunch and got a bedroom upstairs in a house. I put five up in this room and we set up the office in the kitchen. We will sleep five more in the room beside the kitchen. Our A and C-Batteries were firing fire missions in the next field. We all went to work doing back work, Pay Transfer Accounts, and Soldier's Deposits Payroll turn backs. The people around here are partially dressed in Jerry uniforms. We are in Horchheim.

## March 7, 1945
Horchheim, Germany

I heard the whistle blow at 7:45 a.m., so I got up for breakfast. Everyone was more or less surprised to see me at breakfast. This is about the fourth time I've eaten it in two months.

I got all my material ready and with Linscott, Charlie, and Staff, I left at 8:45 a.m. We went through Niederberg, Düren, Eschweiler, Stolberg, Zweifall, and then to Division Rear. Düren is beat up and practically all rubble. It was sprinkling and hard to see through the windshield because of the mud sprayed on it by the passing vehicles. It took us a little over two hours.

I did my business at the Adjunct General and then went to Finance where Colonel Hargy counted my turn backs. I had the clerk count my Pay Transfer Accounts and Soldier's Deposits. I met Chief Warrant Officer Phil Moyer and another Warrant Officer from Ordnance there. We walked over to chow with the colonel. We left, to return about 1 p.m.

We went to Aachen as Linscott wanted to drop in at an Ordinance Unit. We went toward Eschweiler and took the super four-lane highway (Autobahn). It runs between Aachen and Düren. We made a wrong turn somewhere and were headed for Cologne. The sign said 20 km, and we could see the tall factory chimneys plainly. We finally got back about 4 o'clock.

I cleaned up and went to chow. Captain Healey is here as he was hit with a little piece of shrapnel in the knee. He will stay with us for a while. I came back to the office and cleaned up the day's work. Later I fried a couple fresh eggs in butter. I read and wrote.

Düren, Germany.

## March 8, 1945
Horchheim, Germany

I lay in bed until 10 a.m. Sergeant Garner came in and said we wouldn't move. I got up and had an egg, toast, jelly, and butter.

I cleaned up a lot of work that was on the desk. It is sprinkling, or

213

rather like a drizzle out. I worked all afternoon on various things, wrapped the perfume to send home, checked papers, censored mail, and wrote correspondence.

After supper I did a few things, cleaning up the work. We heard that the 47th Infantry got across the Rhine. They went across on a railroad bridge.

I sewed my combat pants and wrote a letter. We are to move tomorrow morning, so I got things together. Battalion Supply wanted me to play the piano. I told them, I only fooled around with one hand. They insisted I play, so I did for a while. I came back to the office and had some fried chicken. Joe King and Jack Markowitz had got them in the nearby hen house. They wrung their necks and cooked them.

**March 9, 1945**
Horchheim, Germany

The whistle blew at 4:30 a.m. but I didn't get up for breakfast, instead I got up at 5:30 a.m. I packed my equipment and rolled up my bedroll, folded my cot, and threw them on top of Rusty's truck. The gang loaded the trailer and then Rusty's truck. We hitched up the trailer and Rusty pulled out. Kanousky's truck came in and we put the rest of the stuff on it. We moved out about 7 a.m.

We went through Euskirchen to Rheinbach. Fourteen truckloads of German prisoners came by. We saw three men in Jerry uniforms coming across the field. They were probably soldiers coming to give themselves up. No one has the time to bother to investigate. We went to Vettelhoven. There were a lot of vehicles stuck on the shoulders of the road. We got stuck on a side road, but got out and pulled into the town of Beller. We found rooms here and there. It is a farm town. There are Polish forced laborers here.

I took George and we went looking for Division Artillery. We went to Oeverich, then to Gemmingen. Our own Battalion was just arriving here so we drove up the road to give them time to get set up. We went

214

on to Heppingen and then to Bad Neuenahr. It was a resort town, large hotels, stores, and shops. The Second Infantry doughboys are moving through. There are soldiers in town with arms full of liquor; a few were drunk. As we went up the road a Messerschmitt dropped bombs just in front of us. The ack-ack was heavy and men fled in all directions. We just sat.

We got to the Battalion, did our business, talked, and then went to Division Artillery where we did the same. We came back to Beller, read, wrote, and talked. The 99th Infantry Division (Checker Board Charlie) has moved into this town.

## March 10, 1945
Beller, Germany

I didn't get up this morning until 10 a.m. Tony Tooley came in and left a message for me. I had coffee and toast. I brought in the Regimental desk and set it up beside my bed.

The 99th Division doughboys are all over the town. We have some Medics upstairs.

After dinner I went to the Battalion Command Post with Captain Tooley and Captain Healey. They are near the Rhine River. I was in S-3 room for a while. The Battalion is firing at a hill across the Rhine. It is interesting to listen to them contact the Cub plane and then fire on the target.

I stopped in at the Medics and then we came back to Beller. There was a lot of traffic on the road. We stopped off at the 60th Infantry, Service Company, outside Bad Neuenahr. Some planes came over; they were P-51s. They zoomed around and then dove over the east. One of them came circling above and everyone fired on him, for what reason?

There are many people on the road, freed French soldiers, Moroccans, Russians (Ukrainians, Mongolians), and Poles. There is a lot of stuff moving on the road, bridge pontoons, tanks, ack-ack, and engineers. We were held up a bit coming back because of this.

We got back about 4:30 p.m. Father Connors was here. He was going to say Mass at the Chapel here but they were cleaning it up for tomorrow, for a transient priest. So Father Connors said Mass in our office.

After supper, the people here came in for a while. I worked, read, and wrote.

## March 11, 1945
Beller, Germany

I didn't get up for breakfast but got up at 9 a.m., had some coffee, butter, and toast. I worked on correspondence. The Germans here in the house went to Mass at 9 a.m. When they came back they fried us two eggs each. They even brought us in plates, knives, and forks. They must have fried 20 in all.

I worked most of the afternoon. Colonel Beets and the rest that were on pass to Paris, dropped in. They ate supper in our room. Captain Tooley, Healey, Warrant Officer Bob Ramsdell always eat here as the kitchen is next door.

I am going back to Division Rear tomorrow. I counted money for Pay Transfer Accounts. I worked in the evening. We are having quite a time here giving directions. Everyone coming by seems to be lost. We printed signs. We even go out of our way to ask them if we can help them.

## March 12, 1945
Beller, Germany

I got up at 7:20 a.m., ate breakfast, and collected things together. Linscott, Carter, and I left here at 8:15 a.m.

We went to Ringen, then towards Rheinbach. They wouldn't allow us to continue on this road, so we wandered around the country roads. We finally found ourselves in Euskirchen. We had quite a job, as the traffic was heavy. The liberated workers are all along the road hiking and pushing carts. We went to Düren and then toward Stolberg. We cut off and finally got to Division at 11:35 a.m. I left the Pay Transfer Accounts and checked with the Adjunct General. I ate dinner here and did a few more things. Then I had Linscott drive me to Rott where I talked with Frank Page.

We came back to Stolberg and then returned to Beller. We made pretty good time coming back. It was muddy and slippery out. We saw freed slave laborers in three covered wagons drawn by horses and oxen. We got back at 5:30 p.m.

I talked outside the house. We learned that a sniper killed Lieutenant Bernie Wilensky, the professional piano player from Dorchester, Massachusetts, yesterday. Ledford and McFatter from A-Battery, Webb, and Lieutenant Crabbe from C-Battery, and Morrison from Headquarters Battery, were all wounded. Gordon from B-Battery died of injuries received when he was thrown off a truck. In the evening we read, got mail, and ate.

Lieutenant Edward S. Cholmeley-Jones from Westport, Connecticut, Lieutenant Stephen Birofka from New York, and Lieutenant Bernard L Wilensky from Dorchester, Massachusetts (KIA)

## March 13, 1945
Beller, Germany

I slept until 9 a.m. and lay in bed until 9:30 a.m. I got up, washed, and had coffee and toast. I cleaned up the work on the desk then wrote correspondence and endorsements.

There was a lot of traffic on the road; the trucks are bumper to bumper. There were four truckloads of Krauts outside. I had Lawrence take a picture. The lady upstairs threw apples and chocolate candy (candy they probably got from us) to them. The Military Police yelled at them. It is a serious thing to feed them.

It turned out to be a wonderful day. The sun was shining later in the afternoon. I got a three-fourth-ton truck and with Skoczylas and Bob Ramsdell we went to Quarter Master, who are just beyond Bad Neuenahr. I left off the personal effects of the dead and Skoczylas had his typewriter repaired.

A German Jet-propelled airplane, first we've seen, came streaking down the valley. Everyone was shooting at it, four P-38s were behind him, up high, but they were too slow. It was a sleek, streamlined job. It was low and not very far away.

We stopped in Bad Neuenahr. It is quite a town. It is full of hotels and cafes. All the G.I.s are roaming around. We got back for chow. We loaded the trailer as we move tomorrow. Willie (Donald) Williams is around; he is having his jeep fixed.

They brought in Lieutenant Wilensky's personal effects. He had an accordion, which we played for a while. We watched the 90 mm ack-ack firing for a while. In the evening we listened to the radio, read, and ate.

## March 14, 1945
Beller, Germany

We got up at 5:15 a.m., ate, and rolled up our equipment. We moved out at 7 a.m. and we rode with Turner.

We went to Ringen, Heppingen, and into Sinzig. It is foggy out. We got in what was once a very nice house now beat up. The bathroom even had an ultra-ray lamp. The boys are cleaning up some rooms. An armored unit occupies the cellar and two rooms upstairs. The boys set up a stove, strung up wire, put in lights and had a radio playing.

We had dinner and it turned out to be a great day. I took a stroll up town and met a few of the boys prowling about. We investigated the brewery. It is drained now and the G.I.s are wading in liquor. They had bored holes in the kegs and they then couldn't stop it, so it ran out onto the floor. They had filled their helmets full and anything else they could

218

find. You can smell alcohol a half mile away. There is a foot of wine and cognac on the floor.

In the afternoon we set up part of the office. The German Jet-propelled planes are trying to knock out the Railroad Bridge over the Rhine at Remagen. They started coming over, they are Messerschmitt's 262s. Our P-38s and P-47s are cycling in patterns over the bridge as guards. The Jets came sliding in, low. The ack-ack is terrific and the P-38s hang on the outside trying to get them after they pass through. The Jets go right in and let their bombs go and the ack-ack doesn't seem to bother them. We watched the bomb come right out of the plane and I saw it explode. The second plane's bomb didn't explode. There were six or eight over in a half hour. You can watch for about two minutes and then run for cover as what goes up must come down and some of the spent bullets hit the side of the house.

Charlie came back from the Battalion Command Post at Linz. He said the first bomb had killed eight tankers in a tank and burned three trucks killing some ack-ack men and Medics. The other bomb landed 20 feet from our Battalion Command Post, knocking a tree down and dirt around. It was a dud, likely.

After supper we talked outside until dark, came in, read, and wrote until 11 p.m. I decided to go to Division Rear, with Willie (Donald Williams), who is still with us, tomorrow.

## March 15, 1945
Sinzig, Germany

I lied awake and finally got up at 8 a.m. I made the fire, fixed the ration report, got things together, and had some coffee.

Willy and I took off for Division Rear. It is misty and foggy. We headed for Remagen, as the other roads are one way. We decided to chance that the road to Bonn is clear, as it is a good road with no traffic. We went right along. It is a swell road and we could see the water of the Rhine as we drove along beside it. You could not see the other side of the river however, because of the fog. We were stopped at all roads by the Infantry of the 7th Armored Division and asked the password. We are about the only vehicle on the road. We took one of the main roads but there was an overpass bridge lying on the road. There wasn't even a sign to say the road was blocked or closed, as yet. We could hear fighting on the other side of the river and incoming shells. There are barges from Rotterdam, ferries, and sightseeing boats all tied up.

We didn't see many G.I.s for a while and then we came to the edge of a town. The people stared at us. At a cross road, a green uniformed man shuffled and fumbled. I thought that he was a German soldier reaching for his gun and I almost did the same thing. It was a policeman in a green overseas cap and a long coat and boots dressed the same as the Jerries. He saluted me. This is a wonderful town. It is an elaborate, large Rhine resort town with well-dressed people, and even some of our Military Police all shined up. It is Bad Godesberg.

We went on to Bonn, a 1st Infantry Division town, and it wasn't too badly shot up. It is large and nice. We got to the edge of Cologne, but you couldn't enter without a pass. The fog is too thick to even see it. We did see the two impressive spires of the Cologne Cathedral. We finally got to division near Zweifall at 12:40 p.m. I ate and did my business and went over to Rott and dropped a radio off for Frank Page. I came back to Division Rear and met Frank who was also here on business.

We came back via Aachen, Stolberg, Eschweiler, Düren, and Euskirchen. There was too much traffic, so we cut to the Rhine and followed it by the bridges (iron and pontoon). It is a nice sight driving along. Got back at 7 p.m. I ate, read, worked, and wrote.

## March 16, 1945
Sinzig, Germany

I got up at 10 a.m. and had a piece of toast to eat. I worked most of the morning. I am kept busy.

After dinner I took a walk around town. I didn't go too far. I came back and did some work. The fellows, tankers in the other part of the house, found seven cases of wine and rum behind the coal pile. Murray and Fabre and the gang had red and white wines. They know where there are 500 gallons. My boys visited them and all were rosy. I read, wrote, and worked in the evening.

## March 17, 1945
Sinzig, Germany

I lay in bed and got up at 9:45 a.m. and had a piece of bread. I washed and then did a little work.

I went down to Service Battery and got a Typhoid shot. I had a bottle of ginger ale there. It is made locally and is pretty good stuff. The guys had got a few cases at a factory. I came back and wrote some correspondence, signed reports, and mailed official business. I hung around and worked after dinner. It was chilly out after dinner. I am kept busy lately.

Service Battery kicked a lot of the civilians out of the houses. An eight-inch Howitzer outfit is moving in. They arrived about 4 p.m. and fired until about 11 p.m. They knock the plaster off the ceiling.

After supper I worked on overseas marriages.

## March 18, 1945
Sinzig, Germany

I lay in bed but the others got up. All morning long the fellows were coming and going. I could hear civilians chattering about. Every now and then a girl's voice and someone would open the door and say something about "Soldat schlaf." I got tired of this, as in the first place they aren't supposed to be in here. Secondly they aren't supposed to be taking things out after they leave. There was a girl and a man with Harry, I got up and dressed and they came in the door. I told them emphatically "No" and to get out, "Raus," and kind of slammed the door after them. At first, they came in for a small item and end up taking beds. No one even knows if they lived here.

It is a nice day. I took a sponge bath, shaved, and changed underclothes. Afterwards I cleaned up some work.

After dinner I took a walk and watched the Second Division boys playing softball by the church. They have some of the new Negro doughboys and some of them were playing ball. I watched the people go to church (Sunday). I met a Chief Warrant Officer from the eight-inch Howitzer outfit, and he introduced me to Doc Copleman's brother, who is a clerk here. I had a drink with the Chief Warrant Officer. I came back, had supper, and we talked by the front of the house, came in and read, ate, and wrote.

## March 19, 1945
Sinzig, Germany

I slept fairly well, despite the eight-inch Howitzers firing nearby. They shake the plaster off the ceiling and it is all over my bed, it is on the chair I use to work on, and it falls down my neck. I got up at 9:30 a.m. and took a sponge bath in the bathroom, changed clothes, and even shined my shoes. The fellows all went up to the corner and took a shower at a mobile unit.

After dinner I took a ride in a Liaison jeep. We went to Division Rear at Remagen, did some business, and then went to Bad Neuenahr. It is a wonderful day. We stopped at III Corp to shower but it was crowded. We went to V Corp shower. We took off our jackets with insignias, as we are not in V Corp now. I changed clothes but did not take a shower.

We came back and the gang was loading up. We are moving tonight. We loaded most of the stuff and then ate. We are all already now and waited for the rest. We moved out about 5:30 p.m. We went across the Rhine River, my first time on a pontoon bridge. We went through the heart of Linz and it is very picturesque. We have houses on the outside of town. We have two bedrooms and a kitchen. We moved all the stuff inside the house, out of the way. We even had the young Jerry kids helping us. We set up in record time, sleeping stuff only. We had air raids starting after dark. We read and ate.

## March 20, 1945
Linz, Germany

I had a fair night's sleep even though there were enemy air raids off and on throughout the night. There was plenty of our ack-ack around, firing. I got up at 9:30 a.m., washed, shaved, cleaned things up and then went outside. It is a wonderful day with sun, and regular spring weather. I started to try and get things set up. I pushed a few tables around and eventually the boys slowly arranged their things. I set up the big desk and started to clean up all the work and there is plenty of it, Add Bonds, After Action Reports, the officer's efficiency reports, correspondence, and censoring mail.

After dinner I worked on all these things. I step outside for a breath of fresh air every now and then. After supper Captain Tooley showed up from leave. He got married to his nurse fiancé.

After supper we, Service Battery and Personnel, all threw the ball around in the street. We had a good time until dark. The civilians all watched us. There are quite a few nice looking girls around here. There is one upstairs in our house, all the boys have been sizing her up, and there is another in the house where the kitchen is. After supper I worked typing, writing, and then had a snack. I even used candles when the lights went out at 11 p.m. so I could keep working.

## March 21, 1945
Linz, Germany

At 4 a.m., enemy shells began whistling over. One or two landed quite close. The rest seemed to go further down the valley. The ones that came close made the house rattle. Shortly after this there was an air raid and there were a few more before dawn. There was a lot of ack-ack fire. You can hear the bombs that the planes drop hit. I got up at 9:30 a.m.

and washed and then went to work.

I worked on the payrolls, wrote, and mailed correspondence. I took occasional breaths of fresh air. I signed some papers while sitting in the sun. I put my bedroll out to air. The street is quite a beehive with soldiers, trucks, dogs, kids, women, girls, and old men. It is like a West End city scene. I found polish and a brush on the salvage pile. I got a swell shine on my shoes, now they look like new.

Captain Prince and a couple of enlisted men are here. They are going to Paris. In the afternoon I sat in the sun and talked with Eddie Osowski, who is here to have his command car fixed. I also did a few things in the office. Eddie's car is ready so he went back to A-Battery.

After supper we all played ball in the street. The girls and people were hanging out of the windows watching. There is a pretty girl by the kitchen. All the fellows are also hanging out of the windows across the way, while others are sitting just looking (it is $65 if you get caught talking). The kids and dogs are chasing the balls. Occasionally you can hear a shell come singing over and crack in the valley. No one even mentions or pays attention to it. We stayed outside until dark, 7:30 p.m. We went inside, read, had a snack, and I passed around some Champagne.

## March 22, 1945
Linz, Germany

I slept pretty well even though the ack-ack opened up once or twice. I didn't hear any shells come over. I got up at 9 a.m., had coffee, cereal, and toast with butter. I worked mainly censoring mail and checking correspondence. It is a great day so I sat out in the sun for a while.

The girl upstairs seems affected by the G.I.s. She is dressed up all the time and manages to keep around outside all the time.

We heard that Edie Osowski was killed last night. He spent all day yesterday with me, as we are old buddies from A-Battery. He left here about 3 or 4 p.m., as his command car was fixed. I kiddingly said to him, "Why don't you hit the motor with a hammer so you can stay another day with us?" He said it's too late, as it's fixed and they need the radio for fire missions. He was killed about three hours later. The command car is back here now and all beat up. The radio is all shot up with blood. I can remember kidding Eddie about living in Montague, Massachusetts. He was amazed that I hadn't heard of the famous Montague fishing poles manufactured there. I said I had only fished salt water and we just used bamboo poles.

I sat around in the sun and talked with various people. I walked over to the Collecting Company and got the official information on Eddie's death for my reports. I played catch, read, took a walk, and then came in when it got dark. I worked until 11 p.m., then read and wrote. I wrapped 70 pictures to send to Helen through the Base Censor. We had an air raid later.

## March 23, 1945
Linz, Germany

I slept fairly well and got up 9 a.m. and it is a great day. I had coffee and some French toast that Harry brought me from breakfast. I did a few things around the desk but decided to get outside. I walked around in the nice air and warm sun. I sat out there and censored mail. Chaplain Lorenz came by and we were talking when Jerry threw in a high burst just beyond us. The smoke drifted overhead.

We have been staring at a blond girl in the house below. We had the glasses trained on her. She is quite aware of it and is jumping about. Every time a girl passes by on the street, the heads come out of all windows and field glasses are trained on them and everyone stares. I enjoyed sitting in the sun. It was great.

After dinner I sat outside and then dropped in at the Orderly Room at Service Battery. There are a few guys in Service Battery, Tobey, Pewee, and Gill, and they are drinking.

After supper I went to the Third Section and took a red-hot bath in the tub. I feel good now. I sat around and then took a walk to the hill overlooking Linz and the Rhine. I came back and watched the fellows play ball until it became dark. I came in and about 9 p.m. when Jerry threw in some shells. They landed very close with a resounding crash. The fellows said that they could hear the gun that was firing them very plainly. Tony Wisniewski is sick, too much vino. I worked until 11 p.m. and read. I then lit a candle and finished up.

## March 24, 1945
Linz, Germany

I didn't sleep very well as I tossed and turned most of the night, still I failed to hear any of the shells Jerry threw in during the night. I got up at 9 a.m. It is another great day and the sun is out strong. I checked a few things at the desk and had coffee and toast.

The fellows emptied the trailers and then took them down to the creek to be washed. There were a lot of trailers ahead of them though. I sat in the sun, talked, read, and walked around.

After dinner I stayed out in the sun, played catch, watched the girls below, and cleaned my pistol. All the German kids were watching us. I took a couple of pictures of the street and the house across the street, with the huge hole through the corner. They say this is where Lieutenant Shaughnessy, 60th Infantry, from Waltham, Massachusetts, was killed.

After supper Skoczylas and I walked toward the Rhine. We took a couple of pictures overlooking the town of Linz, the ack-ack crew there, and the Rhine. We continued on to the next hill, which is the one sloping down to the Rhine. There are lots of ack-ack crews up here and it is a beautiful sight looking down, so I took some pictures. We had quite a time winding the film, as it is a misfit. We watched the vehicles crossing the pontoon bridges; we looked down at the fallen iron bridge, Remagen Bridge, and the river with soldiers riding bikes and paddling boats.

We came back and stood outside until dark. Charlie Nagy, Lawrence, Schwartz, and Paris came along with about 30 bottles of Champagne and five gallons of wine. I went inside and worked and wrote.

Ack-ack Crew. Linz on the Rhine, Germany

## March 25, 1945
Linz, Germany

I got up at 9 a.m. and it is another grand day. All the local people are dressed up for Sunday.

I did a few things this morning in the line of work. I gathered together all the business I will have at Division Rear. We boxed all the personal effects of the dead and then had dinner.

After dinner, Gene Skoczylas, George Neuhardt, Everett Linscott, and I took off. We took pictures as we went along. We went to Quarter Master and left off the effects. We continued on to Remagen and Division Rear. I met Frank Page at Finance and we talked for quite some time. I sent a few bonds for the boys, two for $1,000 each, must be a card game winner. We came back and got things together as we are moving tomorrow. I read and talked outside until dark. The boys are all itching to fraternize. I took a walk with Skoczylas.

## March 26, 1945
Linz, Germany

We all got up at 5:45 a.m. Some of the boys had just gotten in at 4 a.m. from night fraternizing. We ate and packed everything, as we are to move. There isn't enough transportation for us to ride on, so we will wait until they come back. We hitched our trailer onto the truck and two of the boys went along.

The people are hustling around, getting odds and ends that the soldiers left behind. We got milk, sugar, and butter ourselves. We hung around and the people are sweating us out. We gave them a few things we couldn't use. We got the three-fourth ton water truck about noon. The people would like us to stay. We could probably give them food, they think, besides we didn't cause them any trouble.

We moved about 10 miles. We are on the side of a ravine but the Battery intends to move again. We ate dinner they had saved for us. We took a walk up the side of the hill. We took a picture of a dead SS Panzer soldier. His knee was shot away as well as being hit in the chest and nose. It looks like he died while trying to bandage his knee.

The Battery moved about 4:45 p.m., after eating supper. We had to wait again as there isn't anywhere to ride. We played catch. After dark they came back for us, and the ammunition they had left here. The moon was bright though. We went about 17 miles. We stopped at a school and then we squeezed into the house next door with the ammunition section. We slept upstairs over two dead Jerries, who died here. The Germans had used it as an Aid Station. The girls of the house are scared to death of us.

## March 27, 1945
Germany

We got up at 6:15 a.m. We had fresh eggs. The people are scared to death of us. We moved out at 7:15 a.m. after we had put our stuff on Rocky's truck. I rode with Lieutenant Planting in the jeep. We passed the Prisoner of War field and there were plenty of German soldiers in it.

Rhine River, Germany.
Skoczylas.

Remagen, Germany.
Ludendorff Bridge and
Rhine River.

The weather cleared up a bit later. We rode on the Frankfort to Cologne Autobahn and the road is littered with debris of the fleeing Nazis. Their equipment is strewn all over the roads and fields. We passed a freed Stalag. There were Russian, French, Belgians, and French Indo-Chinese. We passed a large railroad bridge, intact, but the town flattened. I can't figure out whether they missed the bridge and hit the town or what.

The German people don't show much expression. The forced laborers all wave, smile, and are happy. I saw Lieutenant Potter, 60th Infantry, and he had his ration crew behind us. He had a jeep and tows three or four small trailers filled with hot containers of food. This way the doughboys get a hot meal whenever possible. I took his picture; he was playing a liberated violin as we drove along. We had a good time. The German kids were waving white flags and giving the V for victory sign. I took some pictures.

The roads are crowded with traffic and we traveled about fifty miles. We pulled into Langenhahn about 5 p.m. We ate and then took a room in the house across the road. Eight Jerries walked into Quarter Master at the Railroad station. There were two Jerry planes on the Railroad cars at the station.

We put in electric lights and set up our cots. Jack worked on the morning reports. All houses here have bullet holes in them as the doughs fire in all houses. We rigged up the German's radio and had hot water and hot milk. I had three cokes, our ration. We went to bed at 11 p.m.

**March 28, 1945**
Langenhahn, Germany

229

We had breakfast at 6:15 a.m. and moved out at 7:30 a.m. after the rest, because we had to have a strip of metal welded on the jeep. We just turned the jeep on its side to do this. We hurried along and covered a pretty good distance.

There are wrecked vehicles, dead horses, and equipment everywhere. The tanks ride right over the motors crushing them. We hit heavy traffic. We followed Notorious Forward and Nutmeg signs all the way. We stopped for lunch at a machine shop, as we had run out of signs.

Everyone is scavenging; some of the boys are working on a safe. King found a good trailer. I got welding glasses to keep the dust out of my eyes. The boys found a bicycle, two cases of soda, rifles, and some machine equipment. It looks like we are the first ones here. I think we liberated a town or two as the Armor was searching the last town. The people stare at us and seem surprised. We ate our lunch and took off.

We haven't seen any signs of Captain Tooley yet. We followed the long dusty column of tanks and trucks. There are trucks, liberated foreign soldiers, dead horses, and discarded equipment everywhere. The 34th Field Artillery Battalion is right behind us. We drank some of the liberated soda pop. We finally pulled into a field about 5 p.m. and got ready for chow. Everyone is tired and dirty. The last few towns we passed through were just liberated. There were German trucks smoldering, freshly killed horses, and people scared to death. There are Jerry soldiers just sitting by the side of the road with no one bothering to capture them. There are Jerries in truckloads coming by moving to the rear; in some cases they are driving themselves. We put up pup tents to sleep.

## March 29, 1945
Germany

I heard the rain beginning to fall during the early hours of the morning. The whistle blew at 6:45 a.m. and we had chow at 7 a.m. It was drizzly out. We had fresh eggs and cold cereal, plus the usual coffee and we even had raisin bread.

We moved out about 8 a.m. and went for about six miles. The mud splattered up from the trailer on my back. I had Shad Rak, the motor's dog, on my lap, as this is their jeep. We passed a couple of our Batteries, pulled into Oberwalgern and bivouacked behind Command Post. We are to sit here today. We pitched the pyramidal tent and I washed and shaved. I walked over to Message Center. Jack and Charlie are here to work, as it is warm and has light. I went with Bob Ramsdell to Division Artillery. They are about eight miles back. I saw a prisoner of war enclosure and they all looked like Polish soldiers. After we came back I went over to the Command Post. I talked with Major Williams, Pete Thivierge, and Lieutenant Doc. Graham.

After supper I played catch. Two Jerry planes came by just a little over from us. The guns fired on them as they came back and one of them appeared to get hit. It went behind the hills.

In the evening we talked, Red Schossau brought over his radio to test it, and we listened to it all night. I passed around my one-half bottle of Gin and some mixed cherry soda. Johns of the wire section brought in three Jerries. The boys just go in the woods and fire their guns and the Jerries come out of hiding. We got about 20 today.

## March 30, 1945
Oberwalgern, Germany

I had a good night's sleep even though there were some low flying planes over. I got up for breakfast at 7:30 a.m. and had five pancakes. We don't know whether we will move or not.

The boys reported that 35 jammed truckloads of prisoners went by. I hung around and listened to the radio and talked.

After dinner I walked around and lay down and had a good rest. I dropped around to Service Battery Orderly Room. Tom Gaffney was here visiting, also Captain Gray and Captain Tooley. Tom wants to get back into our outfit. He asked me to write something. I came back, pulled out the big desk, and sat on my bed. I worked writing on his request; through channels, and one direct one. I typed them myself as well as the correspondence. I quit at 11 p.m. I had a little coffee and went to bed.

## March 31, 1945
Oberwalgern, Germany

I had a swell night's sleep and there were plenty of low flying planes again. I lay in bed and everyone was coming in for various reasons. The boys began to get up one by one. Tom Gaffney came in and I told him where he could get his papers. I got up at 9:30 a.m. and had coffee, bread and butter, as all we have is C-rations anyway. I cleaned up all the work on my desk, as we are to move today.

We got orders to turn in winter equipment. I turned in the stove that we used in the tent as requested. Everyone reduced their bedrolls, so I built mine up a bit, as I didn't have enough. We cleaned out all excess equipment and belongings.

Every time the Ammunition Section has an argument, which is often, they seek me out to settle it.

It is an overcast day. We are to move between 6 p.m. or 8 p.m. tonight and go about forty miles. One of the Battalion boys led eight prisoners from the woods, with two G.I.s bringing up the rear.

For dinner I had C-rations and coffee.

In the afternoon I arranged my things and prepared a report for the colonel. We struck the pyramidal tent at 4 p.m. We had C-rations, bread, and coffee for supper. They delayed the move until 11 p.m. I took a walk around the village. All married women wear their hair upswept to a nob. They wear traditional long dresses and black stockings. They remind me of the Normans of old. These people are Hessians. This is Hess. They helped us in the revolutionary war against the British. They are predominantly Lutheran.

We hung around Message Center until 10:30 p.m. We moved out at

11:30 p.m. I rode in the Motor's jeep. Service Battery had a lot of trouble trying to round the sharp corner with their trailers.

# Chapter eleven: April 1945

April 1, 1945 to April 30, 1945

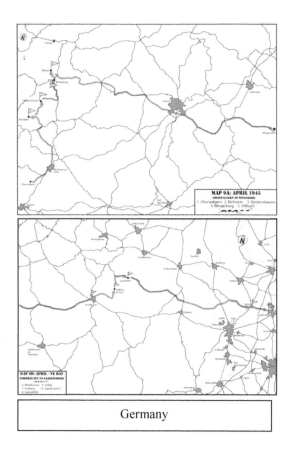

Germany

April 1945 Historical Overview
Month of April 1945 Corps Assignments:
First Army, 12th Army Group
April 1 to April 3, 1945 - VII Corps
April 4 to April 13, 1945 - III Corps
April 14 to April 30, 1945 - VII Corps

234

General Overview

As Germany nears utter defeat, German soldiers are giving up en mass.

From the west, the Allied forces are moving rapidly across Germany. From the east the Russian troops are closing in.

The Ruhr Pocket is closed. The Ruhr Pocket campaign took place during March 1945 and April 1945. Allied troops participated in an encircling maneuver surrounding the industrial rich Ruhr area.

On April 11th the 104th Division and the 3rd Armored Division discovered Concentration camps in Nordhausen. The Nordhausen camp and Dora-Mittelbau camp operated a slave factory producing V-2 Rockets. They found 3000 corpses and 750 emancipated survivors, many who died soon after. The townspeople of Nordhausen were forced to bury the bodies.

On April 28, 1945 President Franklin D. Roosevelt dies. Harry Truman is the new President.

The official meeting of the Russian and Allied troops is recognized as occurring on April 25 1945 at the Elbe River near Togua, Germany.

Italian partisans hang Mussolini

On April 30, 1945 the same day the Russian Army entered Berlin, Adolf Hitler, with his new bride Eva Braun, committed suicide in an underground bunker.


9th Division Overview: To quote Captain Joseph B Mittelman's book *Eight Stars to Victory: A History of the Veteran Ninth U.S. Infantry Division*, the month of April 1945 was "fateful, fast, furious, and victorious."

The 9th Division moved across Germany rapidly until they meet stiff resistance in the Harz Mountains around April 15th, 1945. Remaining groups of fanatical Nazi soldiers defended this naturally fortified area. This sector was secured by April 20, 1945 and the 9th continued onward, southeast into Germany.

On April 14, 1945 the 9th Division encountered Concentration Camps in the town of Nordhausen. The Camps were named Nordhausen camp and Dora-Mittelbau.

On April 26, 1945, a day after the "official" meeting of East and West, a patrol of 60th Infantry Regiment of the 9th Infantry Division made contact with Russian forces

Fraternization defined as, "friendly, familiar, or intimate, contact between Allied soldiers and German nationals" remained a prosecutable offense.

***

### *April 1, 1945*
Oberwalgern, Germany

We stopped and started all throughout the early morning hours. Being in the Motor jeep we stopped three or four times at broken down vehicles. It was a chilly ride and we could hear guns as we neared our destination, which is Richstein. It was after 5 a.m. when we arrived. Jerry was shelling a town a little over from us and it was burning brightly.

We are in a house and I have two rooms for my section. There is one bed - I slept on this and the rest slept on the floor. I took the bed as the cots weren't handy and I don't feel too well. I got to bed about 5:30 a.m. and slept until noon. I feel lousy with a cold and a stuffed head. I went back to bed until 1:15 p.m. I feel terrible and I had to lay down every few minutes, so I decided to go to bed.

The Ammunitions Section, which is the further one down from us, was standing around the fire when two Jerries came out of the woods and gave themselves up.

It is Easter Sunday and my birthday at that. I am 28 years old. The civilian kids downstairs are having a colored egg hunt. If I had known it, I think I would have hunted with them. After eating C-rations, eggs would taste pretty good. The boys brought me coffee, and eats. The Pill Rollers (Medics) came over and gave me nose drops and aspirins.

About 5 p.m. the fellows in the room here spotted some Jerries coming down the side road with a white flag. Skoczylas, who had been sitting in the field, borrowed a gun and went toward them. A couple of Service Battery guys followed. They brought them in, eight in all. They searched them and brought them to the Orderly Room. They were taken away in the three-fourth ton truck. I got up out of bed to watch all of this by looking out of the window. I feel a little better. This makes 14 prisoners that Personnel have had a part in taking. I stayed up for a while and wrote.

## April 2, 1945
Richstein, Germany

I had a good night's sleep and we are supposed to move this morning. Jack had the women in the kitchen cook our breakfast. We then gathered everything together.

We aren't going until the second load, so Skoczylas and I went on our scheduled prisoner hunt. We started out down the valley floor. It is drizzly out, clearing every now and then. We passed the few houses below and then walked along the road. We saw two figures on the hill. They were two Jerries: one in a green coat and the other in a dark coat. We yelled and beckoned to them and they stood fast. We cut cross-country, keeping them in view but when we arrived at a certain point we split. We had to lose sight of them for a few moments until we ascended the height. When we got there they were gone. I went down to look at the low side of the hill, but they weren't there. We figured they had run back into the woods. We fired our guns into the woods and yelled but to no avail. We yelled, "Kommen jetzt hier, Deutsch Soldat." We gave up and checked a nearby farmhouse. The people were scared to death. The young fellow showed us his papers and that he had been discharged some time ago. We left and practiced firing our weapons. We fired at a wild duck that had just left the little pond below. Skoczylas dropped it with his carbine at 100 yards.

We came back to the group of houses and the Service Battery guys, Brock, Eisenstein, and Tony, were checking them for a Jerry Lieutenant in civilian clothes, who is supposed to be here. Skoczylas and I talked with the friendly blond Fraulein in French for a long time.

We went back and I had to go to Division Forward to get the Battalion pay. I spent some time counting and then talking with a cute Russian slave laborer and Colonel Hargy. We came to Service Battery's new location in the town of Didenshausen. I then went to the Battalion area and paid some officers, including Colonel Beets. I came back to Personnel, Service Battery area, and we are in the tent, in the rain.

## April 3, 1945
Diedenshausen, Germany

I slept pretty well and didn't get up until 10:30 a.m. I had C-rations for breakfast, cereal, coffee, and crackers. We have a wood fire outside the door, that's all we have to heat the place or keep warm and dry. It is still raining, although it clears every now and then.

Yesterday was a miserable day, raining, and I had to pay the Battalion under such undesirable conditions. Tony Tooley said that one of my boys was fraternizing and that we were complaining. Naturally my boys were browned off, as we have to set up a tent in the rain, have no stove, and have to do office work, such as typing, when most of the others are in houses. Even the Ammunitions Section are in houses, in fact all but us, the Kitchen, and the Orderly Room, are in houses. There isn't anywhere to work. We have nine sleeping here in the tent and it is cold and wet. Everyone's shoes and feet are all wet. I changed mine for dry ones.

I rode up with Joe King to the Battalion to try and pay off the rest of the Battalion. They were packing to move as I got there, so I came back. It is wet and rainy out. We are still eating C-rations. The ground is softly wet. We hung around and talked. Some of the boys went in the house and played cards. I went to bed at 8:30 p.m., as it is the only warm and dry place. Once again, we who have to do the important work - office work and payrolls - in a cold/wet tent while all the other are billeted in houses, and playing cards.

## April 4, 1945
Diedenshausen, Germany

I slept a little chilly, as it was really cold out. No one got up in the morning as it was cold and raining and there is not a way of keeping warm and dry. We all slept until about noon. I was the first up and I had cereal and then heated water for coffee. The rest then got up. We found out that we are to move as soon as the trucks return.

We assembled all our stuff and loaded the trailer. It rained and hailed as we worked loading. There is snow on the tops of the surrounding hills. We struck the tent and waited in the house until the trucks came. We had to have the trailer winched out of the muddy field by Battalion Motors. We then had to wait until Rusty had two flat tires fixed before we could pull out.

We passed Division Forward and Noisy and moved into an already overcrowded house at Liesen. We make the people crowd together in other rooms, take out their stuff, and start a fire. We have two beds upstairs that had belonged to two girls. We let them have use of the kitchen and they can sleep downstairs. We have two more beds and a couch here, as well as a single bed in the office room. I set up my cot and then had them set up the office. We had the lights put in and hooked up the radio. We heated our rations and did some work in the evening. I passed out the various jobs and we worked until the lights went out at 11:06 p.m.

## April 5, 1945
Liesen, Germany

I had a good night's sleep and got up at 9 a.m. I had coffee, crackers, and cereal. I have a terrific amount of work. I started in writing correspondence, recommendations for awards, answering questions, reading poop sheets, passing out work, and addressing letters.

I went up to Battalion; it was about 12 miles up from here. The 7th Armored Division is on the road. There is plenty of destroyed Jerry equipment, staff cars, trucks, autos, and a Nebelwerfer, a six-barrel screeching mortar. The Battalion is in buildings and the Command Post is beside an office. They are near a radio (Radio-fabrik) factory and a typewriter factory. Everyone has nice new radios, right in the crates, and nice portable typewriters. I left the Officers' pay up there. This is Winterberg, the place where the Jerries captured most of C-Company, 60th Infantry, and some of our guys. They got Lieutenant Stacey, Jankowski, Stepp, and Wood. They also captured Major Waters, a good friend of mine. He had been Personnel Officer of the 60th Infantry for a long time.

I came back and went to work. Everyone is around today and we are all busy working. We are still eating C-rations. I took a little walk around the town and back. I worked all afternoon and evening.

## April 6, 1945
Liesen, Germany

I had a fair night's sleep and got up about 10 a.m. and was the second one up at that. It is one of those sleepy mornings.

Father Connors came to Service Battery. He had Rosary and Communion. It is sprinkling and miserable out. I worked writing award recommendations, correspondence, and checking records. I haven't much of an appetite for C -rations. I took a sponge bath and washed some clothes. I took a short walk in the evening, then worked and wrote two letters.

## April 7, 1945
Liesen, Germany

I slept pretty well and didn't get up until 9:50 a.m. I had a little snack

240

for breakfast. The kitchen is now feeding B-rations again. I would have had to get up at 7:30 a.m. to get it.

The sun is finally out but it is cool. I took a walk by myself after doing quite a lot of work. I walked along the stream to a few knocked out vehicles. I picked up a chair to use at my desk.

I didn't eat much for dinner. We had fresh meat, potatoes, and gravy. In the afternoon I did some work. Then I took a walk all alone up the road along the wadi. I set up a bottle on the stump and practiced firing at it and then came back. I took my barracks bag and tidied things up.

I ate supper and then walked over to pick up some ammunition. I cleaned up my mess kit and washed up. I read, stood outside, wrote, and worked in the evening. The boys brought back some eggs, about 24, they sort of shook down the civilians for them. We got some potatoes and had them boiled, so we can have eggs and fried potatoes for breakfast tomorrow. I worked the rest of the evening.

## April 8, 1945
Liesen, Germany

I was cold as it was chilly last night; actually it was cold. I got up 8:30 a.m. so I could go to mass at 9 a.m. I washed and dressed. The other boys are getting up to cook their eggs and potatoes.

Skoczylas, Delli and I went to church. There was frost on the ground from last night. As we entered the local churchyard - it's a little country church - two girls ahead of us were obviously scared or nervous. They probably thought we were following them. They opened the door and the priest could be seen on the altar. They were relieved to find that we were going to Mass and not there to loot or snoop. It was crowded but there were only about four other G.I.s. The people say the Mass out loud.

We came back and I fried potatoes and eggs. It was a delicious breakfast with coffee, bread, and butter. I worked a bit and then took a walk before dinner. We are to move after dinner so I walked down to the cross roads - where there's a pond - to tell Jack and Tony

Wisniewski. They were there fishing with hand grenades. We packed and then ate.

Charlie and I walked up the valley and fired our guns a bit. We sat outside in the sun all afternoon, and then went inside. The kids in the house made their first Communion today and were pesky. We fried a batch of spuds and later some beef and had coffee, in the people's kitchen. We talked with them. One young woman, with a baby two years old, whose husband was a prisoner of war in America, was a real Nazi. The older women shushed her every once in a while. They can't understand our point of view toward them.

We moved out about 12 miles to Silbach. We are in a school. By the side of the building the trailer got truck. I have a private room. I worked and ate.

## April 9, 1945
Silbach, Germany

I had a good night's sleep in my private room. I was awake and Angelo Ricci, B-Battery, came in. He is going home as well as Norder of Headquarters Battery. Ricci is from Quincy, Massachusetts, and he and I and a few others were the first ones drafted into the service from Quincy. I told him to drop by my house and say Hello and tell them everything is okay. I gave him a letter to mail locally when he got back.

I finally got up, washed, got my fire going, and took a sponge bath. I sent my clothes out with Skoczylas; he is having some Polish slave laborers do it, as he speaks the language. The Poles in turn are having the Germans do it.

It is a nice day. I worked all morning and Tony Wisniewski is counting and checking money. I checked Cohen's (from B-Battery) money, as he is turning it in for conversions to Marks. I was busy all morning but had time to wash some clothes.

We had 10-in-1 rations for dinner. After dinner I was busy except for a little time out to fool with the drum, piano, and violin. I took a short walk.

We had 10-in-1 supper, which is better than C-rations. I walked around town just looking around. All the people stare at you. I then worked and talked until the lights went out. I wrote by candlelight until 12 a.m. I am going back to Division Rear at Korbach tomorrow.

## April 10, 1945
Silbach, Germany

I slept well and got up at 7:25 a.m. and had breakfast. I made a fire, heated water, washed, and shaved.

I came downstairs to get things together, as I am going to Division Rear. While there I am sending my Brother Wally some German cigars. We are bringing a couple thousand dollars in Pay Transfer Accounts, Soldier's Deposits, and Bonds, and a few thousand dollars for conversion from Belgium Francs to German Marks. We had the command car stacked with boxes. Linscott drove and Tony Wisnieski, who had counted and organized the money, came along with Staff and Dougan. We tore up the road in true Linscott style.

It is pretty country. I checked the route and kept us on the right roads. We went to Medebach and then to Korbach, which is a fair sized place. There are a lot of Russians, Poles, and other forced laborers being evacuated. I stopped at Finance and turned in the payrolls, while Tony Wisniewski took the Pay Transfer Accounts. I stopped at the Adjunct General and they were all after me for Morning Reports. I walked to the Post Office and mailed my things. I ate at the Officer's mess; it is in a nice set up in a Hotel. I dropped in and talked with Frank Page. I went back and talked with Ricci, who is still here, waiting to go home. I did a few more things at Finance and talked to various people. We left at 3:30 p.m. and came back.

After supper Charlie Nagy and I took a walk. Lieutenant Planting went with us part of the way. We went up to the top of the hill. We found a hunting lodge and huts. We fired our guns and then we met Brush and

Zutke from Service Battery. We all shot our guns at trees, German helmet, and grenades.

In the evening I wrote, read, and worked.

## April 11, 1945
Silbach, Germany

I didn't sleep too well as it was hot. I lied in bed till 9 a.m. I got up, cleaned up, and washed out a couple things, after having started a fire. I came down about 10 a.m. and fried two eggs, and had coffee and bread.

I was busy answering payroll questions, writing correspondence, reading, checking poop, and typing reports. Major Elliot dropped in and he is now Division Assistant G-4 at Division Forward. He is sweating out the G-1 job. He came to close out the Battalion Fund.

It is a great day and the sun is out. I aired my bedclothes. In the afternoon I worked steadily on various things. In the afternoon Captain Thivierge, Captain Gray, Captain Tooley, and Sergeant Nix dropped in. We are quite busy with payrolls and efficiency reports.

After supper someone saw a P- 47 go down. I saw the smoke coming up. I walked straight up the hill and along the path by myself. It was tiresome as I am not in condition. I wandered thru the woods to the firebreak and the clearing. I couldn't see any traces of the plane. I wandered up a ways and down another firebreak. There are lots of hunter blinds. I walked to a shack looked around and then came back to the first firebreak. I fired my pistol at the marked trees, 20 shots. I am improving a bit. I came back and talked with the Medics outside for a while. A young fräulein has been leering at me. I wrote, read, and cleaned up my pistol.

## April 12, 1945
Silbach, Germany

I slept pretty well and got up at 9:15 a.m. I cleaned up and came downstairs. I had to borrow a cup of hot water for coffee from the kitchen, as no one had built fires.

It was overcast and sprinkled. I sat at the desk all morning and worked. I have much to do and I am busy all the time. I bought a pair of slippers from Shipe; he gets them thru the Abercrombie and Fitch catalog, and I am sending them to Dad for a birthday present.

After dinner I worked steadily and occasionally went out for a breath of fresh air. The ack-ack officers were around at supper. There was Captains Baine, Tex, and a new fellow with Service Battery.

After supper I stood outside for a while watching the boys stare at the local fräuleins. I came in as it started to rain. I worked until 11 p.m. counting money, signing papers, and reports. I am going to Division Rear tomorrow, at Korbach.

The majority of Service Battery was around at 11 p.m., getting ready to take off, as they have to drive the 39th Infantry on a long trip. They are going to the other side of Hanover. I went to my room at 12 a.m. and jotted this note.

## April 13, 1945
Silbach, Germany

I got up at 7:25 a.m., had breakfast and then got everything ready to go down to Division Rear. I changed my mind as I have a lot of work to do, so I sent Jack Markowitz. I was terribly busy. I wrote the important parts of the Battalion History, correspondence, typed a few notes, and answered questions all morning.

Tom Collins, 34th Field Artillery (from Swampscott or Lawrence, Massachusetts), is here with other Paris pass men. They are to leave from here. I talked with him for a while. I was very busy all afternoon. The boys went for a walk and the daily shoot. I took an occasional breath of fresh air.

After supper I worked, sent Skoczylas to Division Quarter Master to send personal effects, wrestled with Lieutenant Obeldobel, talked, and then had some French potatoes that the boys had fried in my room. All day and night the radio is bemoaning President Roosevelt's death. He died yesterday sometime. It must be quite a blow to the home people. It is just another death to the G.I.s. No prediction, by me, of the future, I don't even recall what the Vice President, Harry Truman, looks like.

## April 14, 1945
Silbach, Germany

I had to close the windows during the night; I had them wide open to clear the air out after the kitchen had fried potatoes in here. I got up at 9:30 a.m., had coffee and two fried eggs. I went right to work. I am still busy on payrolls. We received word that we are to move tomorrow. We will move about 160 miles. We cleaned up all the work we could.

In the afternoon I took an occasional breath of fresh air, watching the G.I.s watching the fräuleins and fraus. The fräuleins are making goo-goo eyes all over the place. Some of the trucks came back from their trip to Hanover.

After supper, we loaded the trailers and hauled them to convenient spots. The fellows, from Hanover, brought back some fireworks. They had slept in the factory last night. They fired off a whistle-bomb. It had some of the guys looking for a foxhole at first. Roman candles, skyrockets, aerial bombs, and firecrackers rent the air. They were setting them off on the side of the hill. The boys, being a little tight, helped out the situation. They had a little battle against each other with Roman candles. The civilians, especially the kids, got a big kick out of it all, saying, "Sehr" and "Wunderbar" as they went off.

I read and then went to my room, cleaned up, wrote, and read.

## April 15, 1945
Silbach, Germany

I didn't sleep much, got up at 4:20 a.m., dressed, and went to chow in the dark. I came back, made a fire, and got my things ready. We loaded up, the trucks lined up, and we moved out about 6 a.m. We have

162 miles to go. It began to sprinkle.

The Service Battery Guys were throwing firecrackers around. Some people said that someone was sick; the guys just threw more firecrackers at the house. They sent a whistler after a man on a bike; he looks like a clergyman. He dropped the bike and ran. He ran up the hill, and they sent a skyrocket after him. He took off again.

It is pretty riding. We got a second flat tire and got behind the convoy. We caught up at the lunch stop. It got dusty. We passed Nordhausen, which is flattened. We had previously passed camouflaged oil tanks and V-2 rockets on a train. Nordhausen was flat and there were thousands of forced laborers fleeing. They don't look any too well. We could see the graves of the 3,500 starved political prisoners.

We ran out of gas. We finally pulled into Stolberg-im-Hartz. We have two rooms in houses on either side of the street. As we passed the corner pulling in here, a Jerry came walking up the street with his wife and kid, past the Military Police and Road Marker. We yelled at them and they stopped him and began to search him. In front of our house I almost bumped into three of them coming down on bikes. They had taken their hats off but the Military Police stopped them. The 9th Divisions trucks brought truckloads of Jerries by.

## April 16, 1945
Stolberg-im-Hartz, Germany

I slept pretty well but didn't get up until 9:15 a.m. I went across the street and had coffee and cereal. I washed and shaved over there. I brought some of my work over. I signed the morning reports and payrolls.

It is a great day so we stood outside and then sat for a while. There are a lot of good-looking fräuleins around. We had a K-ration dinner.

After dinner I took a walk up the street, and then climbed the hill. I saw two girls going up the path in the woods. I followed them a bit and then found two guys from Service Battery lying on a blanket nearby. I put two and two together and came back and hung around outside the house.

After supper, which consisted of crackers, with butter and jam, a couple of the boys and I took a walk to the other part of town. We came back and saw a girl, she must have been mental, looking around corners and running up and down the street. There were some nice looking fräuleins around. In the evening I had a snack, did some work, and wrote.

## April 17, 1945
Stolberg-im-Hartz, Germany

I didn't get up for breakfast but had coffee across the street. I washed up over there and hung around outside. Lieutenant Van Leuven dropped in and left some Bronze Star recommendations to be written up. We talked for quite some time.

After dinner I took a walk; it is interesting just walking around. People stare at you. The girls give you a look that entices. I walked up towards the place where the fellows fish. I saw a girl along the road. She was hiking along. I stopped to look at the creek. She went on and turned in a path labeled "Hartz Garden." She sat on a bench. I walked by where she was reading and up a path. I reached the top of a little hill and she still sat (by not going – she was inviting). I came back and she looked up. I said "Hello," and then spoke a few words. She answered "Heiß." I sat down and said a few things and sized up the situation. I decided I better return to our area, as it is time to eat. I said I would see her here at 2 p.m. tomorrow. I left.

After supper, I hung around outside and then walked down to the fence at the T road. I sat on the rail, talking with a few fellows. The forced laborers go by, they have been streaming by all day. They are Poles and Russians, and they all wear striped uniforms, like convicts.

In the evening I stayed inside and went to work on writing Bronze Star recommendations.

## April 18, 1945
Stolberg-im-Hartz, Germany

I had cereal and coffee across the street, at our other place over there.

I sat at my desk, by sitting on the end of my bed, and did some work. I took a short walk. All the people here say they made alcohol at Nordhausen. We know they made V-1 and V-2 rockets underground.

We saw them burying the dead. Some of the boys --my gang --went down in the tunnel underground where they made them. They found it like a production line, with Gestapo Posts every so often. There were nice blockhouses overlooking the lines of workers. Ten thousand worked 12 hours and another 10,000 worked the other 12 hours. An average of 40 died every day. They were worked until they fell of weakness and then they were put in a pen outside to die, 3,500 had already died. They were fed one meal a day, usually consisting of a bowl of watered down soup with fish bones in it.

I took a walk and went down where Archie Dougan was fishing. I watched him catch a trout. The girl I was supposed to meet at 2 p.m. was coming by. I did not want to meet her, as she was a hustler, I felt. I told my one of my friends, so he followed her and later he talked with her. He borrowed a key for a vacant house at the Schloss (Castle) and they went inside.

In the evening I talked outside, walked down and sat on the rail of the fence, at the T road. We talked and watched the people go by. The girls are all man conscious. Most of Service Battery have been drunk for two days and are all shacking up. There are some pretty girls around. I worked after dark.

Nordhausen

## April 19, 1945
Stolberg-im-Hartz, Germany

I got up and had cereal and coffee across the street. I worked on a few things and then sat outside in the sun.

In the afternoon I took a walk up the road where they fish. A man and two girls at the Stone Arch called me and said, "Ruski-hose-?" They meant the Russians were stealing their stockings and clothes. I said, "Nicht verstehe," as the easiest way out of it. I circled the town and came back. One of my friends took the place of my other friend with that girl. This town is a strange place. The people don't have very much to eat. The Russians and Poles are moving through all the time, sometimes stealing and molesting. They are a motley looking crew. There are disabled Jerry soldiers around. There is going to be trouble yet. The Counter Intelligence Corps (C.I.C.) is going to check the town soon. The guys are all getting rifles, shotguns, and cameras, from the Bürgermeister. In most of the towns the Bürgermeister collects all guns for safety and safekeeping. Everyone in Service Battery is drunk and staggering around. They have women in the Ammunition House. De Rosa is hanging out the window and ringing a hand bell, like the town crier. He keeps saying, "Bürgermeister says, alle Frauen gehen schlofen, Fräuleins, kommen jetzt hier." All the people are laughing.

A nice blond, with a wonderful figure, named Sonja, came by. She stopped to pat the puppy I had. She cast eyes. Later we walked by her house. She flung the window open. We spoke but there were too many people around.

Everyone is drunk tonight. Charlie and Freddie Murray had a guy out on the sidewalk at 1:30 in the morning doing close order drill in his long underwear. A little later I could hear German voices on the street nearby somewhere.

**April 20, 1945**
Stolberg-im-Harz, Germany

I got up at 9 a.m. and had coffee and crackers. I got some correspondence in today's delivery; Bronze Star recommendations were among them. I put everyone to work typing his own Batteries. I wrote one for Lieutenant "Doc" Graham, so we were all busy this morning on these.

Shortly after dinner Captain Pete Thivierge came down to get some dope on a Court Martial. It is a case of rape. I got Harry Hammer on the case, as it is in B-Battery and he has the Service Records. George drove me and we followed them to Battalion. We got out and I went to Pete's room while they waited for the Military Police. We went down to the house. The woman, 38 years old, with one child, told her story. We got the information for a report. We came back to Battalion and I made out the report.

Captain Thivierge then found out that General Howell, of Division Artillery, wanted the case investigated tonight, so we just prepared to

251

stay. I went to B-Battery and got the charges, came back to the Regimental Headquarters, and talked to Mr. Wood, Warrant Officer. I started Harry on the charges at 9:15 p.m. We worked, Harry typing, me writing and answering questions. We worked till 12 midnight, then Pete brought in the witnesses' statements. Harry worked steadily all through the night. I stayed with him and made some French fried potatoes, and ate crackers. The case involves three men. The charges are rape, fraternization, breaking safe guard, threatening a sentinel, and absent without leave (AWOL). It is all mixed up. The case of rape is being struck and fraternizations used.

## April 21, 1945
Siptenfelde (Battalion Headquarters), Germany

All through the wee morning hours I sat beside the table, Harry typing and answering questions, and me nodding. The rest of the people involved in the case found spots in the room to sleep in.

About 5 a.m. the colonel called to have the papers ready for him to sign. He came in. I typed some of the forms and he signed mostly blank papers, as did Captain Brown; as they had seen the rough drafts. I worked on one typewriter and Harry on the other. Everyone was calling up about the charges. I had a little coffee and a biscuit. Everyone was here calling about it or answering calls about it.

I dropped in on the Message Center and the Medics, checking on things. I talked with Mr. Woods about it and cleaned up little odds and ends. Skoczylas helped us. The two cases recommended for General Court Martial were sent about 10:30 a.m. Harry and I worked on the Special Court Martial case and finally finished it about 12 noon. We are plenty tired so Harry and I hustled out of here before the case bounced back. We came back to our own area and the gang was packed up, waiting for March Order, they had just left out the cots and beds. We got the word we won't move until tomorrow.

## April 22, 1945
Stolberg-im-Hartz, Germany

I slept pretty well and woke up when the whistle blew at 4 a.m. I ate, packed my stuff, and we were loaded by 5:30 a.m. and moved out at 5:35 a.m. Some of the men even shook hands with the Germans, even after all the non-fraternization warnings.

I am riding in the open front of Rusty's truck with the assistant driver Zutke. It was cold and began to snow. We went to Siptenfelde, where Battalion is. We pulled off the road and waited. The Battalion came along and we followed. It became terribly cold, raining, snowing, and then the sun would come out. The open truck front was very cold. We finally put a shelter half over us and this made a one 100-percent difference.

We moved about 60 miles to Kapelle. The rumors are that we are now only about 20 miles from the Russians. We got a few rooms on the top floor of a house. We brought our bedrolls in. We had dinner and built a fire. For supper we had eggs that the guys got in the hen house outback. There are Poles here, some of them wearing parts of uniforms. They even have parts of American uniforms that they say were given to them by the Red Cross.

I have a little room to myself. In the evening we had eggs and chicken that Jack had killed and fried.

## April 23, 1945
Kapelle, Germany

I slept fairly well but a little too warm. I didn't get up until 10 a.m. and had cereal, coffee, and toast with bacon.

I started handing out the work. The clerks started to bring up their desks. I cleaned up various papers. It is raining, April Showers, off and on.

After dinner Charlie Nagy came back from Battalion after fixing up the Courts Martial. Captain Thivierge dropped down. He notified

253

Captain Tooley that three men from Service Battery were caught breaking the safeguard by the Counter Intelligence Corps. They are to be tried. Then we talked, especially about a method of speeding up the work. I am to go up to Battalion tomorrow and talk it over.

Captain Tooley called a meeting about fraternization and drinking. I worked all afternoon on various things. They are beginning to clamp down on everything. I worked all evening on the cases. I had George as he has Service Battery Records, complete the Charge Sheets and allied papers.

## April 24, 1945
Kapelle, Germany

I got up for breakfast at 7:30 am, ate, washed, and then got various papers together.

At 9:40 a.m. I took the three fellows from Service Battery who are to be tried, and went to the 60th Infantry Regimental Headquarters. I stopped in at Captain Thivierge and he and Sergeant Nix were there. I talked with them about the new Command Post setup. Then the Military Police Office came in with Captain Ryan from 60th Infantry Regiment. They are talking about a patrol that is to go out, with liquor and cigars, to try and meet up with the Russians.

I rode to our Battalion Headquarters while the men awaiting trial were questioned. I came back and picked them up. While sitting there at the table, Lieutenant Cable gave me a couple of nice Eversharp pencils. I came back to Service Battery. We traveled a little way on the Autobahn. It is a beautiful, wide road. The road goes from Leipzig to Magdeburg, I guess.

In the afternoon I worked on various papers. After super Lieutenant Lemire, Observation Post Pilot, took me up in the Piper Cub airplane. It is my first time in the air. It is a great experience. The land is a pattern of squares of different colors. I could see the town that the Russians have burning. We also have a town burning from artillery fire. We circled a Jerry airport at Köthen and landed. There are burned Jerry planes all over the place and a few were Jet propelled. They had been hit by Ack-ack or strafed on the ground. We took off, buzzed the airport and did a few sharp turns. I nixed a loop the loop, or rather my stomach did. It's such a great thrill! We then looked around, passed over Regimental and Battalion Headquarters, and then climbed. I could see the Elbe River and the Mulde River was below. I could see the Russian guns firing. A little smoke rising on the edge of the Elbe here and there probably indicated a Jerry with no place to go. It is a great panorama; I could see rivers, towns, and cities. We got a sudden alert, "Enemy Air Craft in the area." Lemire stood the plane on its nose. All the map cases came down on top of me as we nosed straight for the ground. We hugged the ground, on a zigzag course, scooting between trees until well out of the area. All in all we made two landings and were in the air well over an hour. We landed in a potato field and I thought the plane would shake apart.

Köthen, Germany. Flew from Kapelle, Germany and over enemy lines.

## April 25, 1945
Kapelle, Germany

I got up at 8:30 a.m., cleaned up, and then ate some eggs with coffee. I set up all the things I need to work. I have plenty to do to get records out and writing correspondence.

Father Connors had a Mass out under the tree at 11 a.m. The 34th Field Artillery Battalion, Service Battery, our gang, and some from another outfit were there. The Polish soldiers attended and people watched from the windows.

After dinner I took the command car, George drove, and we traveled cross-country to Radegast. The 60th Field Artillery and 60th Infantry

Regiment have security guards and patrols here. I saw them checking civilian's passes. We continued on to Köthen. It is a nice road and we continued on to the airport. We took pictures beside the planes. We rummaged through the hangers and a few buildings. I found a few coins and insignias.

We left and went to Division Forward. They are set up in a building protected by Tank Destroyers. It is a nice city, rather large and good-looking girls who kind of give you the eye. I picked up the efficiency reports for correction and we came back.

After supper I did quite a bit of work. There are four men going home on 45-days' leave. Going home are Captain Parrish, Pflieger from A-Battery, Murray from C-Battery, and Gelders from Service Battery. We got their records ready.

## April 26, 1945
Kapelle, Germany

I got up at 8:40 a.m. I heard a whistle blowing; it was a formation at Service Battery. I had coffee and a couple of eggs.

I have a lot of work to do and three more of our men are on road guard today. I worked on correspondence all morning. Our telephone is pretty busy. It is a nice day and the sun is out. I talked with the wire section guys at dinner. They asked me if I want any film. They met a civilian who had a hay wagon full of 120 film packs. I got a wooden box from them of 50 rolls. Later Rusty got me a dozen rolls of 35 mm.

I worked in the afternoon on correspondence. Mike Maher, from the 34th Field Artillery Personnel, dropped in and we talked all afternoon.

After supper Harry and I took a walk and we went up to the windmills. A G.I. brought two German kids, about 19 years old, out of one. We questioned them, examined their papers, and then let them go. We took pictures and walked to the other side of town and back. I did some more work and wrote a letter in the evening.

**April 27, 1945**

Kapelle, Germany

I got up at 9 a.m., cleaned up, cooked some fresh eggs and had coffee. The boys are yelling, as they have to pull 24-hour guard. On top of all this, they are expected to do their work.

We got a notice that they are going to submit more Bronze Star recommendations. We are to get them at 1 p.m. and they are to be in by 5 p.m. I had the clerks relieved from guard. We finally got the things at 3:30 p.m. We all pitched in, I typed some. Headquarters had 15: A-Battery has six: B-Battery has one: C-Battery has one: and Service Battery has five. I had to write about five or six of them. I added Gene Skoczylas and Harry Hammer to the lists. We worked until 8:30 p.m. and then sent them up to Battalion. I then tried to clean up the other odds and ends of work.

**April 28, 1945**

Kapelle, Germany

I didn't sleep any too well. I figure I have been doing a little too much work under pressure lately. I go up at 9:30 a.m. and had two eggs and coffee.

I have plenty of work and most of the men are either on guard or going on guard. I am writing recommendations for awards. The phone has been busy all day. We got two new officers in Service Battery; they will replace Lieutenant Obeldobel and Lieutenant Planting, who went to A-Battery and C-Battery. Lieutenant Tracey will be Motor Officer and Lieutenant Kuisisto will be Ammunition officer. Gene Welch came back from the Hospital and picked up his effects. I had them in my room ready to send out. I worked all afternoon. Various agents and others dropped in all afternoon. I worked after supper until 9:45 p.m.

## April 29, 1945

Kapelle, Germany

I got up at 9 a.m. and had three fresh eggs and coffee. I am still as busy as ever.

I collected things together so that when I got to Division Rear, I'll know what I had to do. I fixed the Pay Transfer Accounts and bonds. I'm going after dinner.

The Safe Guard brought in a Jerry soldier. He didn't come when called and started to run, so one of the men shot at him. He hit the Jerry once through the shoulder.

George drove me and Tony Wisnieski came along. We went to Division Rear at Köthen. I completed my business, talked with Frank Page and then later met Joe Devine. He dropped down from VII Corp. He says he is going home next week. He said the First Infantry is in Czechoslovakia. He said we might also go there. I came back and brought two casuals, returning from the hospital, with us. We took a couple of wrong roads and cut across country. On a rural road, two partridges ran in front of us. I shot at them twice.

We had a late supper and were told we are to move tomorrow. I collected a few things together and we loaded the trailer. In the evening, I took a walk before dark. I wrote and fried a couple of eggs, had some of my champagne and made some pancakes.


## April 30, 1945

Kapelle, Germany

I got up at 6:30 a.m. and went to chow. I came back and packed up. We cleared out of the house. Rusty's truck wouldn't start so he had it towed. We moved out about 7:35 a.m. and it is cold riding as the wind comes across the open fields. It sprinkled a bit but actually feels more like snow.

At various spots on the level ground you can see factories, their tall smoke stacks rising above the outlines. The film and camera factories

(AGFA) are just on the other side of the Autobahn, a little ways over.

We traveled on the Autobahn for a few miles. We turned off and headed for Bitterfeld. We stopped off and then turned into a schoolhouse yard at Sandersdorf. We are all in one wing of a Deutsch Jugend High School. We cleared two classrooms. We sleep in one and work in the other. We have city electric power and they fired the furnace. The kitchen has a nice setup. I did some work and talked with Charlie Nagy for a while.

After supper I played softball with Service Battery and we had a good game. I came in and cleared up some work and then wrote.

# Chapter twelve: May 1945

May 1, 1945 to May 31, 1945

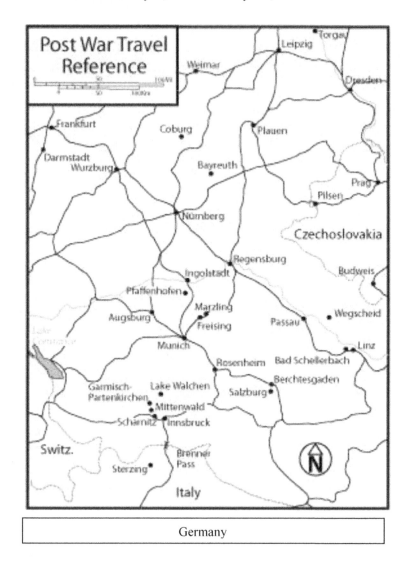

Germany

May 1945 Historical Overview
Germany, Austria, Czechoslovakia, Italy, and Switzerland

260

General Overview

May 8, 1945 marks Victory in Europe (V-E) Day, the official day of the ending of the war in Europe.

The streets are filled with refugees, both German and forced laborers, trying to return home. Some Germans are fleeing toward Allied territory and away from the Russian occupied areas.

Large movements of troops are moved about internally among the divisions.

Preparations are made to transport troops home. The Point system, formally called the Advanced Service Rating Score (ASRS), was used to determine which soldiers were eligible to return to the U.S. Points were awarded according to criteria outlined by this policy.

9th Division Overview: The 9th Division moves to Bavaria and sets up their Occupation Headquarters.

As is happening with other Divisions, many 9th Division soldiers are transferred to other Divisions to work on the new duties of a post-war army.

***

*May 1, 1945*
Sandersdorf, Germany

I had a terrible night last night. I must have a touch of asthma. I was having trouble breathing. I wonder if it was the ballgame or something else that brought it on. I got up and took a big swig of whiskey. I still had difficulty breathing. I was tired when the morning whistle blew. Service Battery has reveille and drill call.

I got up at 7:30 a.m., too late to make it to breakfast. I did get coffee and bread. I came back and tried to keep warm, as the heat is not on. The boys brought up a stove from the cellar and fitted it with a pipe. We got hot water and more important, heat. The central heating system also started up at about the same time.

261

Lieutenant Lynn Freeman came by to get me to go for the pay-money at Finance. I talked him out of me going. He picked it all up. I worked during the morning. I got paid $79.70 for the month.

I worked in the afternoon and then took the shower truck. We stopped at A-Battery to get instructions. We left without Skoczylas, who was talking somewhere. The shower room was good but the water cool. We took a shower and then came back. The Russians and Poles are drunk and roaming around.

I stayed in in the evening and read and wrote. The gang went to the show in Bitterfeld. Hitler is reported dead today by the Germans.

## May 2, 1945
Sandersdorf, Germany

I slept better than last night but still not any too well. I didn't get up until 9 a.m., and then had coffee and toast. I worked all morning and there is a lot to do. It is cold and sprinkling out. I wrote various letters and correspondence. I worked most of the afternoon.

In the evening I worked, read, and wrote. The news sounds good. German troops in Italy and Northern Italy surrendered. Berlin fell to the Russians.

I walked out by the street after supper and three girls beckoned for me to come over.

## May 3, 1945
Sandersdorf, Germany

I slept pretty well and didn't get up until 9 a.m.

I collected things together. I shaved and then had George drive the command car and go to Division Rear in Köthen. We got there about 11 a.m. I turned back the payrolls. I stopped in at Adjunct General and they are all looking at the camera I have. I had a Zeiss-Ikon Super Ikonta, belonging to Freddy Murray. I gave one of the fellows two boxes of 20 rolls of 35 mm color film that Tony Wisniewski had sent him. They were all excited and are going to collect watches and try to trade them at the factory for cameras. You give a Slave Laborer a watch and he disappears to the back of the factory and them comes out with some kind of camera. They looted the place after everyone took off.

I met all the Personnel Adjutants around the area of the Adjunct General. I ate at the Officer's Mess and saw Colonel Beets there. We had a meeting at the Adjunct General at 1:30 p.m.; it was on checking data for completed records. I met Frank Page there. I completed the rest of my business and decided to come back. We made good time as the roads are good. We got back at 4:30 p.m. About 5 p.m. the Adjunct General gang came down looking for the camera place. Tony Wisniewski took them over.

After supper Tony came back and said they got a couple cameras. I hung around in the evening, reading and writing. I sent a $180 Pay Transfer Account today.

## May 4, 1945
Sandersdorf, Germany

I didn't get up till 9:30 a.m. I cleaned up and had something to eat. I had the boys checking the Service Records.

The war is beginning to crumble. The Germans are giving up and are surrendering whole sectors. A European Theater Operations Inspection Team is to check our records one of these days. I had stencils cut for inserts and the men are working on their records. I am terribly busy myself so we decided we couldn't go to a live afternoon show. Instead, we all worked all afternoon.

In the evening Service Battery fellows played softball outside. I worked all evening until 12:30 a.m.

## May 5, 1945
Sandersdorf, Germany

I got up for breakfast as I thought the Inspection Team might be around. Everyone worked steadily all morning. We are to move tomorrow to the other side of town. Everyone is working on their records to get them in top shape for the inspection. I am particularly busy doing a sergeant major's job as well as my own. I worked all evening and up until 12:45 a.m.

## May 6, 1945
Sandersdorf, Germany

I got up for breakfast as we are supposed to move sometime today and also we are still expecting the European Theater Operations Inspection Team. It is a rainy and chilly day. The people, across the way, are all going to Mass. I got all of our things together and sort of closed down the office. We are to move after supper.

I walked over to the new place after dinner. It is only a little distance, on the other side of the main road. It is a large house with plenty of rooms. There are two large rooms, two bedrooms, a large hall, and a kitchen. I sent George over to put in electric light fixtures, as someone had stripped the place. We sent over our stuff on various loads. The boys went over after a while and set up the office. I came over after supper. The girls were sort of circling the area. They are after men. The new area is still worse. I worked all evening on things to take to Division Rear tomorrow, as I plan to go.

## May 7, 1945
Sandersdorf, Germany

I got up for breakfast this morning, as I plan on going to Division Rear. I got everything together and have George as a driver and Tony Wisniewski along. We took a load of personal effects. We made good time going and got there about 11:30 a.m. I went to Quarter Master, but the Personal Effects man was out to lunch. I came back to Adjunct General and talked there until lunchtime. I ate at the Officer's Mess up the road a ways. I came back to the Adjunct General to finish business and then dropped in on Frank Page, he is Personnel Sergeant Major of the 15<sup>th</sup> Engineers. The European Theater Operations Inspection Team was here. I talked with Frank and the European Theater Operations Inspection Team Sergeant. I gave Frank some film.

I went to Finance and completed my business. Some Military Police and Adjunct General boys are to follow us and go to the AGFA film factory. We stopped at the Autobahn and left Tony Wisniewski off to escort them. When we came back, the Radio announced that the Germans had surrendered, unconditionally, effective tomorrow. Everyone was jubilant. We ourselves don't have much to say or do about it. As a matter of fact to go out and talk to a civilian, i.e. get caught, would still cost us $65 or more.

I worked on many things that have piled up. After supper I fooled around with the movie projector used by the Hitlerjugend. It is a 16 mm, Siemens, worth about $125. I worked and read until 12:45 a.m.

## May 8, 1945
Sandersdorf, Germany

I was going to get up for breakfast but didn't. The special messengers came down and I gave them instructions on how to get to Division Rear. I got up at 8:30 a.m. and had a bit to eat.

Today is Victory in Europe Day, called VE Day. They are celebrating all over the world but we are doing our work as usual. I guess we have been at it too long; it is over two and one-half years in the combat area. People were coming and going all day. It is a great day. I wrote Dependency Discharges and a letter of condolence during the morning.

In the afternoon I decided to go to Battalion. I worked for a while and then got George to get the command car. He had to get a push to get it going. I stopped at Message Center and then walked to the Command Post. They live and work in a mansion. Captain Thivierge showed me around. It is a beautiful tiled-roof house, with extravagant fixtures and appliances. It has a small swimming pool heated by encircling pipes.

There is a violet-ray lamp in the bathroom. I sat in the S-1 office and talked. The German girls across the street are in bathing suits and lounge around or rather flaunt. They change clothes by the open window.

We came back to Service Battery area, worked, and talked until supper. I hung around and then took a walk with Harry Hammer. The girls are hanging out the windows across the way making hand signals. I stayed up reading and Captain Tooley dropped in with Sergeant Garner, checking who was in and who might be out. I sort of half thanked heaven that all my men were in and half proud that at least Personnel was all present and accounted for.

## May 9, 1945
Sandersdorf, Germany

I got up at 8:30 a.m., washed and shaved and had a little coffee.

Captain Tooley caught 17 of his men Absent Without Leave (AWOL) last night and two fraternizing. I was busy on various things. Lieutenant Young dropped in and I helped him fill in his questionnaire. It is another great day. It is hard to believe that the war is over here in Europe and they say we may get a chance to go home. We are quite busy making out requests for Dependency Discharges. Service Battery fell out and went to a special speech by the colonel.

In the afternoon I worked and had plenty to do. I took a nice shower at 4:30 p.m. and it sure felt good.

After supper I hung around outside. Captain Tooley is making a clean sweep of the men that were caught out last night. He broke five G.I.s I know, and a few others, while a few more will be Court-Martialed. He caught one man, with his bedroll under his arm, coming up the street about 3 a.m. He caught two in a house with two girls.

Tonight it is not necessary to have your blackout up. It is a strange sight to see light streaming from a window. I haven't seen this since October 1942.

**May 10, 1945**

Sandersdorf, Germany

I got up at 9 a.m. and washed, shaved, and had some tea, as there was no milk for coffee. I worked most of the morning and kept pretty busy on discharge papers.

After dinner it got real hot. The Red Cross Club Mobile came and the American girls were the center of attention. They gave us lemonade and doughnuts. All the boys, who wanted seconds, said that they were getting the doughnuts for Mr. Lovell. The Red Cross girl looked me up to find out the story.

It is very hot! I took a swell shower after supper and then went to the United Service Organization (USO) show in Bitterfeld. It was in the theater and I had a seat in the third row. It was a G.I. band and French girls and actors. It wasn't very good. I took colored pictures with Tony Wisniewski's camera. When we got back Sergeant Nix was waiting; we have to make a report on overseas duty in regard to the 45-day rest. I am one of the eight officers qualifying. We worked until 1 a.m. to get this done.

**May 11, 1945**

Sandersdorf, Germany

I got up at 8:30 a.m., washed, shaved, and had coffee, toast and doughnuts, which were left from yesterday. I started right in to work, as three men going home are here: Sergeant Sortino, De Naro and Gomes (Gomes from Cape Cod, Massachusetts). I worked on their overseas status reports, also checked and signed the records. I took an accident report from Lieutenant Treacy. I hurried around to get it all done and correct.

I took off at about 10:30 a.m. for Division Rear. It is a hot day. People traveling just sit by the side of the road. Girls think nothing of having their dresses up around their hips. At Division I deposited savings and sent Pay Transfer Accounts. I had the men, who were going home,

Service Records' checked.

I dropped a 16 mm projector, with sound attachments, off at Special Services. Sergeant Cohen and Lieutenant Lindsey Nelson told me that they couldn't use the silent 16 mm projector and hinted I could legally send it home.

I ate dinner at the Officer's Mess. I then finished my business and picked up Fedelli, A-Battery, plus two men from the 60th Infantry who were at the Casual Company returning from the Hospital. We got back about 2:30 p.m. and I stayed out in the air. It is sure dirty around here though, from coal dust. I went for a shower and there was only red hot water. After I had lathered up, I just sponged off; the thing is kaput.

All the girls are sitting across the street or are flaunting by. We loaded up as we move early tomorrow. We are going near Austria. All the boys are waiting for dark to meet up with the girls. Earlier in the day, after I came back from Division, I packaged the movie projector and sent it home.

## May 12, 1945
Sandersdorf, Germany

We got up at 4:45 a.m., ate at 5 a.m., packed, loaded, and moved out at 5:30 a.m. I am riding in the Motors' jeep. A girl bid goodbye and shook hands, but the Motor Officer wouldn't shake her hand. We moved slowly to the Autobahn and it was chilly, we will have to wear jackets all day. We got on the Autobahn and moved right along.

The Autobahn is really a great road. It was built by Hitler to transverse all of Germany, so things can be driven all over the country without interruption. It also serves as airplane runways.

We passed outside Leipzig and headed for Nuremberg (Nurnberg). It warmed up at times as we hustled along. There are thousands of refugees on the road, walking, pushing carts and bikes. It began to get hot.

We stopped at various points to check vehicles with trouble. We passed outside Bayreuth and Nurnberg. The people on the road are sweltering. Girls ride bikes throwing legs all around. They sit down at the side of the road showing everything. They don't seem to care about these things. We finally neared Ingolstadt, on the Danube. There are German soldiers all along the road going home and no one is stopping them. All are pretty well pooped by now.

We crossed the Danube River and it is not blue but a fast, brown, brackish river. We continued on the München, (Munich), Autobahn. We cut cross-country; it is hot, dusty, and tiresome. We have jackets on and are sweltering. I felt sickish jouncing along in the heat and dust. We finally cut across a field to a row of houses. We have a house for Personnel. I feel lousy. I just washed my dirty face and went to bed at about 7 p.m. We traveled about 250 miles and are now in Bavaria.

Autobahn to Munich.

## May 13, 1945
Marzling, Bavaria, Germany

I got up for breakfast at 8:30 a.m., ate, and then cleaned up. We arranged the office and fixed things up. I washed uniforms and clothes. It got warmer during the day.

I walked up the hill following the little stream, and it led to a big river. Some say you can see the Alps from certain locations here. The

Captain Thivierge and Captain Healey.

big river is the Isar River. It is really pretty up here as you have a nice view. All the churches have round domes that are called onion towers. I wasn't able to see the Alps, so I came back and hung out my clothes to dry in the sun. I took some of the sun myself and then took a walk around the village. It is just a farm community, the women in the area all sewed uniforms for the German Army, mostly for the Russian front. They make

269

rabbit hair-lined hats and insulated, reversible jackets, with the white side for snow and the other side multicolored for camouflage. Some of the fellows took a long walk and then went in swimming. I hung around doing odds and ends of paper work.

I went to the Battalion Command Post in the afternoon to see Doctor McFadyen about the Physical Profiling of all men. We ran off some forms on the mimeograph for this. I talked with Captain Thivierge and the colonel. I came back and did some more work. In the evening I stayed around and cleaned up more odds and ends.

## May 14, 1945
Marzling, Bavaria, Germany

We have breakfast at 6:15 a.m. as Service Battery has reveille at 5:45 a.m. We don't stand this, as we are independent of them in most things. After breakfast I worked and then washed some things. We were busy all morning.

In the afternoon the fellows went up to the Battalion for their Physical Profiling. I stayed around, sitting in the sun, and took a walk down by the stream and dangled my feet in. The water is quite cold. I came back and the men were returning from Battalion. We had supper and sat around.

I have a collection of the equipment that the women were sewing. I have fur hats, leather-seated breeches, shirts, hoods, and jackets. All brand new. Everyone is sending the stuff home. It is legal as it is confiscated war material.

## May 15, 1945
Marzling, Bavaria, Germany

I got up at 6:05 a.m., ate breakfast, and then did some work. I went to Battalion with Captain Tooley at 9 a.m. I talked at Message Center and S-1. I hung around waiting for Captain Tooley. General Howell came in. We had to stand at attention while he inspected everything.

Everything is G.I. now.

We found out that we are to move back with Battalion as soon as the Medics move out. There are all kinds of Russians, Poles, English, and other freed prisoners, walking around. In some cases they have been shacking up here with the Germans. One Englishman left in the morning and the Jerry soldier-husband came back from the war this afternoon. The blond child will need an explanation.

We came back for dinner. I ate and then had the boys lay out their stuff for inspection. The General is supposed to visit. The Liaison Officers are also checking equipment.

I went to Division Artillery Headquarters at Nandlstadt. It was a cross-country trip of about 10 miles. I picked up the dope on the point system for discharge. I talked with Chaplain Lorenz while here. We came back as the officers were in our area for inspection, Major Williams, Captain Tom Gaffney, Captain Healey, Captain Welch, and Captain Thivierge, are doing it. The colonel was also around. We got by okay. The colonel was downstairs while the inspection was going on

Left: Captain Welch and William Anderson.
Above: Captain Ted Healey.

271

upstairs. He remarked to Bob Ramsdell that he didn't like moving us back.

After supper I took a walk through the village, came back, hung around, and then did some more work.

## May 16, 1945
Marzling, Bavaria, Germany

I got up at 6 a.m., ate breakfast, and then went to work. It is chilly this morning. The clerks are all working on their payrolls and counting points. We are very busy.

After dinner we continued working. Later it turned out to be a nice day so I washed my blankets. These are the same white navy ones I got from the ship on the invasion of French Morocco after I lost mine. I put them out in the sun.

At 5:05 p.m. we got a call for the total number of men with over 85 points. This is the critical score. We got it in by 5:50 p.m., as the deadline was 6 p.m.

After supper all the clerks worked on counting points until late in the evening.

## May 17, 1945
Marzling, Bavaria, Germany

I got up at 6:15 a.m., ate breakfast, and cleaned up. I started to work cleaning up the things on my desk. We are all busy counting points, making the cards for scores, and making payrolls. In the morning, at some time, I got a call. The kind of call we all have been waiting for, for two and one-half years overseas. They said you could send 70 men out of the Battalion home. We prepared rosters for the Battery Commanders of the 20 highest scores in each Battery. I called them into the Command Post by phone. They let us know later who was selected. It was one happy gang. Some men were out on the road in convoys, so Division will contact them. Some are Nix, Linscott, and Hyland, all the old men, many of whom were drafted and came in with me. We are terrifically busy, as the time is short. All hands are working on their records. I am doing all kinds of jobs. The phone is humming and all operators are listening intently, to get a little news. We sure are busy. I ran up to Battalion for a while and got a few things straight.

After supper we all worked and stayed with it until 12:30 a.m.

## May 18, 1945
Marzling, Bavaria, Germany

I got up at 7 a.m. had some coffee and washed up. All hands were late arising this morning, but were soon hard at work. Agents came and went as well as the phone humming. It sure is busy.

Jack and I took off in a jeep to get the rating cards signed of the men going home. We left off the cards at B-Battery and A-Battery. Then Jack went to Headquarters and I went to A-Battery. I talked with them in A-Battery for a while and then came back to the Command Post. I ate at headquarters Battery Officer's Mess.

After dinner we came back to Service Battery. The boys were still busy. I did some things.

After supper I took a walk and was walking along when the ration truck came by. I jumped into it and went up the road a ways. I got off and walked back, about a mile. I sat on the fence and watched the refugees go by.

I came back to the office only to find out I have to go to Division Forward in Ingolstadt, with Captain Thivierge. It is for a meeting on Officer's ratings. We started out through Freising. We got on the Autobahn and made good time and arrived before dark. We met all the Adjuncts and Personal Adjunctive from Service Batteries. Captain Strong, the Adjunct General, gave out the dope on scores and reports.

We left at 11:30 p.m. and got back about 12:30 a.m. Jack and Delli were working on the records. I worked myself on them until about 4 a.m.

**May 19, 1945**
Marzling, Bavaria, Germany

I got to sleep after 4 a.m. and at 6:30 a.m. the phone began to hum. People came and went and it is a little emotional. These are the guys we have been with for almost five years in the service and almost three years overseas. Hyland came in and shook my hand. I could hear George Neuhardt; he is going to Division with them to do any necessary work on their records.

I got up at 7 a.m. and was too groggy to dress up well. I took a walk, way up on the hill overlooking the rivers. I sat down and rested in the sun and quiet. I came back, washed, shaved, ate a bite, and I feel better.

I took a ride to Battalion in the afternoon. I am having Tony Wisniewski fix up the Officers' scores and cards. I took them with me and left them off for Captain Thivierge, who is to get them all signed. I have 117 points: 85 are all that is needed to qualify to go home. Almost everybody in an outfit like ours has more than the qualifying amount. Some of the Air Observation Post officers have over 200 points and some of the Infantry officers must have almost 300 points. One 60th infantry lieutenant colonel was wounded 12 times (Purple Heart with 11 clusters, two Distinguished Service Medals, Silver Stars, and Bronze Stars). I answered, "No" to remaining in the Service and had an Efficiency Index of 45.2, which is between excellent and superior.

I did odds and ends in the evening, getting to bed about 11:30 p.m., and I am tired.

**May 20, 1945**
Marzling, Bavaria, Germany

I got up at 7 a.m. and had coffee and crackers. I washed and then did a few things at the desk. It has slowed down a bit. Delli is busy working on an information roster on Headquarters Battery, and Jack is helping him. We cut occasional stencils to run off. We all took it sort of easy today, knowing that there is a lot worse yet to come. Every so often we get a call for some other kind of roster or report.

After supper, I went with the Service Battery Officers to the Battalion to have a Physical Profile or as they say a Physical Classification. I declared my nine cases of Malaria, a Concussion occurring in Sedjenane Tunisia, French North Africa from an accident, hemorrhoids, frozen feet from the Kasserine Pass, Tunisia, and an appendectomy operation.

We came back and I took it easy the rest of the evening.

## May 21, 1945
Marzling, Bavaria, Germany

I didn't get up until 7 a.m. and didn't shave; I just had a cup of coffee. I did a few things around my desk. I have a decided lack of interest in work today.

After dinner, I took a jeep and driver and went to the Battalion. I hung around for quite a while doing odds and ends. I then went to Division Artillery Headquarters over at Nandlstadt. It is about 12 miles, and it is a pleasure riding. We went through Moosburg, a well-known Prisoners of War (POW) camp, and it is quite a sight with its freed POWs and laborers. A convoy of Russians went by, about 30 truckloads. I came back to Battalion and talked for a while and then came back to Service Battery. I did some work and then ate.

After supper, I went to the show in Freising. It was raining now. We came back and find out that we have plenty of work to do. The morning reports have to be all changed and in tomorrow.

## May 22, 1945
Marzling, Bavaria, Germany

I didn't awake until 7 a.m. and got up at 7:30 a.m., had some black coffee, no cream or milk available, and washed up. I started doing odd jobs around my desk.

I got a call from Sergeant Logan, Division Artillery, to requisition replacements for all men over the critical score, which is 85. We have

369 men left who qualify, and we are to requisition for a 30-percent overage. This will be a lot of work and it has to be in at 6 p.m. Jack and Tony Wisniewski had rounded up the morning reports which have to be at Division Artillery at 6 p.m. with the survey of scores roster. Tony Wisniewski got the information for the requisition.

We ate early chow and went right to the Command Post. We talked it out with the colonel and Captain Thivierge. They called a meeting of the Battery Commanders. We had them show us all the men they wanted to promote with scores below 85. The rest of the meeting was about the move. I represented Service Battery.

We got away after 3 p.m. and came back to work on the report. The morning reports left at 5 p.m. We tried to call in the requisition at 6 p.m. but the lines were too busy. We all ate and after supper an agent came and took the reports over.

I worked on various small things on my desk. I am making Technician Fourth Grade Jack Markowitz a Technical Sergeant, and am transferring Technician Fifth Grade Tony Wisniewski to Headquarters Battery from B-Battery so he can be made Technician Fourth Grade.

We sat around all night talking.

## May 23, 1945
Marzling, Bavaria, Germany

I didn't get up until 7:30 a.m. and I started a fire, had coffee and then shaved. I did a few odd jobs at the desk and am having Jack take over. I worked all morning.

After dinner I did a few things, typed statements, allotments, and transfers. I took a walk, snapped a few pictures, and later hung around. I sat out back and wrote. Jack Markowitz made a lettuce, egg, onion, and radish salad for me.

The Batteries moved out of Bitterfeld and passed by on their way to a new area. I walked to the road, but they had passed. In the evening I hung around and wrote and worked.

**May 24, 1945**

Marzling, Bavaria, Germany

I got up at 7:30 a.m. and had coffee and went right to work on a few things. We got a notice that we are to send 42 more men home, soon. We worked all morning.

At dinner Captain Tooley said that we should move when the first trucks come back. We tried to clean up the pending work and ran stencils off. Sergeant Garner came in and said that the first truck was outside. We all hustled about, gathered everything up, and were actually loaded in a little over one hour.

We moved out through Freising to the Autobahn. We went along it for quite a distance and then turned off. We arrived at the new location, a railroad station in Strasshof. The civilians were still in the section that we are to occupy. We moved them out.

We have a nice set-up for offices. We set up our stuff and used one room for five beds. The rest of the boys will sleep in the office room. We have electric lights, clocks, running water, two sinks, and office desks. I took my personal things over to the Officer's quarters. This is located in the beer hall and Hotel section. I dropped in at the S-1 and S-2 offices downstairs. I then made an inventory of all Service Battery property and typed some of it up. I had stencil cut on the form, and we worked till 11:30 p.m.

**May 25, 1945**

Strasshof, Bavaria, Germany

I didn't get up for breakfast and I am pooped. I got up about 8:45 a.m., came to the office and started putting things together. We are busy completing the records of the 42 men that are going home.

After dinner I worked steadily and we are as busy as we have ever been. The powers-that-be changed their minds and wants the roster of the men going home turned in. We started it. I had just been to Division Rear and returned and nothing was said, they were only talking about

277

arranging a meeting tonight of all Adjutants and Personnel Adjutants.

We went up to the Battalion. The rosters from the Batteries are going to take time. We just had to wait for them, as we have to have them when we return to the meeting at Division Rear tonight. The meeting was at 6:30 p.m. Pete and I got there at 7:30 p.m. We had to stay after the others left so we can get details of the meeting. It was about the clothing of the men returning home. We got back about dark and I worked on various records and reports until 11:30 p.m. or so.

## May 26, 1945
Strasshof, Bavaria, Germany

I didn't get up until 8:45 a.m. and went to work in the office. We have oodles of work and I can't seem to make an impression on it. I have Advanced Service Rating Scores (ASR), allotments, records, reports, and correspondences.

I worked until dinner then had Message Center pick up clothing records at the Adjunct General.

We worked all afternoon and evening up until 11:30 p.m. I took a hot bath and went to bed.

Skoczylas missed out on this quota. He has 112 points but they drew them out of a hat.

## May 27, 1945
Strasshof, Bavaria, Germany

I didn't get up for breakfast, as I am pooped these days. Everyone noticed that I just come and go and they hardly see me these days. I worked all morning on the work that has piled up here. The records are going to have to be ready to go tonight. Sergeant Eddy Rouse, now Master Sergeant, will take them. We worked on them and I signed and initialed away. I got through about 11 p.m. Eddy came around and picked them up. I went to my quarters, took a hot bath, and went to bed.

**May 28, 1945**

Strasshof, Bavaria, Germany

I got up 8:30 a.m., came to the Rail Road Station, cleaned up, and had a cup of coffee. I did various things. The 42 men left for home this morning.

I walked over to the Command Post, which is quite a distance from us now. I found out that we are getting 3 to 4 replacements and that we are to send 20 more men home. I decided it is time for a few of us to walk away from this for a short while. I rode back to Personnel, called Pete, and arranged to go on a little sightseeing tour. Before going, I walked over to the Command Post again and it is hot out. The Battalion has 24 Jerry prisoners for details now.

I got George to drive, and took Delli and Skoczylas, and we set out in the open command car. We went to Pfaffenzhofen and around the by-pass to the Autobahn. It is a great day and we whisked along.

As we neared Munich (München,) we could see the snow-covered Austrian and Swiss Alps. It was a pretty sight. As soon as the first G.I.s here saw the German signs for München, they coined the expression, "How about Luncheon in München?" We drove up the main Munich drive. The place was hit pretty badly. We saw people swimming on the outskirts of town. We passed the Government buildings and stopped at the far end of the Mall. We took pictures and decided to hustle on towards Austria.

We took the Salzburg Autobahn and passed many camouflaged airplanes by the side of the road, which used the Autobahn for a runway. We stopped and took a picture of a jet-propelled plane. We neared the Alps and came into prettier country. The homes are designed as Chalets. We turned off the Autobahn and passed through local communities. The people appear a little different. They are evidently more Austrian. They dress more Tyrolean style. We are right beside the mountains, so I took some color pictures. We went into Rosenheim, a fairly large city. We went a few miles beyond, 25 miles from Austria.

We decided to come back as it would take too much time to go and return. We ran into the whole German First Army, which is moving toward Munich from Italy. They had surrendered en masse. We were right in the middle of their convoy. The German Military Police and road markers were dumbfounded but waved us on with the Germans. People waved and yelled to the Germans but as they started to wave at us, it dawned on them, and they dropped their hands and made believe they were scratching their heads. A German Officer and Military Policeman waved us on and saluted.

We cut out of their column and stopped at the old 79th Field Artillery, 240 mm, formally from our old stamping grounds, Fort Bragg, North Carolina. They are now the 658th Field Artillery. We had a chicken supper and a very hospitable time. We came back to Munich and ended up in a couple dead end streets. The rubble is still blocking some streets. We arrived back home about 8:45 p.m.

## May 29, 1945
Strasshof, Bavaria, Germany

I didn't get up until 8:15 a.m. and then went to the office and cleaned up some work. I worked all morning, as we are busy on the new replacements. I have quite a problem trying to get a clerk or two. All the new men seem to be farmers. All the Batteries are to train a cadre and the men must have less than the critical score, I worked all afternoon on it.

## May 30, 1945
Strasshof, Bavaria, Germany

I got up at 8:30 a.m. and went to breakfast. Breakfast was from 8 a.m. to 9 a.m., as today is a holiday, Memorial Day. I went to the office and signed the routine stuff. I sat around the office all morning and cleaned up a few matters.

At dinner I was informed that I was to be in the parade. I talked Major

Williams out of it. I have too much work to do. I got one of the new men from Service Battery for a driver and went to Division Rear at Ingolstadt. The Danube River was a bluish-green today. I completed my business, talked, and came back. I worked until supper and then sat in the quarters and wrote.

## May 31, 1945
Strasshof, Bavaria, Germany

I didn't get up until 8:15 a.m., came to work, and had a cup of black coffee. I worked on routine and new business. I got a new assistant clerk for Delli. I don't think he is too interested in being a clerk.

Captain Brown bawled out Harry for trying to get a clerk out of the Battery. George got an assistant clerk today. It rained all day.

I worked all afternoon and got paid $81.15 for a month. George is going to the Riviera, from Service Battery.

# Chapter thirteen: June 1945

June 1, 1945 to June 30, 1945

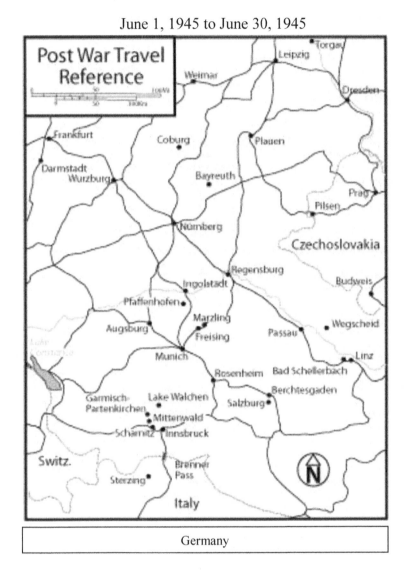

Germany

June 1945 Historical Overview

General Overview

Massive internal troop movements occur to accommodate the new needs of a post- war occupation army.

The enormous task of returning U.S. troops home continues.

The U.S. Army duties are now that of an occupation force in post-war Europe.

9th Division Overview: Large movements of personnel into and out to the 9th Division continues. Some are returning home to the U.S., some are being transferred to other divisions: for some they are being sent to where their skill set is needed, for others it is to be deployed home sooner.

The After Action Reports are no longer written. Instead, travel itineraries of the surrounding areas are given out to 9th Division troops

*** 

## *June 1, 1945*
Strasshof, Bavaria, Germany

I got up and had breakfast; it consisted of a little cereal, pancakes, and coffee. I went to work and was busy all morning.

The B-Battery assistant clerk and five assistant clerks showed up this morning. The clerks are all busy getting rosters and records ready for the men going home. I worked all afternoon and discovered, after all, that the rosters don't have to be in today.

After supper I worked on the records. Archie Dougan, Freddy Murray, and Don Williams were in to say good-bye. We all had a last coffee together (Nastrovia). I passed around the remains of a bottle of Scotch, we shook hands, and they left. These were good friends, fellow draftees, together for almost six years. They are to fly by plane, from La Havre to the United States.

Skoczylas heard today that his father died. I went to the office and signed the morning reports and then went to bed about 12 a.m.

283

## June 2, 1945
Strasshof, Bavaria, Germany

I was quite tired this morning and I didn't get up until 8:30 a.m. I went to the office to work. The colonel stomped in with his inspection team. He blew up a storm because no one called "Attention" immediately. He asked a few questions and stomped out. We were quite busy all morning.

After dinner I took the command car with a driver, and went to Division Rear at Ingolstadt. I did a few things there and picked up a replacement. We had trouble starting the command car and we finally got back about 4 p.m. I hung around doing odds and ends.

After supper I sat on one of the freight car flats and wrote.

## June 3, 1945
Strasshof, Bavaria, Germany

I got up at 11 a.m. this Sunday after a good night's sleep. I went to the office and washed up, then I came back and ate.

After dinner Lieutenant Treacy and I tried to get bicycles, to go for a ride. We couldn't, so we took a walk. We walked to the bridge, along the creek, to the mill, by the Command Post, and then came back. Later I strolled off by myself and followed the stream the other way. I met Bob Ramsdell and his brother, who is in another unit of the 9th Division. I went to the little dam where the kids are swimming. I sat down, took off my shirt, got some sun, and watched them. I strolled back after a while, ate supper, hung around outside the Officer's quarters, and then went over to Personnel.

## June 4, 1945
Strasshof, Bavaria, Germany

I got up at 8 a.m., had breakfast, and then went to Personnel. I worked on the papers that were on my desk. About 10 a.m. I fried two eggs and had coffee.

After dinner, I took one of the new men, Levine, and took a jeep with Gill as a driver. We dropped Levine off at Division Artillery Headquarters at Pfaffenzhofen. I continued on, going back to the Autobahn, and then went to Division Rear at Ingolstadt. The Danube River is a greenish blue today. I completed my work there. It began to rain, but Gill the driver and I decided to go back anyway. It was wet but moving along seemed to keep it at a minimum. My right arm was real soaking wet. We made good time coming back. I stood by the fire for a while.

I got a Staff Sergeant in today to be Personnel Sergeant Major. I went to my quarters and took a good hot bath and then went to eat.

After supper I hung around the quarters and the Personnel Office.

## June 5, 1945
Strasshof, Bavaria, Germany

I got up at 8 a.m. and went to the office. I met the new Staff Sergeant. I talked with him and told him what he was to do. I did a little work and had coffee. I came back to my quarters and washed my underclothes.

I returned to the office and talked with Captain Thivierge who was here. I stayed around all afternoon and did various odds and ends, and then went to dinner with the captain.

After supper I played around with the accordion and later I fried some eggs, and then had an egg and lettuce sandwich.

## June 6, 1945
Strasshof, Bavaria, Germany

I got up just before 9 a.m. and in time for breakfast. We had fresh eggs. I washed and shaved. It is a holiday today, Anniversary of D Day, the Normandy invasion. I walked over to the Battalion Command Post and checked a few things and talked with them for a while. I walked back and went to dinner.

After dinner I took the Service Battery truck on the swimming detail. There were three men and a driver. I went to Pfaffenhofen and then down the Autobahn. We decided to go to the furthest point down before crossing over the Freising Highway. We could see the Alps and were close to Munich before we crossed over. We went through Freising. All along the way people were in the fields, raking hay or wheat. We went through Marzling and to Moosburg.

We got to the pool; there were two pretty girls sitting outside as well as the G.I.s sitting around looking at them. We met Lieutenant Kraft and Lieutenant Crabbe there. I swam around and took a few dives. The pool is a large square, with an alcove for diving. I sat around for a while and then everyone began to leave. I took off about 4 p.m. We took the short way back.

After supper I played catch with Lieutenant Kraft. I wrote and talked during the evening.


## June 7, 1945
Strasshof, Bavaria, Germany

I got up and had breakfast, but I could hardly eat anything as the food was cooked terribly. I went to work and kept busy all morning. I decided to go to Division Rear to deposit money. It is a hot day.

After dinner I was going to have George drive but they wanted him in a parade. So to get him out of the parade, I had him continue his work, and had Tony Wisniewski drive the command car. It is open and the sun is hot. We took our time, taking in all the sights. We watched the travelers and workers.

We got to Division Rear at Ingolstadt and completed our business. Then we drove the Adjunct General boys over to the brewery, until they got their beer, and then we brought them back. Colonel Beets stopped us to see if we knew where his driver was. He found him sleeping. We met Chaplain Lorenz here also.

We drove along and after cussing the Danube River - no crossovers-

we turned off at the Lake. We watched the people swimming and the G.I.s just mingled in. They swim in their shorts in front of everyone. The girls change clothes right at the edge of the woods, in sight. They all seem fairly attractive. We moseyed along and it was very hot. We got back and watched the Battalion parade in the field below the Rail Road Station.

After supper I went to the movie in Pfaffenhofen. It still is very hot.

## June 8, 1945

Strasshof, Bavaria, Germany

I got up about 8 a.m. this morning and went to the office. I shaved and then did some work, mainly writing correspondence. I made myself a cup of coffee.

I made plans for a trip to Division Rear, as I have to sign some rosters there. I had George drive the command car. It was a nice hot day as we rolled along in the open command car. The people along the road are fatigued, and many stop and go in swimming. I went into Adjunct General and completed my business. I came out and looked for the Leather Shop. I saw the sign saying, "Off Limits", so I stopped the search.

We came back but took our time. We just took in all the sights; travelers, and swimmers. When we got back, I did a little work, and then went to eat.

After supper I sat around, went to the office, and fried some eggs. I came back to my quarters and went to bed.

## June 9, 1945

Strasshof, Bavaria, Germany

I went to work a little after 8 a.m. after having breakfast. Everyone tidied up in case they inspect here this morning. We worked all morning and I was very busy trying to get a couple Officers records out, Lieutenant Sagle, who is sick, and Lieutenant Stacey, MIA, (Captured).

I also had a lot of correspondence.

I decided to take the afternoon off; it is a half-day anyways, as it is Saturday. I walked around in the afternoon. I went to the Battalion Command Post and tried all the musical instruments there. They will give them to the band but they are all old and beat up. I talked, picked up my mail, and then came back to Personnel.

After supper I went to the show with Captain Gray, Lieutenant Van Leuven, and Lieutenant Freeman. The picture was terrible. I hung around the quarters and went to Personnel for a while.

## June 10, 1945
Strasshof, Bavaria, Germany

Sunday, I just lay in bed, half awake, and half asleep. I didn't get up until 11 a.m. I walked to the office and shaved.

I came back and ate dinner then took a walk. I walked up the tracks and saw a G.I. with a girl but ignored it. I walked to the next town and back as there isn't anything to do. I should have gone to church but it is too late. I hung around all afternoon and evening and it is boring.

## June 11, 1945
Strasshof, Bavaria, Germany

I got up about 8 a.m., went to work, and got things together. I had George drive me to Division Rear in Ingolstadt. It was raining on and off and we stopped at the leather factory. The girl that speaks English showed me upstairs. An English- speaking woman explained the order process to me. I ordered a shoulder holster.

I went to Division and finished part of my work. I ate there and then finished my business. We brought back George Gunter, A-Battery, from the Casual Company, returning from the hospital. It rained on the way back.

The Red Cross Club Mobile is here, giving out doughnuts and coffee.

I talked with one of the girls. She is from Milton, Massachusetts.

I worked in the office until supper. After supper, I hung around and then went to bed.

## June 12, 1945
Strasshof, Bavaria, Germany

I got up at 8 a.m. and went to work at the office. It is raining off and on. I worked all morning writing correspondence.

In the afternoon I gave Lieutenant Young my dry cleaning, a camera, and some notebook rings to have leather covers made. We got a new kid in today to work on the files and mimeographs. This makes 15 men in all.

After supper I hung around. It is raining off and on and there is nothing to do. The movies in Pfaffenhofen are broken. I hung around reading and listening to the radio.

## June 13, 1945
Strasshof, Bavaria, Germany

I got up at 7:50 a.m. and had breakfast and then went to work about 9 a.m. Colonel Beets called and said that Colonel Barton, Inspector General, was on his way down to inspect Personnel records. We fixed things a little. He sat at my desk with his Technician Fourth Grade and checked 10 Service Records and Classification cards from each Battery. He asked various questions in between. I took him to lunch and I sat at the Staff table. Colonel Beets and Major Williams came in.

After dinner we walked back to Personnel. He checked more records and then he left about 2 p.m. He said the records were okay and that he would send down a letter. He was formerly a First Sergeant in the First Division and has 27-years of service.

I did some odds and ends, and then watched part of a ball game, then came back to Personnel. I ate supper and then hung around the quarters. It rains off and on.

## June 14, 1945
Strasshof, Bavaria, Germany

I got up, had breakfast, and worked all morning writing correspondence. The clerks all have been busy on payrolls. I signed and checked a couple of payrolls.

After dinner I worked on various things. I stayed there all afternoon and then went to supper.

After supper I played catch with Bob Ramsdell and then we went to Pfaffenhofen to the movies. It was a good picture, but true to form, the sound failed and the movie was not appreciated.

## June 15, 1945
Strasshof, Bavaria, Germany

I got up for breakfast and went to work doing various things all morning. I have to be Duty Officer at the Battalion Command Post today. They are presenting awards at the parade at Division Artillery. A lot of our officers and men are to be decorated, so the rest will have to march.

I ate dinner and hustled down to the Command Post. I stayed there, as no one is coming back here after chow. They will dress and go to the parade. I had Jack Markowitz send me the remainder of the payrolls that hadn't been signed. He ran them to Division Rear and turned them in to Finance. I hung around talking to Charlie Nagy, walking around, reading, and then sitting out in the sun by the stream. We sat there, talked, and watched the people come and go. A farmer came by and traded eggs for cigarettes. Charlie gave the eggs to me, 10 in all, for a couple bars of candy and a pack of cigarettes.

About 5:45 p.m., Lieutenant Dougher came down and relieved me, so I came back to my quarters. I dropped over the office after supper for a while. I came back to the quarters and hung around talking.

**June 16, 1945**

Strasshof, Bavaria, Germany

I got up, had breakfast, and reported to work about 8:20 a.m. I did a few things but was restless and walked to my quarters and back again. I sat at my desk sort of listless, until 11:20 a.m.

I gave Jack Markowitz $50.00 and Tony Wisniewski gave him $150.00, to go to Paris. He is to see his brother who is also on pass.

I got up to leave about 11:30 a.m. and the old circulation in my fingers was going. I knew immediately that I had another attack of Malaria. I walked to my quarters and went to bed, chattering with the chills. I couldn't get warm. Lieutenant Kraft came in and put a blanket over me. I had taken a Quinine pill prior to going to bed. I had the chills for quite some time. I told them not to call the doctor, as I knew what it was and would probably handle it okay.

I began to sweat and ran a good temperature. I tossed and turned. I sweated up a storm and then got sick. I almost threw up in the room. Later I threw up in the toilet. I feel miserable. I have the headache and all my bones are sore. I got one of my Atabrine pills and took that. All during the night I tossed and sweated.

**June 17, 1945**

Strasshof, Bavaria, Germany

I felt fairly well this morning but quite weak. I drank plenty of water and rested fairly well.

In the afternoon I got up and dressed, but was very weak. I walked to the edge of the ball field and back, about 200 yards. I came upstairs and flopped into bed. I am not well and stayed in bed. I just lied there all day. Everyone came in and looked at me and asked inquiring questions of my roommates.

I took Atabrine and drank water. I didn't eat a thing. Jack, Tony

Wisniewski, and Harry dropped in to see me.

## June 18, 1945
Strasshof, Bavaria, Germany

I feel miserable this morning. My stomach is bound. I asked Lieutenant Lynn Freeman to call Doctor McFadyen. He came in and examined me. I did feel hot and had a temperature of 101. He told me to drink at least three quarts of liquid and juices.

A Medic came up and gave me Atabrine and Codeine. I am to take the Codeine every 4 hours. He checked my temperature. It was 102 and then a little later 103. I was sweating up a storm. Skoczylas, Lawrence, Delli, and Harry dropped in to see me. I believe my temperature was at least 104 at times. I put in a miserable day. I drank water and orange juice. I took all the pills and drank all day. My fever was breaking when the Doctor came in. I felt pretty good later. The bed is getting pretty hard now.

## June 19, 1945
Strasshof, Bavaria, Germany

I rested pretty well and am feeling pretty good, but weak. I only had juice for breakfast. I rested all morning.

In the afternoon I got up and walked to the edge of the ball field, where the Officer's ball team was practicing. I talked with Doctor McFadyen and he gave me instructions. I came back and rested on my bunk. I am too weak to walk around.

Tony Wisniewski is going to a meeting at Division Rear with Sergeant Slota, in place of me. He came back later and told me they said we were Occupation and that XX Corp was to draw the men to go home by Special Serial Number. We have to be prepared to lose all men with a critical score of 85 or over, in 20 to 30 days.

I rested and went to bed about 10:30 p.m.

## June 20, 1945
Strasshof, Bavaria, Germany

I slept well, with the aid of that sleeping capsule. I got up about 9:30 a.m.; I took a bath and dressed up.

I have to go to the Battalion Command Post and tell them the dope put out at last night's meeting. I had Tony Wisniewski get a jeep and we rode down. I went over the plan with Pete Thivierge. We are now in category one, Occupation. The men may be gone in 20 to 30 days and will be called by XX Corp and by Special Serial Numbers.

I came back to the quarters and flopped on the bunk fatigued. I rested until noon. I didn't eat dinner. I had some orange juice. I hung around in the afternoon, mainly on my bunk.

I made supper and was welcomed to the dining room, as I was such a stranger. After supper I rested and hung around the room. I went to bed about 10:30 p.m.; I didn't take any sleeping capsule.

## June 21, 1945
Strasshof, Bavaria, Germany

I didn't sleep well at all, as I was tightened up and nervous. I got up about 9 a.m. and cleaned up. I had Thrasher get me breakfast. I gave him two fresh eggs to cook. I had a swell breakfast of orange juice, toast with butter, jam, coffee, and eggs.

I rested on my bed. Tony Wisniewski was in a couple of times about the report, Inventory of Specialists, which had to be in by tomorrow. I am going to shuffle Personnel a little. I am shifting Smith to Service Battery clerk, Remer to files, and am going to get a replacement for Marlof in B-Battery.

I was talking with the officers for a while before I realized they had eaten dinner, so I went down and ate alone. Tony Tooley sat with me talking.

In the afternoon I rested on my bed. I consulted with Tony

Wisniewski on the report and current business. Later I wrote three letters.

The officers are getting ready for a retreat parade. Lieutenant Kraft came back from the clothing Post Exchange near Nuremburg. He bought me a khaki shirt, Poplin, 22 marks, or $2.20.

I ate supper. Tony Wisniewski came over and we cornered Captain Prince in his room, and Captain Brown and Wilson in the dining room, and had them go over the report with us.

I came upstairs and rested. I talked with the gang and listened to the radio. Before going to bed I took vitamin tablets, Atabrine, and Codeine.

I got a German Gas Mask box for a footlocker. They are as large as our metal ones but are made out of wood. We haven't had any since ours were stolen somewhere in transit. Lieutenant Kraft brought them back from the Battalion Command Post. I got my camera case, made out of leather, from Lieutenant Young. It is wonderful workmanship and cost $2.20.

## June 22, 1945
Strasshof, Bavaria, Germany

I slept fairly well but a little cold as I slept in the G.I. bedroll rather than the Officer's bedroll. I didn't get up until Captain Tom Gaffney came in about changing his marital status. I got up and took a bath, dressed, and then called for breakfast. I gave them two fresh eggs to cook and I had toast, butter, and coffee. I put salt in the coffee as that is what they sent up, thinking it was sugar.

I tried to get a haircut but couldn't find a barber. I came back to my room and wrote. I am still listless. I'm taking vitamin pills as well as Atabrine. I rested all afternoon just lounging around. Malaria seems to have cycles, almost every 24 hours you are sure to have a bad spell, in between you have good spells,

After supper I got a haircut at the Medic's. I can always depend on Barzy (Barszewski, Northampton, Massachusetts). I came back to the room and rested. They began to fry eggs, so, I fried myself three and then went to bed at 9:30 p.m. I kept getting up to tune in the radio as I lied there. I finally quit and shut it off.

## June 23, 1945
Strasshof, Bavaria, Germany

I didn't get up until 8:30 a.m. Shorty Cole came in and asked me what I wanted for breakfast. I told him toast and coffee. I got up and washed and the cook brought me up a tray with coffee and toast. I shaved and washed my hair.

The colonel is inspecting Headquarters Battery in rank, outside. He chewed them out for not having haircuts. I started to go to Personnel a little later, but saw the colonel inspecting Service Battery. I came back to the quarters and read for a while, and then I went to Personnel. It felt funny to be back. This is the first time since last week, at about the same time. I sat there and talked and went over a few things. I stayed until 12 noon and then went back to eat.

After dinner I rested while the Batteries and the Officers went to a compulsory movie at Division Artillery. It was "On to Tokyo." I just rested all afternoon.

After supper the Officers started getting ready for the dance. The captains were all drunk and they were wrestling and throwing stuff around. The colonel had to speak to them. They finally staggered out to the dance. I rested all evening and went to bed early.

## June 24, 1945
Strasshof, Bavaria, Germany

I got up at 8:45 a.m. and ate. I had all intentions of going to church, as this is Sunday. I talked Lieutenant Crabbe and Lieutenant Burns into a trip to Innsbruck, Austria. We ate early chow and took off.

We made good time to Munich. We wandered around town, trying to find the Innsbruck toad. We found it and hustled on. It was beautiful out. We put down the top and enjoyed the sight of the distant snow covered Alps. We went down to the valley floor and the towns are quaint. They are picturesque and the homes are of the Chalet style.

We met a G.I. truck full of Italian prisoners; they are headed for the Brenner Pass and Italy. We stopped at a mountain stream; it came down with great force and threw spray around. It was a raging tumult.

We neared the Alps and came upon a beautiful scene. It was a lake, surrounded by green mountains. It was Lake Walchensee. Gondola-shaped boats are on the lake and boathouses are in the water. It was a great sight.

We continued on to Mittenwald and on to Scharnitz, which is just over the German border into Austria. We were right in between the Alps. One Mountain soared into the mist and clouds, it was snow covered. We went back to Mittenwald and took a left fork to Garmisch-Partenkirchen. This is where they hold the winter sports for the Olympics. On the green mountain were a ski jump and a stadium below. It is a picturesque town.

We stopped off outside town and ate in a beautiful Bavarian-style home. The 10th Armored Division is here and we ate with a Warrant Officer from Service Company of the Infantry Regiment here. He said there was a cog railway to the mountaintop. They have skiing exhibitions up there.

We hustled on but it was threatening to rain and the storm was all over the mountains. We sped along back to beat it. It began to sprinkle but we ran out of it into good weather. We saw another section of Munich. En route back we picked up two doughboys and gave them a lift to our area. We were back by 8:15 p.m.

The Alps, Austria.
Italians en route to Italy.

296

## June 25, 1945

Strasshof, Bavaria, Germany

I got up at 7:45 a.m., ate breakfast, cleaned up, and went to the office to work. I signed a few papers and wrote some correspondence.

I left about 11 a.m. and went to eat and rested a little. I wandered over to Service Battery to the ball field to watch the Officers play the 84th Field Artillery. The 60th lost, they got beat. I hardly recognized anyone. They are all new Officers. I spoke to Lieutenant Craig and a few others. This is the team that the colonel wanted me to manage and play for. I just didn't have the physical strength after Malaria.

After the game I went to Personnel. I signed a few papers. I went back to the quarters and rested. I worked on my footlocker and completed it. I put my clothes and odds and ends in it. I got my shoulder holster today. It is pretty nice, 16 ½ marks, or $1.56.

## June 26, 1945

Strasshof, Bavaria, Germany

I got up about 7:50 a.m. and ate breakfast. I went to the office and cleaned up the routine work.

I signed papers until 11:45 a.m., then came back to my quarters, ate early chow, and left with C-Battery officers to see the USO Show. It is the Jack Benny show at Augsburg. It was a long trip and quite dusty. We went in convoy. We pulled into an airfield and the show was held in a hanger. The 9th Division, 45th Division, 1st Division, and 80th Division were here. The show was pretty good; it was Benny, Adler, the harmonica player, and Martha Tilton, the singer.

Afterwards we got out of the traffic tangle and sped along. As we neared a town, a column of smoke rose into the sky. We stopped. The people were running around. It was a huge barn and combination house on fire. The people were removing furniture. It was a raging inferno. The slate was falling from the roof and people were crying. Some G.I.s were even helping to remove furniture. We came back to quarters and had supper. I hung around the room and went to bed at 9:30 p.m.

### June 27, 1945

Strasshof, Bavaria, Germany

I got up about 9 a.m. then went to work. They don't feed breakfast after 8 a.m. anymore. I worked all morning. I came back to quarters and had a cup of coffee.

I worked after dinner; this is, after having a one and one-half hour rest. I came back to quarters about 4:30 p.m. I rested and then ate supper at 5:50 p.m.

After supper I lied around and rested.

### June 28, 1945

Strasshof, Bavaria, Germany

I got up about 8:30 a.m. and then went to work. I came back to quarters about 10 a.m. and had a cup of coffee. I worked until 11:30 a.m., came back to quarters, and rested until 12 p.m.

I ate and then rested until 1:30 p.m. I worked all afternoon until 4:15 p.m. I came back and rested until 5:30 p.m.

I ate supper and hung around the quarters. I am getting as much rest as possible to try and gain weight. That Malaria really knocked me for a loop; it saps all your strength and seems to affect you for a month.

### June 29, 1945

Strasshof, Bavaria, Germany

I didn't get up until 9 a.m. and went to work. I finished up routine work and then came back to my quarters.

I talked with Major Williams and he said we are to lose all men over 85 points. He is to have a meeting of all Battery Commanders and me at 1:30 p.m. I lay down for a while and then went to the meeting at the Staff Headquarters. We have to get all records ready to go of men with over 85 points. We will lose them all by July 5th. There are 38 men to go directly home, these will be mostly compassionate cases. The rest are to be transferred to a No IV unit, which is to be disbanded at a later date. Skoczylas' and Harry's names were turned in.

I went to Division Rear at Ingolstadt to smooth everything out. I wanted to find out about Skoczylas and Harry. They are both classified as Specification Serial Number (SSN) 405, clerk typist. They said, "No 405 is to leave the theater," and they are checking for juggled Specification Serial Numbers. I spoke to the Adjunct General and the Inspector General and then came back. I had Skoczylas and Harry make out compassionate leave papers. Major Williams is to call General Howell tomorrow about it.

After supper I gathered things together for a trip I have arranged for tomorrow.

### June 30, 1945
Strasshof, Bavaria, Germany

I got up about 8:30 a.m. and went to work about 9 a.m. I cleaned up the work. The clerks are getting all the records of men with over 85 points ready for transfer.

I walked over to the Battalion Command Post and talked with them. I am leaving at noon on a trip I have had in the back of my mind for quite some time, with Lieutenant George Obeldobel and Lieutenant Kuisisto, for Munich, Innsbruck, Austria, Brenner Pass, Italy, and back to Austria and Hitler's home at Berchtesgaden.

Major Williams is going to call General Howell about getting Harry and Skoczylas home on compassionate reasons. I ate chow and got all my stuff together. We took off in a Service Battery command car with a driver after gassing up. It was windy and a bit overcast but nice just the same.

We moseyed along to Munich and we saw the famous beer hall where Hitler was almost killed. I directed them to Route 11. We took the scenic route, it was pretty, and I pointed out the spots of interest, having been

299

here before. We passed over the Austrian border at Scharnitz. The old Alps rise up on both sides and we went right up into them. The peaks soared on all sides of us.

We came to Innsbruck, which is in the floor of the valley between the huge mountains. There was snow on top of it. We went south and we climbed and could look right down on Innsbruck with its mountain background. It was beautiful. We came to the Brenner Pass after running along the side of the mountains. The ravines ran far below.

We got stopped three times at the pass. They had gates. We entered Italy and went to Vipiteno (Sterzing), which is about 20 miles into Italy. We inquired and got rooms at the Parc Hotel. Arlene showed us the rooms. She speaks a little English. We got a supper of eggs, potatoes, red wine, bread, and a salad. It seems familiar to hear the people speaking and singing in Italian. A group was singing in the Café.

I walked uptown with Lieutenant Kuisisto and the streets are narrow, like Sicily. Italian soldiers are all around as are our G.I.s fraternizing. We came back to the hotel and who shows up but Bob Ramsdell. He is conducting a convoy of G.I.s who are on tour.

George Obeldobel and I walked around town until it got dark. We can see lights trickling up the mountainside. We sat on the outside veranda, sipped wine, and talked. We could hear someone, with a good singing voice, singing, and the sound drifted up the side of the mountain as the little lights twinkled in the night air.

Brenner Pass, Italy. Lieutenant Obeldobel and
Lieutenant Kuisisto

# Chapter fourteen: July 1945

July 1, 1945 to July 31, 1945

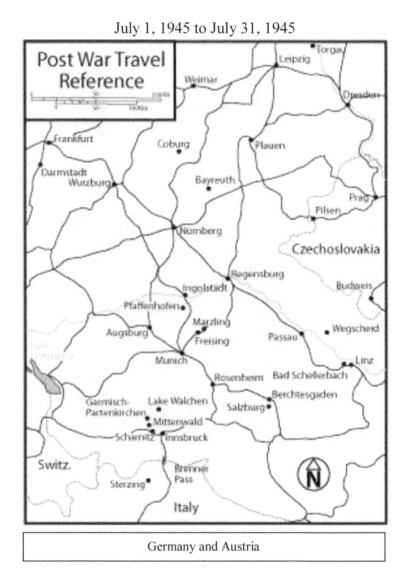

Germany and Austria

July 1945 Historical Overview
Germany, Austria, Czechoslovakia, Italy and Switzerland

General Overview

The former German Reich territory is divided into 4 occupation zones, governed by 4 of the Allied powers; America, England, France, and Russian.

The U.S Army functions as an occupying force in the U.S. section of occupation.

Massive internal troop movements occur to accommodate the new needs of a post- war occupation army.

The enormous task of returning U.S. troops home continues.

9th Division Overview: Large movements of personnel into and out to the 9th Division continues. Some are returning home to the U.S., some are being transferred to other divisions: either where their skill sets are needed, or that will result in a return to home sooner. In the latter case, many soldiers were transferred to units that are to be permanently disbanded, thus making their discharge to home occur sooner than it would they had stayed in their own divisions.

666th Field Artillery Battalion Overview

On June 23, 1945 the 666th Field Artillery Battalion, as part of the War Department's Redeployment Plan, was designated a Category IV. This category meant that the unit would be disbanded and all personnel discharged.

The 666th Field Artillery Battalion was formed on February 21, 1944 and distinguished themselves in action in the Ardennes, the Rhineland, and Central Germany.

***

*July 1, 1945*
Vipiteno, Italy

I slept fairly well in a soft bed. I got up at 7:30 a.m. and shaved with cold water. We had eggs, bread, and coffee for breakfast. We paid 200 Italian Liras each, which is for three of us Officers, plus paying for the driver.

We left about 8:30 a.m. after talking with Arlene, the girl in charge. She is going mountain climbing with her husband. This seems to be a ritual with these people in the Tyrol: going to church on Sunday, packing a lunch, and climbing the Alps.

We went back through the Brenner Pass to Innsbruck. We climbed the mountain, in the command car, driving past the 103 Division Command Post, to the tramway. We ate a little and then took the 11 o'clock tram up the mountain. It was a grand sight - we can watch people hiking up the mountain, sometimes whole families. We climbed and climbed and we passed the down tram at the half-way mark. We arrived at the little house. There is snow in the ravine. There are skis and poles so I tried them out. I fell the first time, as the snow is sticky, but the second time I came all the way down.

We took the 11:45 a.m. tram back to the mountaintop. We have to stay up there until 1:45 p.m. I am tired after skiing and find it hard to get my breath, as the air is so thin. The top is 2,340 meters or 7,200 or so feet. We walked to a knoll; there is snow all around so I took some pictures. From here you can see, Germany, Italy, Austria, Switzerland, and the cities of Vienna and Munich very plain. It is beautiful as we look down on the rocky part of the mountains and the towns below. I am pooped from the thin air but at least it wasn't very cold. We came down and then caught the other tram to the bottom.

We took off for Berchtesgaden and ran along the mountains. It is a grand sight. We ran into a shower but it wasn't bad. As we neared Berchtesgaden it was pretty; mountains, pine trees, and rivers. We parked on the street below and climbed to Hitler's Headquarters. We went inside. We came down and went into Hitler's house. He had a huge window overlooking the mountains and the valleys. We couldn't get into the subterranean home as only majors and above in rank were allowed in. This was the same with the Eagles Nest. We saw Goring's home, the SS Barracks, garage, and stable. I took some pictures of

Hitler's house.

We came back toward Salzburg. We took the Autobahn to Munich. We were caught in a storm at Munich and we arrived home about 10 p.m.

## July 2, 1945
Strasshof, Bavaria, Germany

I was tired this morning. About 8:30 a.m. Jack Markowitz called and said there was a lot to do and so on. I got to work about 9 a.m.

All the men with more than 85 points are to be transferred to some Corp Artillery Unit. We will receive 323 men replacements in the afternoon. There are all kinds of reports to make. Tony Wisniewski has been busy all Saturday, Sunday, and today. I made various calls. My whole section is going, even though they can't leave the Theater. This is because they are clerk typists, Specification Serial Number (SSN) 405, and they are vital to the whole transition process. I came back to the quarters and shaved and then had a cup of coffee. I walked over to the Battalion Command Post and talked with Captain Thivierge and Major Williams.

After dinner, I checked the money the Division Artillery units had turned in to me for conversion to French Francs, for the men going to Paris on pass. I signed papers and checked things out. When the guys returned from Finance, I counted and separated the French Francs.

I ate supper and then I called Jack Markowitz. I gave him a quart of Gilbey's whiskey for a last celebration with the gang. I don't know how I will make out without them.

Major Williams had called General Howell about Skoczylas and Harry. The General called Division Headquarters. Division Headquarters, in turn contacted European Theater of Operations United States Army (ETOUSA). ETOUSA said, "No SSN 405 leaves this Theater, under any circumstances."

**July 3, 1945**

Strasshof, Bavaria, Germany

I got up at 7:30 a.m., as I want to see the fellows off. I ate and went to the office and the fellows were packing and lugging their stuff out. Most of Service Battery was already loaded and emptying the beer keg. I shook their hands as Skoczylas, George, and Lawrence left. Jack and Tony Wisniewski are going in the jeep and Tony is coming back to give us the low down.

I worked in the morning getting the records ready of the 38 men who are to go home directly.

After dinner I worked, then walked over to the Command Post and talked. I rode back to the quarters with Captain Thivierge and Lieutenant Kraft. Pete got a call that 22 men came in from the 45th Infantry Division. I rode back to the Command Post with him. There were four clerks in this group and they will send them down to me. I brought the records back with me. One guy showed up, sent down by B-Battery, a Jewish fellow and Cornell graduate. I had all the records of the 38 men going home ready to go.

I ate supper and then came back to the office. I interviewed the A-Battery clerk that came down, and he didn't want the job. I went back to my quarters. I got a call about 9 p.m. saying that all the records of the 214 men have to go tomorrow. I went back to the office and checked up. We will have them ready to go. I came back to quarters about 11 p.m.

**July 4, 1945**

Strasshof, Bavaria, Germany

I got up at 8:10 a.m., shaved, and went to the office. Delli, Harry, and Jack had come back to do a few things and then packed up. The new clerks are busy on the records. I saw the three off, and I intend to go see them in their new setup this afternoon. I signed and initialed all the records, 214 in all. We had 228 men come in this morning from different

306

outfits. I completed the outgoing records at 11:30 p.m. Sergeant Slota is still trying to straighten out the morning reports.

After dinner, Tony Wisniewski came back with me, and we straightened out the Service Records and then left for the 770th Field Artillery, their new outfit. We went through Munich and it was real cold out. The town was busy. We got to the Command Post, talked with all the fellows, and met their Warrant Officer. The driver and I hurried back to my quarters just in time for supper. I hung around all evening.

**July 5, 1945**
Strasshof, Bavaria, Germany

I got up at 8:30 a.m., cleaned up, and went to work. There are more new men in the office. I did some work and tried to straighten out a few things.

After dinner I went with Bob Ramsdell in an open command car. We went through Munich to the 770th Field Artillery; I talked with the guys and then visited my old gang. They are making out okay and I talked with their Warrant Officer. I went to Munich to the Government clothing store, while Bob tried to arrange a transfer. The driver is new; he almost hit a horse, and then almost hit a woman while driving in traffic. The town is busy and everyone is hurrying about. The streetcars are jammed and the waiting areas stops are mobbed. I bought a couple things and then came back to the 770th Field Artillery.

I ate supper there, in A-Battery with DeRosa the cook. I said goodbye to the fellows and we left. It is sad to say good-bye, probably forever. They are heading for Paris to run a Redeployment Center.

We came back to quarters. I left immediately for the show but it was crowded with all the new men. We came back and I went over to Personnel and checked up on the work. I came back to quarters and hung around.

## July 6, 1945

Strasshof, Bavaria, Germany

I got up at 8:10 a.m., as I wanted to get down to the office so I could get Captain Brown's records ready. He is to leave for the 45th Infantry Division today. I worked all morning trying to find out the correct number of new men and where they are. It is all mixed up. There should be 308 and I can only account 296. I took the papers out of their envelopes and am juggling men around.

There is a new Technician Fourth Grade now to help Sergeant Slota. I worked all afternoon trying to organize things and straighten out the new men. It is beginning to clear up.

After supper I played catch and wrote.

## July 7, 1945

Strasshof, Bavaria, Germany

I didn't get up until 8:30 a.m. It is Saturday. I went to work and spent the early part of the morning counting Pay Transfer Accounts. I had about $1,400 dollars, so I came back to my quarters to await transportation. An inspection is on so all the vehicles and drivers were tied up. I walked to the office and locked the money up until Monday, as Finance is closed Saturday afternoon and Sunday.

In the afternoon I hung around and played catch for a while.

In the evening I hung around the quarters. I talked a couple of officers into a sightseeing trip tomorrow, Sunday. I have had it in the back of my mind to see Lake Constance. It is on the Swiss-German border and near part of Austria.

## July 8, 1945

Strasshof, Bavaria, Germany

I got up early and got cleaned up. I ate breakfast and then Lieutenant George Obeldobel, Lieutenant Don Young, the driver, and I left for

Lake Constance. We made good time to Munich. The driver knew the route so we didn't lose any time. Beyond Munich the road was rough, the terrain flat, and not scenic.

We ate dinner at the 905 Field Artillery Battalion: 80th Infantry Division. We crossed into French Occupational Territory. A Goum, a Moroccan (Arab) soldier, stopped us and said "American?" We said, "Yes," and he waved us on. The French soldiers are all over the villages. We were attracting quite a bit of attention.

We arrived at Lindau about 3 p.m. We drove down to the Lake. It is pretty and you can see Switzerland across the lake. We went toward the Swiss border. We passed through Bregenz. The French are walking arm-in-arm with everyone. We went into a bit of Austria. We came to a bridge two kilometers from the Swiss border. The French border patrol wouldn't let us through without a pass.

We gave two Goums, in white turbans and French uniforms, a lift. In broken French I talked about North Africa, Casa Blanca, and Port Lyautey. We went back to the Lake and parked. We watched the French and Arab soldiers having foot races. The civilians were all around watching. We drove around the Lake a bit. You can see the Alps riding into the clouds as we looked in the direction of Zurich. I looked for old Matterhorn, thinking about Richard Halliburton.

Lake Constance, Austria.
Lieutenant Young from Colorado.

We started back about 4 p.m. We made good time by taking a different route. We are nearer the Alps this way. We ate supper at Company E, 319th Infantry, 80th Infantry Division. We finally got back about 9:15 p.m., and raided the icebox.

## July 9, 1945

Strasshof, Bavaria, Germany

I didn't get up until 8:30 a.m. then went to the office and started to try and catch up on the work. I went to the quarters and awaited transportation to Division Rear. I got a three-fourth ton truck and went to Ingolstadt. I couldn't get rid of the Pay Transfer Accounts before noon, so I ate dinner here. I got rid of the Pay Transfer Accounts and then drove over to the 15ᵗʰ Engineers. I talked with Frank Page for a while. He is going to fly home and is leaving tomorrow. I said goodbye.

I came back to the office and worked until 5 p.m. I ate supper and hung around the quarters all night.

## July 10, 1945

Strasshof, Bavaria, Germany

I didn't get up until 8:30 a.m. I took a bath and cleaned up. I went to the office and started to work. There are a lot of odds and ends to clear up.

I walked over to the Command Post and Captain Thivierge said that I was being transferred to the 666ᵗʰ Field Artillery Battalion, along with Captain Prince, Lieutenant Young, and Lieutenant Crabbe. We are to leave tomorrow. The outfit is in Austria, near Linz. While others are heading to places nearer home they are sending us further away.

I came back to the office and told them. I went back to my quarters and began to pack. I ate dinner and then went to Division Rear. I took Bob Ramsdell along. I said goodbye to the men in Adjunct General, including Whitney and Strong. I stopped in at Division Clearing Company for a few minutes. We came back to the village where Bob has his laundry. We got a couple glasses of beer for the driver and him. We came back and I packed some more.

After supper I fixed a box to mail home some of my heavy clothes. I finished packing and I said goodbye to just about everyone. Then I went over to Personnel and said goodbye to them.

**July 11, 1945**
Strasshof, Bavaria, Germany

Captain Prince awoke us about 4 a.m. I got up and Captain Prince, Lieutenant Crabbe, and I went downstairs and fixed ourselves eggs and coffee as Lieutenant Young joined us. We collected our stuff and took it downstairs. I said goodbye to Bob Ramsdell. It was misty and damp.

We all, including two drivers, had a job taking the top cover off another vehicle and putting it on ours, which is a three-fourth ton truck. We piled our stuff in it and about 5:45 a.m., after much noise we got going. It was getting wetter but I had a nice place. I lay crosswise on the baggage and slept on and off. It was raining now and a miserable day.

We stopped on the Autobahn between Munich and Salzburg. I got in front. It is cold and wet and the water soon seeped through my sleeve and pants. Outside Salzburg we got lost and I got in back again. We went through Salzburg, Austria. It is nice, with a castle on the hill overlooking the town. King Leopold and Queen Astrid are here. They stayed in exile here. We ate with some Tank Destroyers. The local girls waited on tables.

We finally reached the 65th Infantry Division, Division Artillery, in Bad Schallerbach, Austria. The 666th Field Artillery is attached to them and we will be with them. They are just up the street. The Command Post is in a Hospital the Army had taken over. It is on a hill.

We met the officers and the Warrant Officer showed me around. Personnel have a nice set up. I have a room to myself, with a sink, closet, white linen, and maids. I met the two majors, as there are few of the old officers remaining.

There are 15 of us from the 9th Infantry Division. The men here are all agog at the decorations our gang has.

I talked with the Personnel boys. They have a good section and good records but too much red tape. Both the enlisted men and Officers have nice dining halls, with civilian waitresses. They even have a snack bar that is open in the evening for everybody. Captain Prince, Captain Polivy from 60th Infantry, Lieutenant Sheidy, the Air Observation Post Pilot, and me went to the 65th Division Artillery area. We soaked in the sulfur pool for about an hour. It is wonderful, warm, heavy water, slippery, but really relaxing. This was formally a health spa, "Bad" area.

## July 12, 1945
Bad Schallerbach, Austria

I got up when I heard reveille outside. I had breakfast, a novelty for me, and I really enjoyed it, and ate it all. I cleared up a little work in Personnel. There were the rosters of all men with less than 85 points. It is about the opposite of our old group, as almost everyone here has less than 85 points where our old gang almost everyone had more than 85 points. I had it flown to Group Headquarters so they can fly it to XV Corp. I signed the morning reports.

I took off at 9 a.m. with a captain. I was in the back of three-fourth ton truck filled with gas cans. We went to Salzburg. It is about 65 miles. The roads were rough at first but got better. We got there about 11:30 a.m. and went to the captain's old outfit and had dinner. I got a jeep and went to II Corp. It was early, so I went to the Post Exchange, but they had nothing.

I came back to II Corp and saw a Captain Smith about Ardennes credit for the 666th Field Artillery. He sent a Teletype Transmission (TWX) to 9th Army for me. I spoke to a major, G-3, about the transfer order of the unit to the Channel Base Section. I didn't get any satisfaction.

I came back to the area. The captain and another captain named Alexander, from Lawrence, Massachusetts, and I came back in a command car. We sent the three-fourth ton with the gas ahead. We got back about 5 p.m. I checked in at the office and talked with the majors and Colonel Boebel. I ate and then went down and took a Sulfur bath. It is so relaxing.

**July 13, 1945**

Bad Schallerbach, Austria

I got up at 7:05 a.m. and was the first one for breakfast. I went back to my room and shaved, cleaned up, and went to the office. I started to count the money to take to Finance. A Lieutenant came in from Service Battery. He didn't know how much money he had. I totaled it and it came to $3,000 plus a few odd dollars. I counted all morning.

I arranged for transportation at 1:30 p.m. to Finance at the 65th Infantry Division at Linz. After dinner I counted up a storm and I finally finished about 2:30 p.m. I had $13,690; some odd dollars in Marks and $1,000 in Pay Transfer Accounts, and about $2,000 in Belgium Francs, Dutch Guilders and French Francs. I took off for Linz and Finance. They were closed to check stock, as they are changing Finance Officers. I walked up town, with the $16,000 in a ration box under my arm. I met the driver and the assistant driver at the doughnut dugout. We had coffee and we left and came back.

After supper I hung around, had a nice sulfur bath and talked in Personnel.

**July 14, 1945**

Bad Schallerbach, Austria

I got up at 7:15 a.m. and was one of the first down to breakfast. I came back and cleaned up. I worked all morning and didn't go to Linz, as I was waiting for a colonel and major to come and take some men with them. I waited all morning and when I went to dinner, they were there eating. The colonel told me they would be up after dinner so I waited. They came and we went over the Specification Serial Numbers.

After they left I went to Linz. I have about $14,000 in cash. It is a nice trip through the countryside. They said to leave it and I could get it Monday. I told them that most of the men would be gone by then, so they counted it right away.

I rode uptown and then went to the Post Office. I came back to Finance and waited a while and then got the money. I counted it and left about 5 p.m. We got back about 6 p.m.

After supper, I hung around to count the money out to the Batteries. I then walked to the swimming pool and watched the people. I went to the Sulfur bath and stayed about an hour. I came back to the building, sat out on the veranda and talked, and also had a snack. The officers from some of the other Batteries were around and we talked. I went to bed at 12 a.m.

## July 15, 1945
Bad Schallerbach, Austria

I got up at 8:25 a.m. It is Sunday. I ate breakfast and then rushed out to church. It is a nice chapel and was crowded. I stood in the rear. There were about 30 soldiers. The children are cute, with pigtails, clear complexions, blond hair, blue eyes, and tanned. The priest spoke to us in English after his German sermon. I met Colonel Boebel and Major Wilson and walked back to the Headquarters with them. I hung around until dinner and we had chicken.

After dinner we all talked in the captain's room. They all went swimming.

## July 16, 1945
Bad Schallerbach, Austria

I didn't get up in time for breakfast, for the first time. I got up about 8:20 a.m., cleaned up, and went to the office. We have to requisition men. I puttered around until dinner.

After dinner I spent time at the swimming pool and got a pretty good burn. The gang just assigned to the 65th Infantry Division, from our old gang of 60th Field Artillery, dropped in to see us. There was Captain Tom Gaffney, Captain Gray, Lieutenant Kraft, and Captain Gene Welsh.

314

After supper Captain Gray called up to get oriented on the place. I met him and we walked to the swimming pool to watch them swim then walked up the road. We met Captain Polivy from 60th Infantry and Captain Doctor Rumore. The Doc joined us and we walked, ending up at my place. It looked like rain so Captain Gray went back. We sat around and talked and I even went into Personnel for a while.

## July 17, 1945
Bad Schallerbach, Austria

I got up at 7:20 a.m., had breakfast, and then went to the office at 7:50 a.m. I signed reports and then shaved. I came back, talked, and did a few odd jobs during the morning. We completed the requisition for Personnel by 10:30 a.m.

I went with the pilot Lieutenant Herb Sheidy, to Wels by jeep. We took the cub plane and flew to Schärding to deliver the list. It was a nice trip. The land looked like a pretty pattern with rolling hills. The Alps were in the distance on the left. The air was a little bumpy as it was overcast at times with low dark clouds. We ate at the 880th Field

Bad Schallerbach, Austria. Our Billet.

Artillery Battalion. We waited for the messenger and then flew back. I took some pictures of the Danube River, the Hotel we are in, and the swimming pool.

We came back from Wels and I walked down to the swimming pool. The pool was being drained and cleaned. I came back and talked until supper. After supper we all went to the show. We

315

then walked around until we came to the Gasthof, by Division Artillery, 65th Field Artillery. We drank wine, egg cognac, and talked with the Frau and Herr. We wandered back. We met two nurses but they just walked away and went home. We came back and had a snack, eggs, bologna, Coke, and coffee. We talked in the major's room until 11 p.m.

## July 18, 1945
Bad Schallerbach, Austria

I got up for breakfast and went to the office about 8 a.m. I checked and signed a few things. I got a jeep and the C-Battery clerk and we went to Salzburg. It is a pretty long ride and we got there about 12 noon. We dropped over to the 975th Field Artillery Battalion and ate. I talked with Captain Alexander, formerly of the 666th Field Artillery.

I left about 1 p.m. and went downtown, stopping at the Post Exchange and bought a few things. I went to G-1, II Corp, and talked to a Lieutenant there and left a message. We came back. On the way we saw some of the 39th Infantry, 9th Division, on their way to Linz, to join up with the 65th Division. We got back about 4 p.m. and I went swimming.

After supper Lieutenant Young, the pilot, and I walked around. We went to Service Battery and had a glass of wine. We came back to our place and had a snack and talked for a while.

## July 19, 1945
Bad Schallerbach, Austria

I didn't go to breakfast this morning and instead got up about 9 a.m. The water is shut off for repairs. I went to the office and sat on the veranda reading circulars. I did a little work and talked with a visiting officer.

After dinner I went to the swimming pool and got a good burn. I talked with the gang. I passed a few words with an Austrian girl. She is the tall, tan girl. I swam a couple times and left about 5:15 p.m.

After supper we went to the show, came back, and talked.

## July 20, 1945
Bad Schallerbach, Austria

I got up at 7:20 a.m. and had breakfast. I went to the office and started counting German Marks for conversion to Austrian Schillings. I finished about 9:15 a.m. I shaved with cold water, as there still wasn't any hot water. I decided to wait until this afternoon to go to Linz.

I had a nice steak dinner. I got a jeep and went to the 65th Infantry Division at Linz. I counted the money and sent a Pay Transfer Account of my own for $125. I went to the post office and got some money orders. I came back to the 666th and distributed the money and receipts to the clerks.

After supper I walked, by myself, around town. I met an Austrian boy, about seventeen, and talked and walked with him for a while. I came back and had a snack at the snack bar.

## July 21, 1945
Bad Schallerbach, Austria

I got up and had breakfast and then worked in the office. We got orders to go to Antwerp, Belgium; we are to find out the details later. We then got a call to send out 87 men tomorrow.

I got the colonel's Chevrolet, a liberated 1940 model, and went to Linz. I changed some money and started looking for the 256th Engineers. I found them and looked up Danny Ryan, from Houghs Neck, Quincy. We were Home Towner's and had played a lot of baseball together. I haven't seen him for four years. I talked for an hour and then came back to Linz and then back to our quarters.

After supper I walked toward to the pool and got called over to the Hotel Victoria by Doctor Rumore and friends. They were sitting outside and we ordered wine and sat around talking and saying, "Was is los?" to the girls. We went inside to a room and sat and got two bottles of egg cognac. After finishing them we talked to the proprietor and proprietress and then came back. We had a snack at the snack bar and then retired.

## July 22, 1945
Bad Schallerbach, Austria

I got up at 8:05 a.m., ate breakfast, and then went to the office. The Sergeant in Personnel is signing my name to all the records.

It is Sunday. I went to the 9 o'clock Mass at St Raphael's Chapel. It was crowded like last Sunday. After Mass I went to the office. The 87 men left for Salzburg to the 42nd Infantry Division.

We had chicken for dinner. It is hot out today. I went to the swimming pool and spent the afternoon swimming and sun bathing. There are a lot of new faces here on Sunday.

After supper we went to the show. It was a terrible picture, so we walked out. We took a little walk and then came back and had a snack. We had a roast beef, onion, and pickle sandwich. We talked out on the veranda of the upstairs room.

## July 23, 1945
Bad Schallerbach, Austria

I got up and had breakfast and did a little work in the office.

We got movement orders; we are to go to Antwerp, Belgium on Thursday. Colonel Boebel and Major Wilson flew to Corps, to check up on keeping the personnel. We are busy bringing the work up to date. To be truthful I have hardly lifted a hand to do the work as thoroughly as I used to, it's a case of too much for too long.

In the afternoon we all (the Officers) went to the swimming pool. The colonel and major came down later. We are to lose all the personnel prior to moving and are to get all men with more than 85 points. It will be some job. I told them that they would have to postpone the movement until after Monday.

After supper we went to the show and it was terrible so we left before it was over. We walked around, and Doc, Young, and I and talked to

318

some old hags. I left, and came back and had a snack at the snack bar.

### July 24, 1945
Bad Schallerbach, Austria

I didn't get up for breakfast but got up about 8:30 a.m. We worked all morning and the clerks are getting all the records ready.

After dinner I went with Major Fisher to Division at Linz, to straighten out this swap deal. They said that we are to get all our men from Division Artillery. That will mean we get 460 men and then give them 237 men. I stopped at Finance and the Post Office. We came back to Division Artillery and made arrangements with a Major Kelly. He is slow and doesn't seem to be experienced in handling it.

After supper I went for a walk, came back, and had a snack.

### July 25, 1945
Bad Schallerbach, Austria

I didn't get up for breakfast but got up about 8:30 a.m. We worked in the morning and the clerks are getting the records ready. The majority of the men will be transferred tomorrow. We will hold a lot of the specialists until the day after tomorrow.

In the afternoon we all went swimming. I had a cold, so I just took a dip.

After supper we went to a stage show put on by the Austrians. It was good. It consisted of a band, girl dancers, singers, and skits. Afterwards we walked and then came back and had a snack.

### July 26, 1945
Bad Schallerbach, Austria

I didn't get up for breakfast but got up about 9 a.m. I cleaned up and went to the office. We have to transfer our men out today. I have a cold, or hay fever in my throat, eyes, and head. I went over a roster of the men coming in with Major Fisher. We assigned the men to Battery by special numbers.

After dinner we completed the job. I went swimming. All the men coming in were in the ball fields by the swimming pool. The men coming in to us from the 65th Division Artillery were pretty well drunk. Some of them were in swimming with their clothes on. They were making passes at the fräuleins. I got into my bathing suit but it was hot so I didn't stay too long. Actually I just took a dip and went to the office, as there would be work to do.

The clerks were busy. The new men are a bit on the wild side, picturing themselves as old combat men. The major and Captain Polivy had a little trouble with one of the new enlisted men. He was indignant because they didn't have bread at the snack bar. This is the only outfit with a snack bar that anyone ever heard of.

## July 27, 1945
Bad Schallerbach, Austria

I didn't make breakfast but got up about 8:30 a.m. I shaved and then went to the office. The clerks are busy closing out the records. I hung around all morning.

In the afternoon I went to the swimming pool. We sat with the local girls. Actually they came from Bratislava and Vienna. We kidded them. The Doc and Lieutenant Young would curse them occasionally as no good Jerries and laugh, knowing they didn't understand.

I left the pool about 4:30 p.m. and went to the 65th Division Artillery barbershop. The gang from the 666th Field Artillery, Doc, and Young were also here. They have girl barbers. I got a shampoo, and it cost 1 ½ shillings, or 15 cents. A haircut cost 10 cents.

After supper I hung around. The old clerks left, except Sergeant Burdick. He will stay until Monday. The new clerks, plus the sergeant major, a Sergeant Baxt, came in. I hung around then walked down to the 65th Division Artillery and listened to the Division dance band play. They were fair. There was a crowd of civilians and soldiers.

320

The gang up in our quarters was drunk tonight. Doc and Sheidy came in and they were feeling no pain. I went to bed at 11 p.m. after talking in Personnel with Major Fisher and Sergeant Baxt. Then Doc and Sheidy came wandering in my room and we talked.

**July 28, 1945**
Bad Schallerbach, Austria

I didn't get up for breakfast but got up at 8:15 a.m. I went to the office and the sergeant major, Sergeant Baxt, and the new clerks were straightening out the records. I did a few odd things. I packed a Val pack and then did some work.

I spoke to the colonel about getting a jeep to visit Czechoslovakia. He said OK. I took off after dinner. The roads were rough and slow. I went to Eferding, I believe Hitler was born and lived here, Peuerbach, Schärding and Passau. Passau is a quaint old city at the joining of the Inn and the Danube Rivers. There were many riverboats tied along shore. We reached here a little late, 3:30 p.m. or so. We ran along the North side, but in Germany. I figured it was too late to get to Czechoslovakia and then back to Bad Schallerbach. We decided to run along the Danube River to Linz.

It was a nice ride for a ways but the road soon cut away from the river, heading north. The road became rough as we cut inland, passing through Wegscheid, Oepping and Rohrbach. We were only about six miles from the Czech border here but I didn't know it at the time. The towns were beat up by bombing and shelling. A heavy rainstorm caught us and we got soaked. We stopped beside a building for a while. We got to Linz about 6 p.m. It was still raining and it cleared up just as we got home. We were given a meal in the kitchen and I went down and had a nice sulfur bath and relaxed.

**July 29, 1945**
Bad Schallerbach, Austria

I got up at 7:30 a.m.; had breakfast, and I was around the office checking the last minute details. I cleaned up a few items and I went to Mass, as it is Sunday, with Doc Rumore, at St Raphael's Chapel. Father Connors said the Mass. We talked with him afterwards. I got the impression he was disappointed in the poor attendance of the G.I.s. It certainly isn't like the good old 9th Division.

We walked down to Division Artillery, 65th, and played Ping-Pong with Captain Gray and Lieutenant Hopkinson. We came back to dinner.

After dinner I loaded my personal stuff on the trailer. The sergeant had all the Personnel stuff packed except the excess junk. I hung around the room resting, took a walk, and then came back. I finished up a little work at Division Artillery and then took a sulfur bath.

After supper I talked with the Officers and then went to Division Artillery. We talked with Father Connors, Chaplain Lorenz, Gene Welch, Captain O'Leary, and Lou Gray. We had coffee and crackers. I came back to the billet. I collected a few things from Personnel and then rounded up my personal things. We are moving out tomorrow. We are to go near Brussels to run a camp for the redeployment of G.I.s to Japan.

## July 30, 1945
Bad Schallerbach, Austria

We got up at 4:15 a.m., ate, and then loaded everything. I am riding in the front of a jeep and we left at 5 a.m. It is chilly.

We passed through Grieskirchen and the roads are none too good. We went to Schärding and through Regensburg across the river into Nuremberg. We saw the Nazi Stadium on the left as we came into town. The place is pretty well beat up. It is a large city and we continued on to Würzburg. We gassed up and all are tired. We have been eating odds and ends all day, such as K-Rations. As we neared the billet area the sign read, Lucky Camp Area. It turned out to be a field. It was cold riding all today.

We had a hot C-ration dinner and coffee. The Air Corps men beside us are going to Germany for Occupation. We just put our bedrolls on the ground to sleep. Some went to the trouble to put up pup tents. It sprinkled about 2 a.m. but I just rolled over.

## July 31, 1945
Aschaffenburg, Germany

We got up at 6:30 a.m. and ate about 7:30 a.m. We had coffee and hot cakes. We moved out about 8 a.m. and it is chilly again this morning. We went through Darmstadt, which is all beat up. It was a large city and is one of the worst destroyed cities I've seen.

We crossed the Rhine River into French occupied territory. There are Goums and French soldiers all around. We bypassed Mainz and continued on to Trier. This is in French territory on the Moselle River. We pulled into a field for bivouac. It was an airfield. The French had one Air-Cobra P-39 here. The people, in droves, came running after the convoy. In five minutes there were a couple hundred people. There were men, women, and children. We had something to eat. There were girls all around.

Aschaffenburg, Germany. En route to Brussels.

After supper the G.I.s took off in all directions, some with girls, and some in search of them. I walked to the river and talked with some Polish kids. I returned to the trucks and made a little shelter out of a blanket and went to bed at dark.

323

# Chapter fifteen: August 1945

August 1, 1945 to August 31, 1945

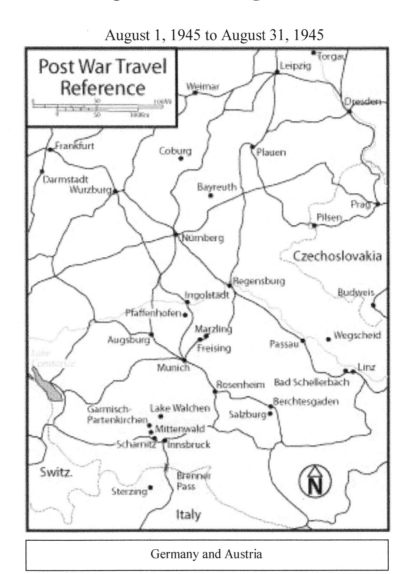

Germany and Austria

August 1945 Historical Overview
Germany, Luxemburg, Belgium and France

General Overview

The massive deployment of U.S. troops home continues.

The U.S. Army is now acting as an occupation force in the American Sector of post-war Germany.

August 6, 1945 the first Atomic bomb is dropped on Hiroshima, Japan.

August 9, 1945 the second atomic bomb is dropped on Nagasaki, Japan.

The Point system, formally called the Advanced Service Rating Score (ASRS), was used to determine which soldiers were eligible to return to the U.S. Points were awarded according to criteria outlined by this policy.

*** 

*August 1, 1945*
Trier, Germany

We got up about 7 a.m., had coffee and cereal for breakfast, and left about 8 a.m. It is chilly out again.

We went to Luxembourg and the city is very nice. The buildings and the homes are attractive. It is a fairly well-off place. The store windows are stocked with goods. The people are well dressed. We passed through, and then gassed up on the outskirts of town.

We went to Arlon in Belgium and then on to Bastogne. This was beat up and is where the 101st Airborne held out in the Battle of the Bulge. Answer to the German demand for surrender, "Nuts." There is equipment along the road, tanks, and vehicles. The people are repairing their homes.

We came to Namur and the people are nicely dressed and have attractive homes. Namur is a large city and we don't have far to go now. We reached Brussels about 4 p.m. and went around the outskirts. We went to a tent city about seven miles outside the city. We set up our cots and bedrolls. I helped unload Personnel. The boys, who were on the

325

advance detail, told us about the town.

We all decided to eat in Brussels and all the Officers got dressed. We all borrowed money and took off, all but one. It is quite a town. We ate at the Allied Officer's Club at the Navy, Army, and Air Force Institutes (NAFFI). We ran all over town going to nightclubs. We talked with the street girls. We danced at the nightclubs.

## August 2, 1945
Camp White Tie, Brussels, Belgium

I got up about 9:30 a.m. and sat in Personnel for a while.

After dinner I hung around, as we have to get in applications for men with 90 and more points and officers with 95 and more points.

We then went into town early and ate at the officer's club. Later we did all the nightclubs. I left them at La Potinière and took in the La Parisiana and Corso.

I was more of an observer than a participant and got a kick out of seeing all the activity. I had about two drinks all night and then came back to La Potinière. The colonel and majors were here also. I danced and talked. Captain Pore was only interested in getting me home to get the men paid. We got out of the club about 2 a.m. The colonel and major picked the lock of one of our 666th's jeeps. With the help of a couple of English officers we managed to steal one of our vehicles to get home. We gave the two English officers a lift to their quarters. We went up in the elevator with them to have a drink. The place was locked up. It was now 3 a.m.

We came back toward town and got lost. I was getting disgusted at this point. We finally found the right road and got back to camp just as daylight began to break. It was after 4 o'clock in the morning.

We are here to run a redeployment camp to send men, with less than the critical score, to Japan. We will receive men as soon as the paper work can be straightened out.

Souvenir postcard in Frank Lovell's collection.

## August 3, 1945
Camp White Tie, Brussels, Belgium

I got up about 10:30 a.m. and feel ragged. I worked in Personnel for a while and after dinner took a little rest. I have done very little work since we have been here.

We went to town and took a Turkish bath and shower, also swam. We then went to the Allied Officers Club for dinner.

Afterwards the fellows did the town. I nosed around the various nightspots with them, dancing and trying not to drink. It usually ends up that I have one or two drinks for the night. We took in the La Parisiana. We ended up in some place on a side street. The street girls are rather attractive as a whole. We came back to camp about 2 o'clock.

## August 4, 1945
Camp White Tie, Brussels, Belgium

I got up at 9:15 am and had a cup of coffee. I did some work in

Personnel, and then I took the Officer's applications to Group Headquarters.

In the afternoon I did odds and ends. We left for town early and ate at the Allied Officer's Club. We had a bottle of Champagne with our meal, it cost about 70 cents. We roamed around town and in and out of the clubs. I came back on the 2 o'clock truck.

## August 5, 1945
Camp White Tie, Brussels, Belgium

I didn't get up until about 8:45 a.m. All the Officers were talking about their dates and experiences. I got dressed and then looked for the chapel, as it is Sunday. I walked all the way to the shower but couldn't find the chapel.

I hung around in the afternoon.

We went to the Allied Officer's Club in the evening and danced and spent the rest of the evening there. We came back on the 2 o'clock truck.

## August 6, 1945
Camp White Tie, Brussels, Belgium

I got up at 9 a.m., washed up, and had coffee. I rounded up the things to go in town to Finance. I took a jeep and a few fellows came along to withdraw their soldiers' deposits. I picked up the Officers' pay vouchers and money. We got back to camp late.

I had dinner and then rounded up things to take to Major Dewey who is in the hospital in Antwerp. We went in the Medics jeep and took a patient with us. It is about 30 miles to Antwerp. We went through the outskirts to the hospital. I left his things off and talked for a while and we left there about 4:30 p.m.

We went to downtown Antwerp and all the signs are in Flemish. The streets are very narrow but there are some nice buildings. The people don't appear so friendly. The girls are not as good looking. We drove around for a while. The houses have nice stained-glass windows and are very attractive.

328

THEATRE

UNDER DIRECTION OF
BELGIUM LEAVE SECTION
CHANOR BASE SECTION

**FREE**

TO ALL ALLIED FORCES
AND LADY GUEST

*Every night*
*Except Saturday night*

FRIDAY AUG. 3rd through THURSDAY AUG. 16th

Brochure for ABC Vaudeville show.

We came back to Brussels and got back to camp about 6 p.m. I ate and then went to town with Doc and Young. We went to the ABC Theater and it had vaudeville acts and a band. It was a good show. We walked downtown with three girls. We were going dancing at the Blue Owl. There was dog racing there instead. We left the girls and stayed for one race. I had never seen dog racing (pari-mutuel) inside a building before. We walked all over town looking in at various clubs. We talked with the street girls. We came back to camp at 11 p.m.

**August 7, 1945**
Camp White Tie, Brussels, Belgium

I got up at 9 a.m. when one of the Battery Lieutenants came in to get paid. I washed and had coffee. I did a few things at the office.

After dinner I did some work, read, and wrote. Later in the day I hung around in our tent, resting, and talking. I went in town early and ate at the Allied Officers Club. They really have a nice place here. There is a bar and tables, a room for dancing which also has tables, and then there is the main dining room. This is a large room with a rotunda. The meals are good and cost 25 francs, about 60 cents. We walked around and later in the evening we had a cold plate at the Canadian Officers Atlanta Club. We came back to camp about 11 p.m.

**August 8, 1945**
Camp White Tie, Brussels, Belgium

I got up about 9:15 a.m. and sort of stalled around doing odd little jobs. I kept busy until noon.

After dinner I did a little work, came back and took a rest, and then left for town early. We ate supper at the Officers Club. We kept chatting with an Auxiliary Territorial Service (ATS) Lieutenant and we had a good time kidding with her. We left and walked around town. We had ice cream sundaes. We stuck our head in all the nightclubs. We chatted and kidded with the streetwalkers. They know us by sight now. We walked some more and ended up in some offbeat places. We sat down for a while and had a couple of drinks. We came back at 1 o'clock in the morning.

## August 9, 1945
Camp White Tie, Brussels, Belgium

I got up about 9:15 a.m., washed, and had coffee. I went to the office about 10 a.m. I signed payrolls and then took a soldier to Finance to withdraw a soldier's deposit. We came back and ate dinner.

After dinner I did a few jobs and then took a rest. In late afternoon we went into town and ate at the Allied Officers Club. We stayed until about 9 p.m. or so, talking, as it is raining out. We then went to the American Officers Club and came back at 1 o'clock. The wind was strong and our combined squad tents were weak. We had to get up and go outside to secure it. The tent is leaking.

## August 10, 1945
Camp White Tie, Brussels, Belgium

It was raining so I remained in bed and got up at 11:45 a.m. There isn't any work planned at Personnel today for me.

I ate dinner and prepared to go to town. Sheidy and I went with Major Jill and we left at 1 o'clock. It is still raining. We went to Finance and I sent a Pay Transfer Account for Sheidy and we then went to Chanor Base Section. A guy stuck his head out of the window and yelled down to us that the war was over with Japan.

We went to the swimming pool. The Women's Army Corp (WACs), from all over, are having a swimming meet. We told one or two WACs that the war was over. The man with the microphone announced that it had just been officially announced that the war was over. The people roared, danced, and cried. The band played up a storm. Sheidy and I began to feel funny as it could be in error.

We took a good steam bath and shower. The showers varied, some shot up from the floor while others completely encircled you. There were two 10-foot square pools of water, one hot and the other cold. You jumped back and forth in them, then go to the Masseur's workout. Then we went into the rest room, a heat-regulated room, and we had towels as large as blankets we wrapped ourselves in, lied down on lounges, and slept like babies for one and one-half hours. We dressed and were ready for anything the night could offer.

We ate at the Allied Officers Club and then went to the show downtown. We came out and went to the American Officers Club. I danced and talked French with the people. I made arrangements to come back with a jeep. I waited until everyone had left the club at 12:45 a.m. I got a lift from the corner to North Station. I caught the jeep there and got back to camp about 2 a.m.

**August 11, 1945**
Camp White Tie, Brussels, Belgium
Captain Fleckenstein and Lieutenant Crabbe awakened me. They want me to go down to Chanor Base Section headquarters in the Shell Building. We stopped in the enlisted men section of the Adjunct General section and got the story. We then went to the Officer's section. We got to the bottom of a shady deal. They have pigeonholed our papers and were sending their own people home. Their people just barely had enough points to qualify, mainly due to the fact that they had stayed in the States, got married, and had children, which gave them points. We had earned ours overseas fighting in North Africa, Sicily, France,

Belgium, and Germany. Some cases had some 100 points more than required. We got some papers and filled them out and instigated some action. We are to return in the afternoon to find out how many Officers can go home. There are about 50 enlisted men eligible to go home.

The colonel and a few others went back to Chanor Base Section after we had come home to explain everything. They came back later saying that all Officers with over 100 points would be going home. All are happy. Everyone got ready to have a party, to sort of celebrate the good news.

Brussels, Belgium. Me and Admiral Donitz mace and diamond studded Iron Cross. He signed the surrender terms. (Mistakenly identified: Spanish Cross)

We left before supper and ate at the Allied Officers Club. We watched the dancing. We then went to a café about 9 p.m. and were the first ones there. This was where the celebration was to happen. It was a clip joint. I left with Lieutenant Crabbe shortly thereafter. We went to the Red Cross Club, then to the American Officers Club, and finally returned to the Red Cross Club, where we met Major Fisher. We then came back to camp at 11 o'clock.

## August 12, 1945
Camp White Tie, Brussels, Belgium

The guys awakened me about 9 a.m. They aren't entirely sober as yet. The Lieutenant from the Merchant Marines, who they drank with last night, is still here. I got up and went to the 10 o'clock Mass, as it is Sunday, at the chapel tent. I then went to Personnel and did a little work.

After dinner Sheidy decided to fly so I went with him. We took an L-5 Stinson. We took off from camp here. We flew to Antwerp and it sure was a nice day. The sun was out and the sky fairly clear. We flew all over Antwerp, the canals, the river, and then to the sea. It is a large city. We flew over people swimming and boating and then came back. We did some wingovers and my stomach is a bit affected. We sort of followed the streets and canals as we went along. We flew over Brussels and it is huge. We flew over parks, the King's Palace, and City Hall. We came back after buzzing a pond of swimmers and people fishing. We buzzed a small group having an outing. My old stomach isn't right and I am sweating. I think it is due to the hot sun and lack of good fresh air. We landed and I am a bit woozy. I came back to the tent and took a nap.

After supper we went to the show in town. We had a couple of ice creams and came back on the 11 o'clock truck.

## August 13, 1945
Camp White Tie, Brussels, Belgium

Everyone got up this morning so I did, too as we are supposed to. I ate breakfast for the first time in this area. I planned to go to Chanor Base Section and Finance. I learned that someone was already there, checking on our orders. I called Finance and learned that the men would be paid tomorrow. In the meantime Lieutenant Young came back from Chanor Base Section and said that my name was the only one on the order. I have to be at the 16 Reinforcement Depot, Compiegne, France, on the 17t[h]. The rest of the gang is humming mad. We are going after dinner to see about the rest of the order. The Officers are talking mad and pacing the floor.

Sheidy and I went to town after dinner. We went to the Red Cross and shaved. We then went to Chanor Base Section. The captain gave us a song and dance about the quota. He said all would not go this time. We went to the Post Exchange and then came back. I hung around the tent. I tried two or three times to get my orders but they are not in yet. I hung around in the evening getting things ready.

## August 14, 1945

Camp White Tie, Brussels, Belgium

I got up about 9 a.m., had coffee, then went into Finance and picked up the enlisted men's pay roll. I got back, ate, and then gave the Battery Commanders the money for their men. I hung around in the afternoon.

We went to town after supper. Most of the men are headed in with their money. We took in a show, ate at the Canadian Officers Club, and came home on the 11 o'clock run.

## August 15, 1945

Camp White Tie, Brussels, Belgium

I got up about 9 a.m., had coffee, and then went to the office tent. I want to go to Paris in the worst way, prior to reporting to the Reinforcement Depot.

I took all the completed payrolls and went with Herb Sheidy to town at 2 o'clock. I turned in the payrolls at Finance. We then went to the Red Cross and took a bath. We ate at the Navy, Army, and Air Force Institutes (NAFFI) Allied Officers Club. I went with one of the Officers to see his girlfriend. We sat in the room for about an hour. I left by myself, as three is a crowd. She is some character; she must be a dope addict as her arm is full of marks from a needle.

I came back to the center of town and to the American Officers Club. I didn't stay here but went down to the railroad station. I came back on the 11 o'clock truck. I got my things gathered together as I take off for Paris tomorrow. I will be eternally grateful to Colonel Boebel and Sergeant Burdick for consummating this arrangement. The compassion of the colonel, knowing that in almost three years overseas, mostly in combat zones, I only was authorized three days of official leave. Then there was Sergeant Burdick's drafting of the official order authorizing it, which the colonel said would permit me to travel anywhere. I got my things gathered together as I take off for Paris tomorrow.

**August 16, 1945**

Camp White Tie, Brussels, Belgium

The alarm went off at 6:50 a.m. and I got up about 7 a.m. I awoke the first sergeant to drive me and we ate breakfast. I got my things together and found out that the first sergeant isn't going, so he got two other men instead. It delayed me almost two hours.

I said goodbye and took off. The roads are rough. We changed our money at Finance in town. We traveled right along to Halle, Mons, and into France to Saint-Quentin. We ate dinner here at the transient mess. It was raining a bit. We hustled on to Compiegne.

We got to the Paris outskirts about 3:30 p.m. I can see the Eifel Tower in the distance. We traveled all over Paris looking for the Opera and Seine Base Section. We finally found them. I got a room at the Hotel Splendid Lafayette, recommended to me by the Base Section.

I walked to the mess building at Place Saint-Augustin. I took the Metro, Underground, to Montmartre. I then went to the Eiffel Tower and walked under it, looking at the airplane exhibition there. I walked up the other way and looked back down at it all lighted up. It was pretty. I walked to the Champs Elysees and the Arc de Triomphe. I took the Metro back to Saint-Augustin and came back to the Red Cross Club at the Opera House area and had coffee. I then came back to my Hotel, had a glass of wine, talked with the people, and then went to my room.

**August 17, 1945**

Paris, France

I got up at 7:50 a.m., washed, and dressed. I went to the American Red Cross Club and had coffee. I then took a tour of the city. We saw the Louvre Palace, Arc de Triomphe, Eiffel Tower, Cathedral of Notre Dame, Sacred Heart or Sacre-Coeur, Invalides or Napoleon's Tomb, Pantheon, and Sorbonne University. We stopped and took pictures. We had the various sights pointed out and explained to us as we went. I really enjoyed it.

We got back about 12 noon. I took the Metro to Saint-Augustin and ate. I came back to the Opera House and walked to the Hotel. I met the driver there. We took off and gave a lift to a couple of men. We made Compiegne in about an hour. We gassed up and then went to the 16th Reinforcement Depot. I reported in and had an orientation speech. I located the rest of the boys and my stuff was there. I set myself up and rested until supper. After eating we saw the picture here, and then came back to our quarters. We had coffee at the Dugout here. We all went to bed early.

August 17, 1945. Me and the Eiffel Tower.

## August 18, 1945
Compiegne, France

I was one of the last to get up. I had breakfast and came back to the area. I cleaned up and arranged my things. I fooled around the ball field and wrote. I hung around all afternoon. I slept most of the time.

In the evening, after supper, we took in the show. We all went to bed early.

## August 19, 1945
Compiegne, France

I got up for breakfast and then wrote two letters afterwards. I went to the 9:30 a.m. Mass at the Chapel Building. We, most of our gang, i.e., 9th Division Officers plus our roommates, played the 82nd Airborne enlisted men in a game of softball. The umpire was one of their men. We won the game, mainly due to the umpire. After the game, one of the 82nd guys took his pants off. At this point my little bit of professional baseball experience seems long gone.

After dinner we hung around resting.

After supper we walked down town and there is nothing there. We sat in a café, where a little boy and girl, about 11 and eight years old were playing the accordions as entertainment. We went to another place, had some ice cream, and then walked back. We turned in early.

**August 20, 1945**
Compiegne, France

I got up last and had a late breakfast. There was a colonel here from the 3$^{rd}$ Division who was wearing the Congressional Medal of Honor.

After dinner we got the call to go to the Holding Company. We sent our equipment out at 1:30 p.m. We are to go at 3 p.m. A gang of enlisted men came in, formerly from the 9$^{th}$ Division Artillery. I met one of our gang, Tony Wisniewski, and some others. We, the Officers, left at 3 p.m. and went to the 88$^{th}$ Battalion, 219$^{th}$ Company. We set up in squad tents.

After supper we watched a baseball game, had coffee and doughnuts, and came back and went to bed.

**August 21, 1945**
Compiegne, France

It was raining all morning, so I stayed in bed until Captain Birum awoke me for dinner. I ate dinner and hung around for a while then walked up town and toured around. I went into Napoleon's Palace. It contained a rather large collection of transportation items such as coaches and bicycles. The rooms were rather beaten up, but pretty. Many things such as paintings and chandeliers have been removed for safety during the war, and

Compiegne, France. Embarking on trains for Le Havre, France.

not yet returned. We walked up town and then came back to camp.

After supper we went over and got some ice cream. I came back as I am duty officer tonight. I hung around the area.

## August 22, 1945
Compiegne, France

I got up about 6 a.m., ate breakfast, and then came back to the tent. I straightened things out. Herb Sheidy and I borrowed bicycles from the Cadre and took our laundry down to the laundry.

After dinner we saw a show at the grandstand. In the evening we watched a baseball game at the diamond.

## August 23, 1945
Compiegne, France

I got up about 10:30 a.m. I saw where the railroad car used to be, the one where the Germans signed the World War I surrender papers. Hitler used the same railroad car and had the French sign the surrender papers in 1940, and then had the car destroyed.

I hung around the rest of the afternoon and evening, just going for ice cream and cokes. I had 12 scoops of ice cream during the day. We had coffee and doughnuts at the Red Cross in the evening.

## August 24, 1945
Compiegne, France

I got up at 10:30 a.m. and waited until dinner to eat. Actually I hung around all day.

In the evening we got ice cream and cokes. Our orders finally came out. We are going to La Havre.

## August 25, 1945

Compiegne, France

I got up about 8 a .m. and got ready to go to Reims to the Post Exchange. It is a long ride; we left at 9 a.m. and got there a little after 11 a.m. I didn't buy anything. We went to town and ate at the transient mess. It was good.

We walked around town and it is fairly nice. We visited the famous Cathedral and it sure is huge. It is reputed to be the world's largest. There is a famous statue of Joan of Arc out front.

Reims Cathedral, France.

We walked around the stores. We got haircuts, shaves, and a shampoo for 80 francs, or $1.60. We went to the Red Cross and there are quite a few nurses around, as they are being redeployed. There was music, cokes, coffee, and paper. Also there are places to write letters.

We ate supper at the transient mess and then caught the truck back at 7 p.m. It was a rough, speedy, ride back. We came through Soissons again. We were here chasing Jerry a few months ago. There was a couple of 1918 cemeteries here, also a monument to the 4th Division (1918). We had coffee and doughnuts and then went to bed.

## August 26, 1945

Compiegne, France

I got up at 10 a.m. and went to Mass, in the grandstand. I hung around until dinner.

We went to a show in the afternoon at the grandstand. It was a local show and was terrible.

After supper we walked over for ice cream, cake, coffee, and doughnuts. We all went to bed early.

## August 27, 1945
Compiegne, France

I got up about 10 a.m. and got a lot of my stuff packed. It is very hot and after dinner we hung around. I took a shower.

After supper we played the enlisted men in two games of softball and beat them in both. We went for ice cream and then came back to the tent, cleaned up, and went to bed. We are to move out tomorrow to La Havre.

## August 28, 1945
Compiegne, France

The gang, yelling and threatening, awakened me. Two of them dumped me out on the ground. I got up a little later and gathered a few things together. I went down and had coffee and doughnuts.

We had a meeting at 10:30 a.m. where we got some information and our 66-1 forms. We got our equipment ready, ate dinner, and then put our stuff outside to be picked up. I wrote for a while, waiting for the time to leave.

We left by truck about 3 p.m. It is hot out as we rode to the train. We have a coach for our group. Our group is two colonels, two majors, two captains, two first lieutenants, and me. The men walked down, it is very hot, and they are all wet with sweat. I sat with the colonels and majors. We pulled out on schedule and were off about 5:30 p.m. We are apparently going in a circle. We passed through Noyon and stopped at a transient mess.

About 9 p.m. we had a hot meal. We rode all night and I didn't get any sleep, as I had to sit up. I dozed from time to time. The seats are wood and hard. We had a breakfast stop at 3:30 a.m. We passed through Amiens and arrived in La Havre at 9 a.m. It is raining and we walked to the trucks and semi-trailers. We rode to Camp Wings. It is a fair camp and we will sleep in pyramidal tents. I washed up and made out the morning report. The day was spent assigning jobs. I got my baggage and

340

went to sleep before it got dark.

## August 29, 1945
Camp Wing, La Havre, France

I got up about 9:30 a.m. and turned in the morning report and did a few other odd jobs. I bought my Post Exchange things.

The colonel of one of the units nailed me to collect all the morning reports. I helped him arrange forms for a meeting at 1300 hours. I made out an Officer's voucher to collect 850 francs ($17.15), gratuity pay from the French Government to compensate for inflation. It will be for all soldiers. In the evening I helped them count money and then went to bed early.

## August 30, 1945
Camp Wing, La Havre, France

I got up at 9 a.m. and made out the morning report. I cleaned up and did a few odd jobs. I talked with the fellows. It looks like we may get a chance to go home soon, as they froze the Category 11 units here. There was a meeting in the afternoon. I went to bed early in the evening.

## August 31, 1945
Camp Wing, La Havre, France

I got up about 8:30 a.m., washed up, and took the morning report to the Orderly Room. I am supposed to collect them all. There wasn't anyone around so I went to the S-1. I checked up on two delinquent ones and finally rounded them together.

I attempted to take a bath a couple of times, but it was too crowded. I hung around in the morning.

In the afternoon I watched a ballgame and then took a walk to the beach, about 500 yards away. We sat on the 200-foot cliff and watched the boats, fortifications, and sea. It would have been suicide to attempt a landing here at La Havre. The cliffs are sheer and covered with pillboxes, gun emplacements, and coastal guns. We came back to the airfield.

After supper I played a game of volleyball and then a game of softball. I went to bed early.

# Chapter sixteen: September 1945

September 1, 1945 to September 14, 1945

France, Aboard Ship, and Home

All above photos are of the ship, Costa Rica Victory, en route home to US.

General Overview

The enormous task of returning U.S. troops home continues.

September 2, 1945, the war is officially over in Japan. Known as V-J Day, Victory over Japan.

***

**September 1, 1945**

Camp Wing, Le Havre, France

I didn't get up for breakfast but got up about 7:30 a.m. and took a shower. I rounded up the morning reports, which depended upon the Public Address system to get the last two. I hung around in the morning. I watched the various sports being played and the airplanes. I talked with various people. I washed my soiled clothes and rested.

After supper I went to the show and then went to bed.

*September 2, 1945*

Camp Wing, Le Havre, France

I got up about 7:30 a.m. and had breakfast. I rounded together as many of the morning reports as I could. There were about six missing at the appointed hour. I checked some more, and found four. I left the remaining two up to the Public Address system.

It is Sunday. I went to Mass in the double squad tent at 11 a.m.

We got corned beef for Sunday dinner, as they ran out of chicken. After dinner I watched the men play ball, watched the airplanes, did a few odds and ends, and rested.

After supper I went to the show, talked with people, and took a short walk toward the beach. I went to bed early.

**September 3, 1945**

Camp Wing, Le Havre, France

I got up at 7:30 a.m. and ate breakfast. Afterwards I sat in the colonel's tent and collected morning reports. I rounded up a table and two chairs for the tent. I had a Jerry soldier, a prisoner, carry the stuff and arrange it.

I hung around until dinner. In the afternoon I rested and then did a little typing for the colonel. It rained in the late afternoon.

### September 4, 1945
Camp Wing, Le Havre, France

I got up for breakfast. They had fresh eggs flown in from Denmark. I hung around the tent most of the day. I got my personal things sorted out and arranged.

I read all evening in the reading room.

### September 5, 1945
Camp Wing, Le Havre, France

I got up for breakfast and they had fresh bananas no less. They must be flying them in from Spain or someplace further south.

I rounded up the morning reports and then rested for a while. I washed a few things. I watched a German helicopter come in. The British are taking it to England for examination. I hung around all afternoon and did some reading. We heard what we have been waiting for, for years. We are to board the Victory ship Costa Rica tomorrow and head for the States. We had a few meetings.

In the evening I hung around.

### September 6, 1945
Camp Wing, La Havre, France

I didn't sleep well at all and the rest didn't either. We actually were chilly even with blankets. After breakfast we all got our things together. We hung around waiting.

We ate dinner at 1000 hours, gathered up our stuff, and joined our respective groups. It had been drizzling all morning. Our group was the first on the trucks. We loaded on semi-trailers; there were 60 of us with our equipment. The fellows on the trucks, as they went along, yelled at the girls and Military Police, as all are happy. We passed pillboxes and cement fortifications, they are all over the beaches, docks, and hillsides. The dock area is leveled of buildings.

We saw our ship, the Costa Rica Victory, and it looks fairly large. The Santa Rosa, sister ship of the Santa Paula, is behind it. We had been on the Santa Paula, a former Grace Liner, from Sicily to England.

We were given coffee and doughnuts and we were the first group to go aboard. The fellows from the 16th Reinforcement Depot are already on as they came from another camp. All the lieutenants and warrant officers are in the forward hold. I got a top bunk and we then watched others come aboard, even some from the Air Corps. The Air Corps were overloaded with equipment and liquor. The G.I.s kidded them. Some fell down and got a big cheer.

The Officers have a card game going already. I took a shower and shaved. There are about 225 Officers in this forward hold. We waited quite some time for supper but it was worth the wait. I came back to my bunk, read, wrote, and then retired.

### September 7, 1945
Aboard Ship Costa Rica Victory
En route to the U.S.

I awoke after a good night's sleep. It was warm sleeping. We had breakfast at 8:10 a.m. The food was good.

We all were on deck. The ship finally left the dock at 9:30 a.m. We pulled out into the stream. They opened the lock ahead and we steamed out about 10 o'clock. La Havre soon faded from view. There wasn't anything to be seen. We are traveling right along. It is a great day.

I retired early in the evening.

### September 8, 1945
Aboard Ship Costa Rica Victory

En route to the U.S.

I had a good night's sleep and got up early for breakfast. It was a wonderful day out. The water was a pretty blue. I took in the sun and read and talked. We passed a couple of ships. We are making good time. I went to bed early.

## September 9, 1945

Aboard Ship Costa Rica Victory
En route to the U.S.

I slept well and got up for breakfast. It is a little rough out and the weather is poor.

After breakfast I went up on deck for a while. It was rough and sprinkling. I came back to the hold and slept.

I didn't get up for the usual noonday snack. I am feeling the weather.

I didn't get up for supper and I am now getting sick, no less. It is terribly rough now and many are sick. The huge waves hit the hull with a resounding smash. The prow seems to raise 15 feet and then fall with a thud. This is too much for my stomach. I rose up, grabbed a towel, and started for the head. I threw up at the foot of the ladder. I went to the latrine and threw up some more, even threw up some blood. I noticed many lying all around, sick. I came back to the hold for a while, as I feel better after throwing up. I got sick again. This time I took a blanket and went to the point that I figured was the center of the ship. I figured there would be less pitch fore and aft and sideways. I spread the blanket on the corridor and lied down with the rest of the guys. It was hard to find any space as all you could see were bodies lying on the floor. I feel better.

## September 10, 1945

Aboard Ship Costa Rica Victory
En route to the U.S.

I got out of the aisle and made my way back to the hold. I feel good after a good night's sleep. I ate breakfast and there weren't many there.

I went on deck and there aren't many there either. Most of the people are still sick. It is still rough and stormy. I stayed on deck all day. There are birds flying around. I went to bed early in my regular place, the forward hold.

## September 11, 1945
Aboard Ship Costa Rica Victory
En route to the U.S.

I got up for breakfast. I had slept in my clothes last night. I was afraid it might get rough and I would have to hustle to the latrine.

It was a little rough during the day. Later it began to get foggy and the water calmed down. The sick began to appear. The four-stacker Aquitania passed us about 8 p.m. I turned in early.

## September 12, 1945
Aboard Ship Costa Rica Victory
En route to the U.S.

I got up for breakfast. I stayed on deck all day. Most of the sick came out today, as it is fairly calm and clearing. The sun broke through about 1 pm and it turned into a great day. The crapshooters and card players have been busy during the whole trip.

## September 13, 1945
Aboard Ship Costa Rica Victory
En route to the U.S.

I got up early and had breakfast.

I went on deck. It was raining but fairly smooth. Soon the sun came out and it turned into a great day. We ran in and out of fog banks. We land tomorrow. I read and talked all day. More than one person told me that they never want to set their foot on another ship for the rest of their life. I wrote and read in the evening.

348

**September 14, 1945**
Aboard Ship Costa Rica Victory
En route to the U.S

Eighth and last day at sea.

I got up early, shaved, and then ate. I got all my things ready, so I could be on deck and watch the arrival. We will dock in Boston.

We saw fishermen. It is a bit hazy and we just coasted along. The water is as placid as a pond. Everyone is on deck. I stood on the prow and we could see the fins of sharks. Then we saw some whales, they sure are huge. We saw more fishermen. They blew their whistle and waved. The fellows have climbed up and are all over the rigging.

About 12:30 p.m. we saw the dim outline of land, what a thrill after three years. We could see some boats as we neared it. The lands we can see are the islands in Boston Harbor. I recognized some. I could see Great Hill, Houghs Neck, in the distance, and could almost see our house. I was hanging from the rail on the sun deck. The boats all around us blew whistles, as well as did our ship. It was a thrill.

A tug, with a band and Woman's Army Corp (WACs) aboard, came along side. The band was playing and everybody was yelling and waving. We came in to the Army Base at Commonwealth Pier. The workers all lined the dock. The soldiers lined the rail, shouting and throwing coins. There was a band playing, WACs, and newspapermen. What a thrill, I almost felt like crying.

Our group was the first ones off and I fell on the gangplank and got a big round of cheers and yells. The reporters crowded around and were taking names. A little later we were given a little snack and milk.

We took a troop train to Camp Myles Standish, Taunton, Massachusetts. I just stood at the open door watching the sights. The regular trains all blew their whistles at us.

After we arrived we were oriented and billeted. I took a bath, called home, and retired.

## Maps by Tom Holihan

## References for Historical Overview

Atkinson, R. (2002). *An Army at Dawn: The War in North Africa, 1942-1943.* New York, NY: Henry Holt and Company.

Atkinson, R. (2007). *The Day of Battle: The War in Sicily and Italy, 1943-1944.* New York, NY: Henry Holt and Company.

Atkinson, R. (2013). *The Guns at Last Light: The War in Western Europe, 1944-1945.* New York, NY: Henry Holt and Company.

Baldridge, R., C. (1995). *Victory Road: The World War ll Memoir of an Artilleryman in the ETO.* Bennington, VT: Mirriam Press.

Hopkinson, E. (1998). *Memoirs of a Civilian/Soldier in World War ll.* Chapel Hill, NC: Professional Press.

Lavender, D., E. (2008). *Nudge Blue: A Rifleman's Chronicle of World War ll.* Bennington, VT: Mirriam Press.

Mittelman, J., B. (1948). *Eight Stars to Victory: A History of the Veteran Ninth U.S. Infantry Division.* Washington D. C. The Ninth Infantry Division Association.

9th Infantry Division (United States). In *Wikipedia.* Retrieved February 1, 2107, from https://en.wikipedia.org/wiki/9th_Infantry_Division_(United_States).

| SURNAME | 1st NAME | RANK | COMPANY | HOME TOWN |
|---|---|---|---|---|
| Adams | Clinton | Colonel | 60th FA | Montgomery, AL |
| Dates mentioned in diary: 7/31/44, 8/3/44, 9/20/44,10/2/44, 11/26/44, 1/7/45 | | | | |
| Alexander | Edgar | Captain | 666th FA | Lawrence, MA |
| Dates mentioned in diary: 7/12/45, 7/18/45 | | | | |
| Anderson | ? William or Ernest | Pfc | 60th FA-HQ | |
| Dates mentioned in diary: 2/6/45 | | | | |
| Appelgate | | Captain | | |
| Dates mentioned in diary: 9/5/45 | | | | |
| Bain | | Captain | | |
| Dates mentioned in diary: 4/12/45 | | | | |
| Barhight | Clifford W | Corporal | 60th FA | |
| Dates mentioned in diary: 6/23/44 | | | | |
| Barton | | Colonel | | |
| Dates mentioned in diary: 6/13/45 | | | | |
| Barszewski | Sigmond R "Barzy" | Corporal/ T3 | Medical Detach-ment | Northampton, MA |
| Dates mentioned in diary: 6/22/45 | | | | |
| Baxt | | | | |
| Dates mentioned in diary: 7/27/45, 7/28/45 | | | | |
| Beets | Walter O | Major/ Colonel | 60th FA | |
| Dates mentioned in diary: 8/7/44, 8/10/44, 8/18/44, 8/23/44, 10/1/44, 11/17/44, 11/18/44, 11/20/44, 11/28/44, 4/2/45, 5/3/45, 6/7/45, 6/13/45 | | | | |
| Bennett | Harold J | Pfc | 60th FA-HQ | |
| Dates mentioned in diary: 6/18/44, 6/10/45 | | | | |
| Bergman | | Captain | Vll Corp | Braintree, MA |
| Dates mentioned in diary: 11/2/44, 12/15/44 | | | | |
| Beston | Harold | | | Hough's Neck, Quincy, MA |
| Dates mentioned in diary: 8/12/44 | | | | |
| Bezold | Paul | 2nd Lt | 60th FA-Btry B | |
| Dates mentioned in diary: 8/15/44 | | | | |
| Birum | Leon R | Captain | 666th FA | |
| Dates mentioned in diary: 8/21/45 | | | | |
| Bloom | Clarence T | Lt | 60th FA-Btry A | |
| Dates mentioned in diary: 1/9/45 | | | | |
| Boebel | Earl F | Colonel | 666th FA | |

| Dates mentioned in diary: 1/12/45, 7/15/45, 7/23/45, 8/15/45 | | | | |
|---|---|---|---|---|
| Bonura | Joseph | Pvt | | |
| Dates mentioned in diary: 6/19/44 | | | | |
| Bothsford | Everett E | | 60th FA | |
| Dates mentioned in diary: 7/16/44 | | | | |
| Brightman | George H | Sgt | 60rh FA-<br>Air Ops | New Bedford,<br>MA |
| Dates mentioned in diary: 2/12/45 | | | | |
| Brock | Elmer | Corporal | Service<br>Btry | SC |
| Dates mentioned in diary: 9/7/44, 4/2/45 | | | | |
| Brown | Milton | Lt | Air OP/<br>Pilot | Los Angelos, CA |
| Dates mentioned in diary: 9/23/44, 1/21/45 | | | | |
| Brown | | | | |
| Dates mentioned in diary: 11/25/44 | | | | |
| Brown | ?John T | Captain | 60th FA-<br>Btry B | |
| Dates mentioned in diary: 4/21/45, 5/31/45, 6/21/45, 7/6/45 | | | | |
| Brush | Alfred P | T Sgt | Service<br>Btry | |
| Dates mentioned in diary: 4/10/45 | | | | |
| Bryant | | | 60th FA–<br>Service<br>Btry | |
| Dates mentioned in diary: 3/5/45 | | | | |
| Burdick | | Sgt | | |
| Dates mentioned in diary: 7/27/45 | | | | |
| Burns | | Lt | | Boston, MA |
| Dates mentioned in diary: 6/24/45 | | | | |
| Burns | Sandy | Sgt/ Lt | 60th FA -<br>Motor O/ HQ | |
| Dates mentioned in diary: 10/11/44, 11/17/44 | | | | |
| Burrows | Roy W | Sgt | Service<br>Btry | |
| Dates mentioned in diary: 6/23/44, 6/27/44, 8/25/44, 12/17/44, 12/21/44, 1/7/45,<br>1/8/45 | | | | |
| Cable | Lionel | Sgt/Lt | 60th FA–<br>Btry C | |
| Dates mentioned in diary: 4/24/45 | | | | |
| Cambell | ? Worth G | Sgt | 60th FA–<br>? Btry C - | |

352

| | | | ? Service Btry | |
|---|---|---|---|---|
| Dates mentioned in diary: 9/17/44 | | | | |
| Carter | | | | MA |
| Dates mentioned in diary: 1/2/45, 2/6/45, 3/12/45 | | | | |
| Carter | Robert | Pvt | | |
| Dates mentioned in diary: 1/2/45, 2/6/45 | | | | |
| Carter | | Mail Clerk | | |
| Dates mentioned in diary: 6/19/44 | | | | |
| Caton | | Pvt | | |
| Dates mentioned in diary: 6/29/44, 7,1/44 | | | | |
| Chase | Elvis E | Pvt | 60th FA– Btry C | |
| Dates mentioned in diary: 12/13/44 | | | | |
| Childs | Edwin O Jr | Corporal/ T5 | Battalion Supply Section | |
| Dates mentioned in diary: 10/28/44, 1/16/45, 2/20/45, 2/23/45 | | | | |
| Clark | | T5 | | |
| Dates mentioned in diary: 5/9/45 | | | | |
| Clayton | Roy | Sgt | 60th FA– Btry C | |
| Dates mentioned in diary: 6/21/44 | | | | |
| Cohen | Isreal | Pfc/Sgt | 60th FA – B | |
| Dates mentioned in diary: 2/27/45, 4/9/45, 5/11/45 | | | | |
| Cole | ?Welsley Dates mentioned in diary: E - "Shorty" | Lt | 60th FA– B | |
| Dates mentioned in diary: 12/21/44, 6/23/45 | | | | |
| Collins | "Nubby" | | | |
| Dates mentioned in diary: 1/27/45, 1/28/45 | | | | |
| Collins | Tom | | | Lawrence, MA |
| Dates mentioned in diary: 2/15/45, 4/13/45 | | | | |
| Cominsky | | Lt | 15th Engineers | |
| Dates mentioned in diary: 2/14/45 | | | | |
| Connors | | Chaplain | | Worchester, MA |
| Dates mentioned in diary: 6/24/44, 7/2/44, 7/13/44, 8/6/44, 9/24/44, 10/1/44, 10/29/44, 11/19/44, 12/1/44, 1/5/45, 2/11/45, 2/14/45, 2/15/45, 2/26/45, 3/5/45, 3/10/45, 4/6/45, 4/25/45, 7/29/45 | | | | |

| Copelman | Hyman | Captain-Doctor | | |
|---|---|---|---|---|
| Dates mentioned in diary: 11/26/44, 11/28/44, 3/18/45 | | | | |
| Corbitt | Noah | Pvt | | |
| Dates mentioned in diary: 6/23/45 | | | | |
| Crabbe | Truman G | Sgt/2nd Lt | 60th FA-Btry C | |
| Dates mentioned in diary: 10/12/44, 10/13/44, 10/23/44, 7/31/44, 8/12/44, 3/12/45, 6/6/45, 6/24/45, 7/10/45, 7/11/45, 8/11/45 | | | | |
| Craig | | Major General | | |
| Dates mentioned in diary: 11/1/44, 1/16/45, 2/15/45, 8/19/45, 6/25/45 | | | | |
| Crandall | Vernie | Captain | 60th FA - Service Btry | Cathage, MO |
| Dates mentioned in diary: 2/17/45 | | | | |
| Dalrymple | Gordon S | Sgt | 60th FA-HQ | |
| Dates mentioned in diary: 10/14/44, 2/21/45 | | | | |
| Delaney | Harold K | Pvc/Corporal | 60th FA-HQ | |
| Dates mentioned in diary: 7/16/44, 7/31/44 | | | | |
| Delli Priscolli | Thomas J | Corporal | 60th FA-HQ | Springfield, MA |
| Dates mentioned in diary: Multiple entries | | | | |
| DeNaro | | | | |
| Dates mentioned in diary: 5/11/45 | | | | |
| DeRosa | Savino | T4 | 60th FA-Servive Btry | |
| Dates mentioned in diary: 4/19/45, 7/5/45 | | | | |
| Devine | Joe | | Vll Corp | |
| Dates mentioned in diary: 10/4/44, 11/2,44, 12/15/44, 1/17/45, 4/29/45 | | | | |
| Dewbury | | | | |
| Dates mentioned in diary: 11/19/44 | | | | |
| Dewey | Richard L | Major | 666th FA | |
| Dates mentioned in diary: 8/6/45 | | | | |
| Dixon | | | | |
| Dates mentioned in diary: 10/22/44 | | | | |
| Dougan | Archie | | 60th FA-Btry C | |
| Dates mentioned in diary: Multiple entries | | | | |
| Dougher | Paul | Sgt/Corporal/2nd Lt | 60th FA-Btry B | |

| | | | | |
|---|---|---|---|---|
| Dates mentioned in diary: 9/11/44, 9/12/44, 9/18/44, 3/1/45, 6/15/45 | | | | |
| Draft | | Lt | | |
| Dates mentioned in diary: 8/17/45 | | | | |
| Duncan | | Lt | Div Arty | |
| Dates mentioned in diary: 7/16/45 | | | | |
| Eddy | Manton | Major General | 9th Division | |
| Dates mentioned in diary: 8/19/44 | | | | |
| Edmonds | James | Lt/ Captain | 60th FA-S-2 | NY, NY- (official record – Ottawa, Canada) |
| Dates mentioned in diary: 2/15/45 | | | | |
| Eisenhower | | | | |
| Dates mentioned in diary: 6/12/44 | | | | |
| Eisenstein | | | | Baltimore, MD |
| Dates mentioned in diary: 7/23/44, 4/2/45 | | | | |
| Elliot | Glen F | | | Lincoln, NB |
| Dates mentioned in diary: Multiple entries | | | | |
| ? Emery or Embry | | | | |
| Dates mentioned in diary: 8/9/44, 1/7/45, 1/8/45 | | | | |
| Evans | | | | |
| Dates mentioned in diary: 11/4/44 | | | | |
| Fabre | | | | Brooklyn, NY |
| Dates mentioned in diary: 1/7/45, 1/14/45, 1/15/45, 1/29/45, 1/30/45, 3/16/45 | | | | |
| Fedelli | | | | |
| Dates mentioned in diary: 5/11/45 | | | | |
| Ferguson | | | | Texas |
| Dates mentioned in diary: 6/22/44, 2/17/45, 2/1/45 | | | | |
| Fisher | Paul A | Major | 666th FA | |
| Dates mentioned in diary: 7/24/45, 7/26/45, 7/27/45, 8/11/45 | | | | |
| Fitchman | | Captain/ Pilot | | |
| Dates mentioned in diary: 2/6/45 | | | | |
| Fleckenstein | Robert V | Captain | 9th Division & 666th FA | |
| Dates mentioned in diary: 8/11/45 | | | | |

| Flilpowicz | Joseph S | Pfc | 60th FA-Btry C | |
|---|---|---|---|---|
| Dates mentioned in diary: 8/17/44 | | | | |
| France | Douglas C | Captain | 60th FA-S-2 | Charlottsville, VA |
| Dates mentioned in diary: 1/29/45, 3/4/45 | | | | |
| Francisconi | | Lt | Ack Ack | |
| Dates mentioned in diary: 2/19/45 | | | | |
| Freeman | Lynn | Lt | | |
| Dates mentioned in diary: 7/14/44, 10/4/44, 10/31/44, 3/5/45, 5/1/45, 6/9/45, 6/18/545 | | | | |
| Freud | Windy - ? Edwin or Philip Joseph | | | |
| Dates mentioned in diary: 12/24/44, 1/28/45, 1/29/45, 1/30/45 | | | | |
| Froelicher | Florenz H | T5 | 60th FA- HQ | |
| Dates mentioned in diary: 6/12/44 | | | | |
| Gaffney | Thomas M | Lt | | Danvers, MA |
| Dates mentioned in diary: 6/7/44, 7/5/44, 8/11/44, 9/23/44, 1/9/45, 3/30/45, 3/31/45, 5/15/45, 6/22,45, 7/16/45 | | | | |
| Galfo | Noel D | Corporal | 60th FA-Btry C | Oak Ridge, NJ |
| Dates mentioned in diary: 6/12/44, 7/18/44, 9/12/44, 10/1/44, 12/15/44, 12/16/44, 2/6/45 | | | | |
| Garner | Wilber W | Sgt | 60th FA-First Ammunition Section | Virginia |
| Dates mentioned in diary: 3/8/44, 5/8/45, 5/24/45 | | | | |
| Garre | Peter | Lt/ Captain/ Doctor | Medical Corps | Amarillo, TX |
| Dates mentioned in diary: 10/24/44, 11/2/44 | | | | |
| Garrison | ? Earl | T5 | 60th FA-Service Btry | |
| Dates mentioned in diary: 5/9/45 | | | | |
| Gasic | | | 87th FA | |
| Dates mentioned in diary: 8/15/44 | | | | |
| Gelders | Henri A | T4 | 60th FA-Service Btry | |
| Dates mentioned in diary: 11/9/44, 4/25/45 | | | | |

356

| Gill | | | | |
|------|------|------|------|------|
| Dates mentioned in diary: 6/4/45 | | | | |
| Gleason | James P | Pfc | 60th FA - HQ | |
| Dates mentioned in diary: 2/6/45 | | | | |
| Goins | D V | T5 | | |
| Dates mentioned in diary: 7/25/45 | | | | |
| Gomes | | | | Cape Cod |
| Dates mentioned in diary: 5/11/45 | | | | |
| Gonzales | | Pvt | | |
| Dates mentioned in diary: 6/24/44 | | | | |
| Goodman | Hugh G | Pvt | 60th FA- HQ | |
| Dates mentioned in diary: 2/6/45 | | | | |
| Gordon | ?Thomas D | Sgt | 60th FA– Btry A | |
| Dates mentioned in diary: 3/12/45 | | | | |
| Graham | ? Raymond | Lt/Doctor | | |
| Dates mentioned in diary: 11/15/44, 1/29/45, 3/29/45, 4/20/45 | | | | |
| Gray | Lewis H | Captain | 60th FA- HQ | |
| Dates mentioned in diary: 6/7/44, 8/3/44, 9/21/44,10/20/44, 1/20/45, 2/23/45, 2/28/45, 4/11/45, 6/9/45, 7/29/45 | | | | |
| Griffith | | Pvc | Btry A | |
| Dates mentioned in diary: 7/25/44, 7/26/44 | | | | |
| Guanciale | Bernie | Sgt | 60th FA- HQ | PN |
| Dates mentioned in diary: 1/22/45, 2/25/45 | | | | |
| Gunter | George | | Btry | |
| Dates mentioned in diary: 6/11/45 | | | | |
| Hall | Thomas | Lt/Pilot | 60th FA- HQ | Rosewell, NM |
| Dates mentioned in diary: 8/11/44, 10/14/44, 2/15/45 | | | | |
| Hall | | Lt | 9th Signal Corps | |
| Dates mentioned in diary: 6/7/44 | | | | |
| Hamburger | Charles W | Corporal/ T4 | 60th FA- Btry B | |
| Dates mentioned in diary: 7/4/44, 7/20/44, 7/31/44 | | | | |
| Hamilton | Maurice W | 2nd Lt | 60th FA– Btry A | Wilmington, NC |
| Dates mentioned in diary: 9/23/44 | | | | |

| Hammer | Harry L | Corporal | 60th FA-Btry B | |
|---|---|---|---|---|
| Dates mentioned in diary: Multiple entries | | | | |
| Hardy | James I | Pvt | 60th FA-HQ | |
| Dates mentioned in diary: 9/1/44, 9/2/44 | | | | |
| Hargy | | Colonel | Finance | |
| Dates mentioned in diary: 2/2/8/45,3/7/45, 4/2/45 | | | | |
| Hartley | Raymond H | T4 | 60th FA– Service Btry | SC |
| Dates mentioned in diary: 3/4/45 | | | | |
| Healy – or Healey | Theodore | Sgt/Lt/ Captain | 60th FA– HQ & Btry A | Newburg, NY |
| Dates mentioned in diary: 2/13/45, 2/17/45, 3/10/45, 3/11/45, 5/15/45 | | | | |
| Hefter | Howard J | Pvt | 60th FA-HQ | |
| Dates mentioned in diary: 10/2/44 | | | | |
| Hickey | | Pvt | | |
| Dates mentioned in diary: 11/24/44 | | | | |
| Hines | | | | |
| Dates mentioned in diary: 7/31/44 | | | | |
| Hochdoerfer | Rex A | Major | 60th FA | Cleveland, OK |
| Dates mentioned in diary: 8/3/44, 8/4/44, 102/44 | | | | |
| Hopkinson | Alfred E or Edward | Lt | 60th FA– Btry A | |
| Dates mentioned in diary: 7/29/45 | | | | |
| Horton | James | | 60th FA– Service Btry | |
| Dates mentioned in diary: 9/25/45 | | | | |
| Householder | Robert A | T5 | 60th FA– Btyr C | |
| Dates mentioned in diary: 8/17/44 | | | | |
| Howel | | General | | |
| Dates mentioned in diary: 2/15/45, 4/20/45, 5/15/45, 6/29/45, 6/30/45, 7/2/45 | | | | |
| Humphries | Roscoe E | Corporal | HQ | |
| Dates mentioned in diary: 7/13/44 | | | | |
| Hyland | John C | T5 | Medical Detach-ment | |
| Dates mentioned in diary: 5/18/45, 5/19/45 | | | | |
| ?Jankowski or Jablonski | | Pfc | | |

| | | | | |
|---|---|---|---|---|
| Dates mentioned in diary: 4/5/45 | | | | |
| Jenkins | John C | Lt | 60th FA– Btry C | Savannah, GA |
| Dates mentioned in diary: 7/5/44, 7/31/44 | | | | |
| Jill | | Major | | |
| Dates mentioned in diary: 8/10/45 | | | | |
| Johns | | | Wire Section | |
| Dates mentioned in diary: 3/29/45 | | | | |
| Jones | ?James | Sgt | | |
| Dates mentioned in diary: 10/12/44, 8/17/44 | | | | |
| Kanousky | | | | |
| Dates mentioned in diary: 3/8/45 | | | | |
| Kelly | | Lt | | |
| Dates mentioned in diary: 6/23/44, 7/5/44, 7/8/44 | | | | |
| Kelly | | Major | | |
| Dates mentioned in diary: 7/24/45 | | | | |
| King | Joe | Corporal | | |
| Dates mentioned in diary: 8/7/44, 10/21/44, 3/8/45, 3/28/45 | | | | |
| Kraft | George | Lt | 60th FA – Btry C | |
| Dates mentioned in diary: 6/6/45, 6/16/45, 6/21/45, 7/3/45, 7/16/45 | | | | |
| Krunas | | Sgt | | |
| Dates mentioned in diary: 2/14/45 | | | | |
| Kunisto | | Lt | Ammunitions | |
| Dates mentioned in diary: 4/28/45, 6/30/45 | | | | |
| La Rock | | | 60th FA– Btry A | |
| Dates mentioned in diary: 6/13/44, 6/14/44 | | | | |
| LaMontagne | Fernand A | Sgt | 60th FA– Battalion Motors | NH |
| Dates mentioned in diary: 10/17/44 | | | | |
| Lawrence | Sonald K | Corporal | 60th FA– Btry C | |
| Dates mentioned in diary: 12/16/44, 2/19/45, 3/4/45, 3/13/45, 3/24/45, 6/18/45, 7/3/45 | | | | |
| Ledford | Clarence A | Lt | 60th FA– Btry A | TN |
| Dates mentioned in diary: 3/12/45 | | | | |
| Lemire | Alfred J | Lt | 60th FA– OP Pilot | CN |
| Dates mentioned in diary: 4/24/45 | | | | |

| Levine | | | | |
|---|---|---|---|---|
| Dates mentioned in diary: 6/4/45 | | | | |
| Leymarie | Louis | Pfc/T5 | 60th FA– Btry A | |
| Dates mentioned in diary: 7/31/44 | | | | |
| Lezon | Theodore J | Pfc/ Corporal | Medical Detach-ment | Ipswich, MA |
| Dates mentioned in diary: 1/25/45, 1/26/45 | | | | |
| Link | Harry W Jr | Lt | HQ Btry/ 60th FA- Btry C | IN |
| Dates mentioned in diary: 12/28/44, 2/1/45 | | | | |
| Linscott | Everett W | | 60th FA– Service Btry | Hingham, MA |
| Dates mentioned in diary: Multiple Entries | | | | |
| Lizon | Henry L | Pvt | | WV |
| Dates mentioned in diary: 6/23/44 | | | | |
| Loftin | Alford | Pvt | 60th FA– Btry C | LA |
| Dates mentioned in diary: 6/24/44 | | | | |
| Logan | | Sgt | | |
| Dates mentioned in diary: 5/22/45 | | | | |
| Lorenz | Orville A | Captain- Chaplain | | CA – (official record is Meyersdale, PA) |
| Dates mentioned in diary: 11/29/44, 12/13/44, 2/27/45, 3/23/45, 5/15/45, 6/7/45, 7/29/45 | | | | |
| Lovett | Thomas | Pvt | 60th FA– Btry C | |
| Dates mentioned in diary: 8/17/44 | | | | |
| Macri | Pat | Sgt | | Huntington, WV |
| Dates mentioned in diary: 6/12/44 | | | | |
| Magnum | | | | |
| Dates mentioned in diary: 12/14/44, 1/16/45 | | | | |
| Maher | Mike | | 34th FA | |
| Dates mentioned in diary: 4/26/45 | | | | |
| Markowitz | Jack L | T4 | 60th FA | TN |
| Dates mentioned in diary: Multiple entries | | | | |
| Marlof | | | | |
| Dates mentioned in diary: 6/21/45 | | | | |

| Marston | John F | Sgt | | Dorchester, MA |
|---------|--------|-----|---|---------------|
| Dates mentioned in diary: 2/6/45 | | | | |
| Materavitz | | Major | | |
| Dates mentioned in diary: 2/25/45 | | | | |
| Mathewson | | | 47th ID | |
| Dates mentioned in diary: 6/8/44 | | | | |
| McElhahatton | Howard D | Pfc | HQ | |
| Dates mentioned in diary: 6/12/44 | | | | |
| McFatter | | | 60th FA–Btry A | |
| Dates mentioned in diary: 3/12/45 | | | | |
| McFadyen | Oscar L Jr | Captain/Doctor | | |
| Dates mentioned in diary: 11/28/44, 11/29/44, 2/23/45, 2/28/45, 5/13/45, 6/18/45, 6/19/45 | | | | |
| McNair | | General | | |
| Dates mentioned in diary: 7/25/44, 7/27/44 | | | | |
| Monson | James R | Lt/Captain | 60th FA | NY, NY (official record-Fort Sill, OK) |
| Dates mentioned in diary: 11/18/44, 11/25/44 | | | | |
| Morrison | Carl L | Corporal | Message Center | MI |
| Dates mentioned in diary: 7/25/44, 9/2/44, 9/17/44, 11/6/44, 3/3/45 | | | | |
| Morrison | Carl F | Corporal | HQ | MI |
| Dates mentioned in diary: 3/12/45 | | | | |
| Moyers | | | 84th FA | College Park, MD |
| Dates mentioned in diary: 12/30/44, 3/7/45 | | | | |
| Murray | Frederick L | PFC | 60th FA–Btry C-HQ | |
| Dates mentioned in diary: Multiple entries | | | | |
| Myers | Mike | | | Northampton, MA |
| Dates mentioned in diary: 1/29/45 | | | | |
| Nagy | Charles J | T5/Corporal | 60th FA | NY |
| Dates mentioned in diary: Multiple entries | | | | |
| Nelson | Lindsay | Lt | | |
| Dates mentioned in diary: 5/11/45 | | | | |
| Neuhardt | George E "Bebe" | T5 | 60th FA–Service Btry | |
| Dates mentioned in diary: Multiple entries | | | | |

361

| Nickerson | Edward K | Sgt | 60th FA- | ?MA |
|---|---|---|---|---|
| Dates mentioned in diary: 10/13/44 | | | | |
| Nix | Henry B | Sgt | 60th FA–HQ | |
| Dates mentioned in diary: Multiple entries | | | | |
| Norder | Clarence | Pfc/Corporal | 60th FA–HQ | Munroe, WI |
| Dates mentioned in diary: 7/15/44, 4/9/45 | | | | |
| Noverio | | | | |
| Dates mentioned in diary: 7/1/44 | | | | |
| O'Leary | | Captain | | |
| Dates mentioned in diary: 7/29/45 | | | | |
| Obeldobel | George A | Lt | 60th FA | PN |
| Dates mentioned in diary: Multiple entries | | | | |
| Omasta | John | T4/T5 | 60th FA–Btry C | |
| Dates mentioned in diary: 8/17/44 | | | | |
| Osowski | Edward A | T4 | 60th FA–Btry A | Montague, MA |
| Dates mentioned in diary: 3/21/45, 3/22/45 | | | | |
| Owens | Lawrence W | Pfc | 60th FA–Btry C | |
| Dates mentioned in diary: 3/5/45 | | | | |
| Page | Frank | | | |
| Dates mentioned in diary: Multiple entries | | | | |
| Paris | | | | |
| Dates mentioned in diary: 3/24/45 | | | | |
| Parrish | Ralph B | Captain | 60th FA–Btry C | Titusville, FL |
| Dates mentioned in diary: 6/24/44, 9/14/44, 12/16/44, 12/29/44, 4/25/45 | | | | |
| Patterson | | Lt | | |
| Dates mentioned in diary: 1/21/45 | | | | |
| Patton | George | General | | |
| Dates mentioned in diary: 8/28/44 | | | | |
| Peters | | T5 | 60th FA–Btry B | |
| Dates mentioned in diary: 12/7/44 | | | | |
| Phelps | Robert L | Pfc | 60th F– Btry C | |
| Dates mentioned in diary: 6/24/44 | | | | |
| Piekowski | Jacob – "Jake" | T4 | 60th FA– HQ | |
| Dates mentioned in diary: 2/23/45 | | | | |

| Planting | Earl | Lt | 60th FA– Btry A &C | |
|---|---|---|---|---|
| Dates mentioned in diary: 10/10/44, 11/7/44, 3/27/45, 4/10/45, 4/28/45 | | | | |
| Pfliefer | Herbert J | Corporal | 60th FA – Btry | PN |
| Dates mentioned in diary: 4/25/45 | | | | |
| Polivy | Calvin | Captain | 9th Division 60th Regiment | |
| Dates mentioned in diary: 7/11/45, 7/16/45, 7/26/45 | | | | |
| Pore | | Captain | | |
| Dates mentioned in diary: 8/2/45 | | | | |
| Pottle | | Lt | 9th Division 60th Regiment | |
| Dates mentioned in diary: 11/25/44, 3/27/45 | | | | |
| Powers | ?Richard or Maurice | Pfc/Sgt | 60th FA– Btry A | |
| Dates mentioned in diary: 1/30/45 | | | | |
| Prince | Louis M | Captain | 60th FA– HQ & Btry A | Greenwich, CN |
| Dates mentioned in diary: 7/18/44, 3/4/45, 3/21/45,6/21/45, 7/10/45, 7/11/45 | | | | |
| Pritchard | Tattanal R | Lt/ Captain | 60th FA– HQ | Savannah, GA |
| Dates mentioned in diary: 6/24/44, 10/10/44, 10/11/44 | | | | |
| Prosniewski | Frank | Sgt | | |
| Dates mentioned in diary: 9/20/44, 10/7/44, 11/24/44, 5/9/45 | | | | |
| Quigley | Walter T | Sgt | 60th FA– Btry A | |
| Dates mentioned in diary: 1/30/45 | | | | |
| Ragland | John D – "Johnny" | Lt | 60th FA– Btry A | Alice, TX |
| Dates mentioned in diary: 7/15/44, 7/16/44 | | | | |
| Ramsdell | | | | |
| Dates mentioned in diary: 6/3/45 | | | | |
| Ramsdell | Robert L | WO | 60th FA– S-4 | Wakefield, MA |
| Dates mentioned in diary: Multiple entries | | | | |
| Reed | Herbert B | Pfc | HQ | |
| Dates mentioned in diary: 10/6/44 | | | | |
| ?Remmer/ Remer | Bud F | T5 | 60th FA– HQ | Chicago, IL |

363

| Dates mentioned in diary: 6/21/45 | | | | |
|---|---|---|---|---|
| Ricci | Angelo A | T4 | 60th FA– Btry B | Quincy, MA |
| Dates mentioned in diary: 4/9/45, 4/10/45 | | | | |
| Richardson | | Captain | 4th ID | |
| Dates mentioned in diary: 11/4/44 | | | | |
| Richardson | | Lt | | |
| Dates mentioned in diary: 1/17/45 | | | | |
| Rockwood | William O | Captain | 60th FA– Btry A/ HQ | ?Rochester or Poughkeepsie NY |
| Dates mentioned in diary: 6/6/44, 6/7/44, 7/23/44 | | | | |
| Rousse | Edmond G | Sgt | 60th FA– HQ | VM |
| Dates mentioned in diary: 6/12/44,10/6/44, 10/13/44, 11/15/44, 2/5/45, 2/6/45, 5/27/45 | | | | |
| Rumore | Emmanuel V | Captain - Doctor | 666th FA | |
| Dates mentioned in diary: 7/16/45, 7/21/45, 7/23/45, 7/27/45, 7/29/45 | | | | |
| Rust | Raymond "Rusty" | | | Beverly, MA |
| Dates mentioned in diary: Multiple entries | | | | |
| Ryan | | Captain | 9th Division 60th Regiment | |
| Dates mentioned in diary: 4/24/45 | | | | |
| Ryan | "Danny" | | 256 Engineers | Hough's Neck, Quincy, MA |
| Dates mentioned in diary: 7/21/45 | | | | |
| Sabo | Edward J | Pfc | 60th FA– HQ | |
| Dates mentioned in diary: 7/25/44 | | | | |
| Sagle | Donald H | Lt | | |
| Dates mentioned in diary: 9/12/44, 11/29/44, 1/22/45, 6/9/45 | | | | |
| Sanders | | | | |
| Dates mentioned in diary: 7/1/44 | | | | |
| Schaussau | | | | |
| Dates mentioned in diary: 7/31/44 | | | | |
| Schossau | Paul A "Red" | Corporal | 60th FA– Btry A | |
| Dates mentioned in diary: 3/29/45 | | | | |
| Schwartz | | | | |
| Dates mentioned in diary: 3/24/45 | | | | |
| Senn | | | Message | |

| | | | | Center | |
|---|---|---|---|---|---|
| Dates mentioned in diary: 9/17/44 | | | | | |
| Severson | Robert A | Captain/ Pilot | | | |
| Dates mentioned in diary: 10/14/44 | | | | | |
| Shafer | | | | | |
| Dates mentioned in diary: 7/31/44 | | | | | |
| Shaughnessy | Martin F | Lt | 9th Division 60th Regiment | Waltham, MA- (official listing is Somerville, MA | |
| Dates mentioned in diary: 3/24/45 | | | | | |
| Sheidy | Herbert W | Lt/Pilot | Air Ops | | |
| Dates mentioned in diary: 7/11/45, 7/17/45, 7/27/45, 8/10/45, 8/12/45, 8/13/45, 8/15/45, 8/22/45 | | | | | |
| Shimkowski | Henry | Medic | | | |
| Dates mentioned in diary: 6/18/44 | | | | | |
| Shipe | | Corporal | | Ithaca, NY | |
| Dates mentioned in diary: 10/7/44, 11/6/44, 3/2/45, 4/12/45 | | | | | |
| Shock | | | | | |
| Dates mentioned in diary: 4/21/45 | | | | | |
| Shopinski | | | 9th Division 60th Regiment | | |
| Dates mentioned in diary: 7/16/44 | | | | | |
| Shuttleworth | | | 9th Division 60th Regiment | | |
| Dates mentioned in diary: 11/25/44 | | | | | |
| Siegal | | | | | |
| Dates mentioned in diary: 7/31/44 | | | | | |
| Skoczylas | Eugene E | | | RI | |
| Dates mentioned in diary: Multiple entries | | | | | |
| Slim | | Sgt | | | |
| Dates mentioned in diary: 2/20/45 | | | | | |
| Slota | | | | | |
| Dates mentioned in diary: 6/19/45, 7/4/45, 7/6/45 | | | | | |
| Smart | "Freddy" | | | NH | |
| Dates mentioned in diary: 8/17/44 | | | | | |
| Smith | | | Service Btry | | |
| Dates mentioned in diary: 6/21/45 | | | | | |
| Smith | | Captain | | | |
| Dates mentioned in diary: 7/12/45 | | | | | |

| Smitty | | | | |
|---|---|---|---|---|
| Dates mentioned in diary: 11/4/44, 1/6/45 | | | | |
| Snead | GW | T5 | HQ | |
| Dates mentioned in diary: 7/25/44 | | | | |
| Sortino | Frank | Sgt | 60th FA – S-3/HQ | Chicago, IL |
| Dates mentioned in diary: 10/26/44, 5/11/45 | | | | |
| Staaf | | Corporal/T5 | | |
| Dates mentioned in diary: 9/20/44, 11/8/44, 3/7/45, 4/10/45, 5/9/45 | | | | |
| Stacey | Frank N | Lt | 9th Division 60th Regiment | IL |
| Dates mentioned in diary: 4/5/45, 6/9/45 | | | | |
| Steponik | | | 60th FA  HQ | |
| Dates mentioned in diary: 1/30/45 | | | | |
| Stepp | | | 9th Division 60th Regiment | |
| Dates mentioned in diary: 4/5/45 | | | | |
| Stern | "Doc" | | 15th Medics | |
| Dates mentioned in diary: 2/22/45 | | | | |
| Stokes | John I | Pfc | 60th FA– Btry C | |
| Dates mentioned in diary: 7/15/44, 7/16/44, 7/17/44 | | | | |
| Stoll | Edward | Sgt | 60th FA– HQ | East Hampton, CN |
| Dates mentioned in diary: 1/21/45 | | | | |
| Strong | | | | |
| Dates mentioned in diary: 7/10/45 | | | | |
| Szcygiel | Thaddeus | T5 | 60th FA– Btry C | |
| Dates mentioned in diary: 6/29/44 | | | | |
| Tempesta | Gerry | | 4th ID | Quincy, MA |
| Dates mentioned in diary: 6/14/44 | | | | |
| Templeton | Webster | Pfc/ Corporal | 60th FA– Btry A | Fort Bragg, NC |
| Dates mentioned in diary: 7/31/44, 2/1/45 | | | | |
| Tex | | | | |
| Dates mentioned in diary: 4/12/45 | | | | |
| Thivierge | Philip "Pete" | Captain | 60th FA– S-2 | ?Malden, MA or Rochester, NH |
| Dates mentioned in diary: Multiple entries | | | | |

366

| | | | | |
|---|---|---|---|---|
| Thomas | Richard L | Sgt | 60th FA–Ammunitions | |
| Dates mentioned in diary: 12/23/44 | | | | |
| Thurtle | George | Captain | 60th FA–Btry B | Lincoln, NE |
| Dates mentioned in diary: 7/16/44, 7/23/44 | | | | |
| Tooley | Anthony M | | 60th FA-Service Btry | |
| Dates mentioned in diary: Multiple entries | | | | |
| Tory | | | | Northampton, MA |
| Dates mentioned in diary: 2/25/45 | | | | |
| Tracey | | Lt | Motors | |
| Dates mentioned in diary: 4/28/45 | | | | |
| Trasher | | | | Northampton, MA |
| Dates mentioned in diary: 6/21/45 | | | | |
| Treacy | | Lt | | |
| Dates mentioned in diary: 5/11/45, 6/3/45 | | | | |
| Turner | | | | |
| Dates mentioned in diary: 3/14/45 | | | | |
| Turnipseed | Lawrence L | Captain | Medical Admin Corp | Alabama |
| Dates mentioned in diary: 1/21/45 | | | | |
| Urban | Raymond G | Major | 60th FA – HQ | San Antonio, TX |
| Dates mentioned in diary: 7/16/44, 7/23/44 | | | | |
| " Van Leuvin or Leuven | George G | Major | 60th FA – Btry B | |
| Dates mentioned in diary: 11/25/44, 4/17/45, 6/9/45 | | | | |
| Villereal | | Pvt | | |
| Dates mentioned in diary: 6/22/44 | | | | |
| Voller | | | 9th Division-60th Regiment | |
| Dates mentioned in diary: 11/25/44 | | | | |
| Wade | William W Jr "Wally" | Lt | 60th FA–Btry B/HQ | Durham, NC |
| Dates mentioned in diary: 11/16/44 | | | | |
| Wall | Matt | | | |
| Dates mentioned in diary: 2/15/44 | | | | |

| Waters | | Captain/ Personnal officer | 9th Division | |
|---|---|---|---|---|
| Dates mentioned in diary: 11/15/44, 4/5/45 | | | | |
| Webb | | | 60th FA– Btry C | |
| Dates mentioned in diary: 3/12/45 | | | | |
| Welsh | Eugene V Jr | | 60th FA | |
| Dates mentioned in diary: 9/12/44,11/15/44, 4/28/45, 5/15/45,716/45, 7/29/45 | | | | |
| Westmoreland | | Colonel | | |
| Dates mentioned in diary: 2/15/45 | | | | |
| Whitney | | | | |
| Dates mentioned in diary: 7/10/45 | | | | |
| Wilensky | Bernard | Lt | 60th FA– Btry C | Dorchester, MA |
| Dates mentioned in diary: 11/17/44,11/18/44, 11/29/44, 3/12/45, 3/13/45 | | | | |
| Williams | Donald K "Willie" | Pfc | 60th FA– Btry A | Northampton, MA |
| Dates mentioned in diary: 6/2/45 | | | | |
| Williams | Ralph I "Willie" | Captain/Major | 60th FA– S-3 | |
| Dates mentioned in diary: Multiple entries | | | | |
| Wilson | Keene "Slick" & ? "Red" | Lt/ Captain | | |
| Dates mentioned in diary: 7/15/44,10/10/44, 10/13/44, 11/18/44, 11/25/44, 11/26/44, 11/29/44, 6/21/45 | | | | |
| Wilson | John B Jr | Major | 666 FA | |
| Dates mentioned in diary: 7/15/45, 7/23/45 | | | | |
| Wisniewski | Anthony J | | 60th FA– Service Btry | |
| Dates mentioned in diary: Multiple entries | | | | |
| Wood | | | 9th Division- 60th Regiment | |
| Dates mentioned in diary: 4/5/45 | | | | |
| Wood | | WO | | |
| Dates mentioned in diary: 4/20/45, 4/21/45 | | | | |
| Young | Donald M | Lt | | CO |
| Dates mentioned in diary: 5/9/45, 6/12/45, 6/21/45, 7/8/45, 7/10/45, 7/11/45, 7/18/45, 7/23/45, 7/27/45, 8/13/45 | | | | |

| Zelwanger | Charles F | Pfc | 60th FA–Btry C | |
|---|---|---|---|---|
| Dates mentioned in diary: 7/15/44 | | | | |
| Zimmer | Edward A | T5 | 60th FA | |
| Dates mentioned in diary: 6/29/44 | | | | |
| Zuba | Joseph | Sgt | 60th FA–Btry A | Pawtucket, RI |
| Dates mentioned in diary: 7/15/44 | | | | |
| Zutke | | | Service Btry | |
| Dates mentioned in diary: 4/10/45, 4/22/45 | | | | |

About the editors:

Mary Lovell is a lifelong Boston resident and one of the five children of author Frank Lovell. During the last five years Mary has devoted herself to the transcription and preparation, for general publication, of her father's WWII diaries. As part of the research for this book, she has journeyed to Europe, retracing her father's footsteps as a soldier during WWII. She counts history and travel as her interests

Yuri Beckers has been researching the World War II history of the 9th Infantry Division for many years and has become an authority on this subject. Currently working on several publications about the 9th Infantry Division as well, Yuri also created and maintains the most visited website on the division, www.9thinfantrydivision.net. Having met Mary Lovell through their mutual research, he has served as historical adviser for many of the subjects and pictures featured within these pages. Together with Mary he has visited some of the places mentioned in the book and served as an assistant editor for this publication. Yuri is a Dutch man, currently living in Denmark, with a huge passion for the 9th Infantry Division's history.

Made in United States
Orlando, FL
01 June 2022

18403047R00212